Solidarity in the European Union

Andreas Grimmel • Susanne My Giang
Editors

Solidarity in the European Union

A Fundamental Value in Crisis

Springer

Editors
Andreas Grimmel
Institute for Political Science
University of Hamburg
Hamburg, Germany

Susanne My Giang
Institute for Political Science
University of Hamburg
Hamburg, Germany

ISBN 978-3-319-57035-8 ISBN 978-3-319-57036-5 (eBook)
DOI 10.1007/978-3-319-57036-5

Library of Congress Control Number: 2017942948

Printed on acid-free paper

This Springer imprint is published by Springer Nature
The registered company is Springer International Publishing AG
The registered company address is: Gewerbestrasse 11, 6330 Cham, Switzerland

Foreword

Working for Solidarity: A Key European Value!

To work for more Europe and for more Union in the EU is more important than ever before in EU history. Of course, the EU's development has never been free from ruptures, contradictions, setbacks and negative developments. Time and again, it has experienced serious crises. But this time a lack of solidarity in dealing with the many crises currently facing us is giving rise to doubts as to whether the EU and its member states are capable of overcoming the challenges of our times.

Rather than running after right-wing populists or abandoning our positions, the pro-European forces have to look, especially in a time of crisis, for a more solidarity-based, environmentally friendly and cosmopolitan Europe. Unfortunately, however, we are again and again witnessing a style of politics which focuses solely on national interests and which sacrifices much-needed European action in favour of domestic political benefit. This must change. The EU must no longer be the scapegoat for the failures of national politics and the shortcomings of national or nationalistic politicians.

Even if we are currently seeing a massive rise in social inequality in the member states as a result of wrong decisions and politics, the EU has made a vital contribution to greater prosperity in the past. We Europeans want the EU to constantly deliver anew on this promise of prosperity. This requires greater social cohesion, more efforts for a real social union whose positive effects are felt by citizens and, again, greater solidarity—because solidarity is a key European value. And it is precisely because of this and other values on which the EU is based—respect for human dignity, democracy, individual freedom, human rights, equality and the rule of law—that Europe holds such a powerful appeal for hundreds of thousands of people who are seeking protection from war, terror, dictatorship and persecution. They show us the immense value of what we Europeans have achieved in our Union.

When it comes to our policy towards refugees, there is a massive and unacceptable lack of solidarity. But this challenge will not be solved by building new border fences. What is needed instead is a common, solidarity-based and humane EU asylum policy which places the rights of those seeking protection centre stage. At the heart of such a policy is a fair and permanent refugee relocation system, with all member states gradually coming to participate in a spirit of solidarity—and abolishing the unjust Dublin system which stipulates that you can only apply for asylum in the first EU country you touch soil.

Europe must be judged by its own promises, its aims and values: whether internally, when it comes to solidarity in the Europe-wide relocation of refugees, or externally, for example, when it comes to shaping a fair global trade policy.

Ulrike Lunacek
Member and Vice-President of the European Parliament

Preface

This volume originates from a conference on 'Solidarity and Its Crisis in the European Union' that was held at Universität Hamburg from 2 to 3 June 2016 and was kindly funded by the Academy of Sciences and Humanities in Hamburg.

Solidarity is one of the fundamental values on which the European Union (EU) was founded. However, the EU has experienced a number of crises in recent years, and it appears as if the solidarity among member states is beginning to crumble. At least, the EU's crisis situation has revealed both the need for *and* the lack of solidarity in the context of the EU.

Against the background of the ongoing discussion about solidarity and the challenges in the EU, scientists from diverse disciplines (political sciences, philosophy and law) and different countries (France, Germany, Italy, the Netherlands, Norway and the United Kingdom) came together for this conference to engage in a fruitful discussion about the current state of affairs and the future perspectives on solidarity in the EU.

This volume is the result of these discussions and makes a contribution to our understanding of the concept of solidarity, its meaning and its practical implementation in the EU. It covers multiple perspectives from the angles of different research disciplines on the most pressing crisis fields and the foundations of a meaningful concept of solidarity in the European context.

We wish to thank all the contributors for their important and interesting presentations at the conference, for engaging in critical discussions and, finally, for publishing their research with us. We want to thank the Europa-Kolleg Hamburg—Institute for European Integration and our research assistants, Norma Schemschat and Florian Kommer, for their supporting work, as well as Springer for agreeing to publish this volume.

Our special thanks go to the Academy of Sciences and Humanities in Hamburg, which made the conference and this volume possible with their kind funding, supporting us with many helpful suggestions and also with all the necessary administrative assistance.

Hamburg, Germany
June 2017

Andreas Grimmel
Susanne My Giang

Contents

Contributors

Bengt Beutler University of Bremen, Bremen, Germany

University of Hamburg, Hamburg, Germany

Manuela Caiani Scuola Normale Superiore, Pisa, Italy

Erik O. Eriksen ARENA—Centre for European Studies, University of Oslo, Oslo, Norway

Susanne My Giang University of Hamburg, Hamburg, Germany

Andreas Grimmel University of Hamburg, Hamburg, Germany

Institute for European Integration, Europa-Kolleg Hamburg, Hamburg, Germany

Michèle Knodt Technische Universität Darmstadt, Darmstadt, Germany

Markus Kotzur University of Hamburg, Hamburg, Germany

Europa-Kolleg Hamburg, Hamburg, Germany

Tim Oliver London School of Economics and Political Science, London, UK

Elena Pavan Institute of Humanities and Social Sciences, Scuola Normale Superiore, Pisa, Italy

Justyna Segeš Frelak Institute of Public Affairs in Warsaw, Warsaw, Poland

Ulrich Steinvorth University of Hamburg, Hamburg, Germany

Anne Tews Technische Universität Darmstadt, Darmstadt, Germany

Henri de Waele Radboud University Nijmegen, Nijmegen, The Netherlands

University of Antwerp, Antwerp, Belgium

Catherine Wihtol de Wenden Centre d'Études et des Recherches Internationales (CERI), Sciences Po, Paris, France

Le Centre National de la Recherche Scientifique (CNRS), Paris, France

Chapter 1
Introduction: Solidarity Lost? The European Union and the Crisis of One of Its Core Values

Andreas Grimmel and Susanne My Giang

Never before in its history has the European Union (EU) been confronted with so many conflict-laden challenges—persistent financial turmoil, migration, the rise of nationalist parties, separatist movements and terrorist threats. What all these challenges share is the fact that they call for common solutions—and for solidarity. Many of these challenges even go beyond Europe and call for solidarity not just among Europeans but also with states and people in other world regions.

If we look at the current discussions, it sometimes seems that the end of the European integration project is near. The former President of the European Parliament, Martin Schulz, for example, warned in a speech held on 5 February 2016 at the London School of Economics and Political Science:

> If we Europeans fall apart, laboring under the fond illusion that, now of all times, the finest hour of the nation state has arrived, we should make no mistake about the consequences. We will be left to drift insignificantly into the backwaters of the world political scene.

Of course, Schulz draws a grim picture of Europe's possible future here. It seems rather pessimistic, and it might even seem unlikely. However, even if the EU will not fall apart and will not 'drift insignificantly into the backwaters of the world political scene', it has suffered damage in a sensitive area during the many crises it has faced—namely, to its values. Europeans like to think of the EU as a 'normative power', being able to convince others of the benefits of their way of life by living by example. In many respects, this is right (at least, if we look at the manifold regional integration projects in the world that follow the European model). In the case of

A. Grimmel (✉)
University of Hamburg, Hamburg, Germany

Institute for European Integration, Europa-Kolleg Hamburg, Hamburg, Germany
e-mail: andreas.grimmel@uni-hamburg.de

S.M. Giang (✉)
University of Hamburg, Hamburg, Germany
e-mail: susanne.giang@wiso.uni-hamburg.de

A. Grimmel, S.M. Giang (eds.), *Solidarity in the European Union*,
DOI 10.1007/978-3-319-57036-5_1

solidarity, however—which is one of the core EU values codified in the Charter of Fundamental Rights—the EU and its Member States have recently given a bad example. At least, this is the case if we understand solidarity as not just helping to avoid larger political or economic damage, or saving others to save ourselves. Such a self-centred—and maybe selfish—concept of solidarity seems to be a crucial element of the EU's crises and challenges, rather than a cure for them.

But what does such a lack of solidarity tell us? And what are its implications for the integration project and its future prospects?

Richard Rorty once said: 'Solidarity has to be constructed out of little pieces, rather than found already waiting'. When we take a look at the current state of the European integration project, there can hardly be any doubt that Rorty was right. Solidarity was, quite simply, lacking in any of the recent crises (its absence being most striking in the financial crisis and the refugee crisis)—it was not already waiting for the Europeans somewhere. In other words, solidarity as a value is not to be found out there, but must be created. Rorty could also have said that solidarity is a process, just as integration is a process. It is unfinished and necessarily has to remain unfinished. At the same time, solidarity—and this is certainly true for every value or norm inside or outside the European context—is a concept that has to be practised and made explicit by the deed. Otherwise, it must remain a hollow word. Good intentions and the evocation of European solidarity are not enough. There is no such thing as solidarity unless it is practised, regardless of the underlying definition of what it means to act in solidarity.

In this light, the current crisis situation reveals that solidarity is not lost, but the concept of solidarity that we are talking about in the EU is still a weak one that is rarely practised. In a way, it remains or often becomes an empty phrase. But it is also one that still has the potential to be developed.

In other words, the EU is in a situation in which it is not just facing profound political, economic, legal and societal challenges. Rather, it has to prove that it is more than the sum of its interests and that it is not just an arena used to ensure national advantage. It has to show through concrete actions what solidarity actually means and implies in the context of the EU. In this sense, the many crises that the EU is facing present themselves as a test case for one of its fundamental values.

Against this background, this volume aims to discuss not only the concept of solidarity but also how it is applied in practice. The themes and case studies covered here take on some of the discussions that are currently most debated with regard to solidarity and its crisis in the EU from the points of view of political science, sociology, law and philosophy. This multiplicity of perspectives, at the same time, aims at an interdisciplinary exploration of the subject matter, not just promising a synoptic presentation of the diverse challenges facing solidarity in the EU.

The two parts of this volume reflect these objectives. The first part takes a closer look at the concept of solidarity and its theoretical and practical meaning.

The chapter by *Ulrich Steinvorth* deals with the application of the concept of solidarity to Europe. He starts by analysing solidarity as a virtue, considering individuals who have similar goals, are on the same legal level, reject unnecessary domination and authoritarianism, demand equality, presume fraternity and help each other when one of them is in a plight that none of them is responsible for. Steinvorth argues that this implies that while justice requires me to compensate for a damage D suffered by B only if I am responsible for D, solidarity requires me to help B—as long as I have the resources to help—even if neither B nor I are responsible for D. However, Durkheim showed that, nonetheless, solidarity and justice are compatible, because without solidarity individual liberty will be defeated by authoritarianism, which will always prove stronger than any single individual fighting alone for their liberty. Yet without individual liberty and responsibility, solidarity will degenerate into parasitism. With regard to the contemporary problems in the field, Steinvorth points out that solidarity has been appealed to from the outset of the European unification, but the concept was obscured by (a) the idea that the subjects of solidarity can be nations rather than individuals and (b) the failure to call upon solidarity in a crisis that no member is responsible for. The latter scenario meant that there was insufficient help for the Mediterranean states that were the place of first arrival for most refugees, whereas the former has meant that European unification is most often measured according to whether it helps nations rather than individuals, thus neglecting the interests of individuals and the unemployment that economic unification causes. To prevent this, Steinvorth argues not only for measures to recognise rising unemployment as something that can be good rather than evil (e.g. by introducing a basic income) but also for taking subsidiarity seriously by promoting regionalisation and secessionism and decentralising European administrations.

Bengt Beutler, in turn, sheds light on solidarity as a variable concept that is embedded in the context of a changing integration project. He starts from the diagnosis that solidarity in the European Union (EU) currently seems to be a lost cause—notwithstanding multiple references to it in the Lisbon Treaties. However, by tracing the unique character of solidarity as well as that of the EU, one can find amazing similarities and mutual interdependence, Beutler argues. Solidarity marks the universal groundwork for, as well as the objective of, the survival of humanity, and the EU—for the first time in history—provides the institutional framework necessary for such solidarity, going beyond the traditional notion of a sovereign state and its exclusive mandate to uphold the common good. To make solidarity real in an increasingly fragmented world, Beutler claims, it is necessary to move away from its present abstraction and instead appeal to the intuition of the people when operating within the institutional framework provided by the EU, achieving this through concrete actions—as envisaged explicitly in the 1951 Treaty constituting the European Coal and Steel Community (ECSC).

The chapter of *Markus Kotzur* examines solidarity as a legal concept. Whereas the Treaty of Lisbon contains manifold references to the notion of solidarity, Kotzur argues that a precise meaning of or conceptual framework for this notion is anything but clear. The question of which overall expectations, moral obligations, political assumptions and normative forces can be attributed to 'solidarity' needs, therefore, to be addressed. Against this backdrop, the chapter aims, firstly, to introduce conceptual approaches to solidarity on the national, regional and international planes; secondly, to identify text-based legal substantiations of solidarity within the EU and beyond; and, finally, to frame solidarity as a constitutional paradigm. In doing so, the paper follows a leitmotif once expressed by Jacques Delors in the saying 'solidarity mechanisms are not based on pure generosity, but on enlightened self-interest'.

Michèle Knodt and Anne Tews address the significance, reality and limitations of solidarity in the European multi-level system. They present an effort to conceptualise solidarity in the European multi-level system and develop a typology of four different forms of solidarity: transnational solidarity, supranational solidarity, intergovernmental solidarity and international solidarity. This contribution focuses on the type of intergovernmental solidarity between Member States and explores the possible limits of solidary acts. Knodt and Tews illustrate their theoretical and conceptual considerations with insights from two different EU policy fields: energy and migration policy. In both fields, solidarity plays an important role according to the Treaty. However, both policy fields are characterised by a lack of solidary actions and thus provide some indications of the limits of European solidarity. Debates on energy policy, they show, feature selective claims of solidarity with regard to energy security and a lack of solidarity with regard to sharing the burden of greenhouse gas emissions reduction, whereas migration policy is characterised by a fundamental lack of solidary claims and actions. The analysis indicates that Member States calculate the benefits and costs of solidary acts from a short-term perspective, focus on domestic concerns and fail to link solidarity claims across policy fields.

The second part then turns to the most pressing issues in which solidarity, as a core value of the EU, in one way or another, plays a central role.

Catherine Wihtol de Wenden analyses the implications of the refugee and migration crisis for the EU. She starts with the fact that, at the beginning of the twenty-first century, international migration reached 244 million people (i.e. 3.5% of the world population), with roughly the same number of flows going to the north (south–north and north–north, 120 million) as to the south (south–south and north–south, 130 million). This presents a new situation. Against this background, de Wenden maintains that all regions and countries are, in one way or another, part of the migration process by being involved in either emigration, immigration or transit flows (most of them in all three aspects together). As a result, categories such as 'foreign workers' and 'asylum seekers' are becoming increasingly blurry. The chapter also shows that new types of migrants—isolated women, unaccompanied children, circulating elites and experts—have entered into international mobility. At the same time, de Wenden reminds us that the right to move is among the least shared in the world: global mobility is highly segmented based on nationality, class, gender, race, etc. As well as this, the end of the Cold War and the fall of the Berlin Wall in Europe in 1989 brought about generalisation of the right to exit, with easy access to a passport, even in southern countries, along with more restricted rights to enter OECD countries.

The chapter by *Justyna Segeš Frelak* sheds light on the reaction of Visegrád Group countries to the refugee crisis in the context of solidarity in EU migration policy. Currently, the Visegrád Group (V4) continues to be in strong opposition to compulsory refugee relocation under any scheme. At the same time, the V4 attitude towards migration fundamentally differs from that of several Western European countries. The chapter argues that this is partially connected to the fact that the V4 are among the states with the lowest percentages of foreigners in the European Union. As knowledge about immigration is limited and stereotypes are widespread, Segeš Frelak argues, the refugee crisis has contributed to an increase in negative opinions about immigration. The anti-immigrant sentiment in the region is not based on real experience with non-nationals. In the case of the Visegrád countries, both populists and mainstream right- or left-wing parties have made use of fears over immigration for their political purposes. Furthermore, this has proven to be a very easy political tactic. Although, the engagement of civil society shows solidarity with refugees, these efforts are often overshadowed by an anti-immigration discourse.

In his chapter, *Erik Oddvar Eriksen* takes a closer look at how the Eurozone crisis raises the problem of structural injustice. Eriksen claims that the beneficiaries receive a diverse array of benefits under an enduring social structure, and he studies the type of duties that this structure triggers. Particular actors have directly or indirectly participated in causing some injustices, and some injustices benefit them, some harm them and some do both. However, things may be wrong but not unjust in the sense that it is others' responsibility. Eriksen shows that we are confronted with the normative puzzle of injustice. These injustices benefit some while no one in particular is liable to pay damages. In effect, the Eurozone crisis gives rise to duties, but not in the form of compensatory obligations. Rather, it gives rise to duties of solidarity—to correct wrongs in order to satisfy political justice.

The chapter by *Henri de Waele* takes a critical look at the growing role of different independence and separatist movements in the Member States of the EU by setting out that some of the most profound 'tearing apart' of the fabric that holds the EU together risks emerging from inside the EU. Independence and separatist movements that prove successful in their quest for secession may spark a potential domino effect and an incremental fragmentation of the Union's Member State base. The chapter first underscores that this danger is far from academic and is ever more likely to materialise by mapping the different pushes towards autonomy that can be discerned in contemporary Europe. It equally discusses to which extent the EU itself may be considered to (wittingly or unwittingly) foment these tendencies. The core objective, however, is to canvas how the current crisis of solidarity manifests itself through the rise of separatist and independence movements and indicates what the most credible response would be from a normative perspective. This culminates in de Waele's argument that the EU need not necessarily be very welcoming towards newly independent regions in search of accession—instead, it may justifiably adopt a more evasive stance and (when considering the negative ramifications of a contrary position) is actually well advised to do so.

The contribution by *Tim Oliver* studies the theoretical discussions of Brexit, Grexit and other exit scenarios. Oliver starts from the fact that the UK's vote to leave the European Union has presented the integration project with an unprecedented challenge. What this could mean for the EU has been the subject of increased levels of analysis and speculation, albeit nowhere near as comprehensive as that into what the vote might mean for the UK. One concern is that Brexit signals or could begin the unravelling of the EU, eventually leading to its complete collapse and disintegration. To examine whether or not Brexit will lead to European disintegration, this chapter explores some of the analysis into what Brexit could mean for the EU and then explores some of the theoretical debates about European disintegration.

Manuela Caiani and *Elena Pavan* chose an exploratory approach towards what can be described as 'inconvenient solidarities'. They start from the finding that, in spite of increasing interest in how information and communication technologies entwine with collective participation dynamics, the ways in which their relational and communicational potential is exploited by extreme right organisations remain overlooked. On this basis, they aim to move research in the field forward by focusing on how extreme right organisations and groups employ digital communications to sustain the construction of 'inconvenient solidarities', i.e. systems of relations among actors that oppose and distort current efforts aimed at promoting transnational democratisation, particularly at the European level. By focusing on the websites of extreme right organisations in six European countries (Austria, France, Germany, Italy, Spain and the United Kingdom) and combining digital research tools and social network analysis, Caiani and Pavan explore how these organisations use information and communication technologies strategically to connect in the online space, as well as to construct and distribute materials criticising and envisaging reforms of the current projects of European integration. Their results suggest that information and communication technologies sustain the construction of inconvenient solidarities in heterogeneous ways, supporting different modes of online conversation that, in turn, affect extreme right actors' capacity to propose shared and unified frames of opposition to and reform of the EU.

Finally, the chapter by *Andreas Grimmel* explores the practical dimension of solidarity as one of the EU's core values. More concretely, the chapter scrutinises the recurring use of the concept of solidarity and how it is mirrored by corresponding practices in the EU. By arguing that even though there is a link between the concept and the corresponding actions that define the meaning of solidarity, the density of this link cannot be measured by relying on either the textual or the practical side. Rather, both have to come together to fill solidarity as a concept and value with life and give it a central role in the integration process. The argument is developed by building on the works of Ludwig Wittgenstein and discussing three of his most influential concepts: meaning in use, rule-following and private language. The author claims that such a Wittgensteinian perspective has the potential to arrive at an understanding of solidarity that discloses a major shortcoming of the value in the context of the EU—namely, a lack of commonality in terms of what solidarity practically implies, i.e. what it means to act in solidarity in actual cases. It will be further maintained that the only way to overcome this shortcoming is to follow a somewhat pragmatic agenda in applying the value in concrete cases and, by doing so, making its common meaning explicit.

Following this structure, the volume has attained its self-defined goal if it is able to achieve two things: first, to scrutinise the role solidarity plays and might play in the future of European integration, while also being clear about the limits of this much-debated and sometimes overburdened concept, and, second, to open up the field for more fruitful interdisciplinary discussions on the topic.

Part I
Solidarity as a Concept and Fundamental Value in the European Union

Chapter 2
Applying the Idea of Solidarity to Europe

Ulrich Steinvorth

1 The Concept of Solidarity

The concept of solidarity has found two applications in French and other European nations' civil law that have made the concept a little less vague. *Solidarité* refers to:

> first, enforceable liabilities of individuals for debts which not they but absconded individuals of the same group or nation had run into. Thus, German students could be made responsible for debts some eloped compatriot had incurred. (cp. Engelhardt 1998: 432; my tr.)

> second, an insurance relationship in which the *solidaires* paid into a fund for agreed upon emergency cases, out of which an agreed upon amount was to be paid for the victims of the emergency cases regardless of how much they had paid into the fund. (cp. Metz 1998)

The concept of solidarity has kept these two connotations. Solidarity is still appealed to when justifying measures to alleviate damages by taking money from people and institutions not responsible for the damages, as well as to provide support for partners who have agreed on mutual support for difficulties they have contractually stipulated.

In the present (and perhaps also the former) concept of solidarity, these two connotations stand in a broader context. The idea that people can be made responsible for actions they are not responsible for is connected to the idea that there are relations between individuals that commit them to the provision of mutual help in emergencies, whether or not they have contributed to the emergencies. Workers on strike appeal to the solidarity of all workers to support them in their strike by going on strike as well, or through other means. The West German population was coerced to financially support the East German population with a solidarity surcharge. The idea of solidarity implies that workers are to workers and members of

U. Steinvorth (✉)
University of Hamburg, Hamburg, Germany
e-mail: ulrich.steinvorth@uni-hamburg.de

A. Grimmel, S.M. Giang (eds.), *Solidarity in the European Union*,
DOI 10.1007/978-3-319-57036-5_2

historical nations are to each other as siblings who should follow their common interest rather than different interests. To be solidary I have to take into account that the misfortune hitting you might hit me too.

Solidarity is understood as a bond that makes up a 'we'. Such relation improves the feeling and power of those related but also makes it possible for some to live off the actions of the others without contributing to the shared power. Thus, their behaviour can become parasitical. Yet this vice is balanced by considerable virtues.

First, solidarity includes the idea of a relation between equals who cannot coerce one another unless justice requires it. Unlike fathers and sons, those bound by solidarity are like brothers who are equals to one another. For this reason, in the French Revolution solidarity was nearly synonymous with fraternity; *solidarité* only emphasized that the dependence on mutual help has family-independent reasons (Metz 1998: 172 ff).

Second, solidarity is considered the ideal relation for individuals committed to liberty and equality, requiring them to interact at eye level rather than using force and fraud and other coercive or fraudulent means.

Third, individuals who pursue similar goals, like the workers in the worker's movement, often have no chance of attaining their individual goals unless they act in solidarity. Hence, it is often in their long-term individual interests for individuals to act in solidarity.

Fourth, parasitism can be reduced if we (1) distinguish misfortunes that the needy *are* responsible for from misfortunes that they *are not* responsible for and (2) limit solidary to situations in which only the latter are helped. Such a limitation not only stops misuse but also stimulates self-responsibility.

So, if refusing to call misused solidarity 'solidarity', we may tentatively define it as follows:

> Solidarity is the virtue of equals who help one another in misfortunes they are not responsible for.

Let's explicate the elements of this definition. Solidarity is a virtue that presupposes:

1. Individuals with similar goals.
2. Individuals who are on the same legal level; no one has more legal rights than any other individual.
3. Individuals who reject unnecessary domination or authoritarianism, demand equality and presume fraternity (Freud's myth of the sons killing their authoritarian father gives us a model of people who are equally free and pursuing similar goals, being mutually dependent on one another and acting in solidarity).
4. Individuals who, when they are well off, do not forget that they might easily get into the same miserable situation as another person who is asking for their help.

2 Excursus to Durkheim: Solidarity and Individuality Result from Mutual Social Dependence

Emile Durkheim (1893) explicated the idea of solidarity by making an ingenious distinction between primitive and modern societies. The former, he said, have a *mechanic solidarity* and the latter an *organic solidarity*. Yet, the former isn't solidarity at all but mutual independence. In primitive societies, individuals or their families have the properties necessary to start a society of their own, by hunting or farming a field for themselves. This independence may seem to favour individualism, but it implies a lack of individuality. Individuals can survive their exit from society only because they are more or less like any other individual, much like the cells of primitive organisms, such as polyps, that survive their separation from the rest of a polyp and can start a new primitive organism only because they lack the differentiation that individuality presupposes.

In contrast, modern societies are kept together by a complex division of labour that requires people to develop special talents to perform specialized jobs. Such individuals cannot leave their society without ruining themselves and their society. They are individualists, but for this very reason, humans are mutually dependent and in need of the very virtue we have provisionally defined as solidarity.

Thus, complex societies need individuals:

1. with the common goal of maintaining a complex division of labour
2. to be on the same legal level rather than standing in authoritarian relations
3. to want to remain in non-authoritarian relations
4. to be aware that they too might, through no fault of their own, suffer the bad luck that an individual who is asking them for help is in

Durkheim succeeded in proving that both the idea of individual liberty and the idea of solidarity are required in a liberal society. These ideas can seem incompatible because solidarity can require actions not required by justice. This is because justice requires me to compensate for damage D suffered by B only if I'm responsible for D, while solidarity requires me to help even if I am not responsible for D. This proof is important because, without individual liberty and responsibility, solidarity will degenerate into parasitism; yet, without solidarity, individual liberty will be defeated by authoritarianism, which will always prove stronger than any individual fighting alone for their liberty.

3 Solidarity Mistakenly Appealed to in the Unification of Europe

The founders of a united Europe appealed to solidarity but replaced the individuals presupposed in the idea of solidarity with European nations. They presumed, just as I did in the list above, that the European nations or states would (1) pursue the common goals of liberty and peace, (2) cooperate and want to cooperate on an equal footing, (3) want to live in non-authoritarian relations, and (4) not forget that they might easily get into the same mess that another European state, through no fault of its own, gets into. But they thought it didn't make a difference whether the bearers of solidarity were individuals or nations. This has proved to be a momentous mistake. Nations and states not only don't have the rights individuals have, but, more importantly, what is good for a nation or a state is not necessarily also good for the individual. Nations can profit from a cooperation that individuals don't profit from. Thus, a nation's GDP can increase while individuals get poorer.

Another mistake was that they did not sufficiently clarify the relation of solidarity to the potentially antagonistic idea of individual liberty. They did not point out that solidarity can be reasonably appealed to only by excluding parasitism. Such an exclusion is easily achieved by distinguishing between messes that those who are suffering are responsible for and messes that they are not responsible for. Such a distinction implies not that sufferers who find themselves in a mess they are responsible for should never get help but that they must not rely on getting solidary help.

This deficit in the appeals to solidarity has appeared in recent crises with a vengeance—for example, after the global financial crisis in 2008 and in the more recent refugee crisis.

In the financial crisis, the states that had the means to bail out the financially threatened states accused the messy states of misusing solidarity, whereas the messy states accused the rich ones of lacking solidarity. Had solidarity been explicitly limited to misfortunes nations are not responsible for, some of the current resentments might have been avoided.

In the refugee crisis, the southern European countries most threatened by unbalanced budgets are also most threatened by the immigration of refugees. In this crisis it's obviously not their responsibility that they are the countries first entered by the refugees. It's a mere accident of their geographical location, which situates them on the routes most frequented by refugees. Nonetheless, according to the Dublin Convention, agreed in 1990 and in force since 1997, refugees can apply for asylum only in the country they arrive in (more exactly, where their fingerprints are stored). These countries have been Italy, Greece and Spain in the first place. They were left alone in their efforts to cope with the masses of refugees entering them first. Since they were not responsible for the mess they had found themselves in, they had every reason to appeal to solidarity—the very solidarity that is restricted to demanding help for the unfortunate parties that are suffering but not responsible for their situation. Here, the fact that solidarity is not clearly restricted to solidarity in situations where the suffering countries are not responsible for their situation has put them in the place of suppliants rather than equals.

So, when the Swedish and the German governments opened their countries for refugees without regard to the Dublin Regulation, this was an act of solidarity conforming to national standards of liberty and responsibility. Unfortunately, this act was not followed by more European governments. This would probably have been harder had more people paid attention to the difference between unconditional solidarity and solidarity conditional on national responsibility. However, Germany's demand for an equal distribution of the refugees within the European Union (EU) didn't take account of the lack of experience with immigrants of the eastern European nations and endangered the idea of equality within solidary relations. The early insistence on this condition of solidarity might have helped.

So much to the detriments in European appeals to solidarity. But they had their benefits as well.

4 Solidarity Based on Common Economic Interests

European unification started with the idea not only that European states should act in solidarity but also that there is a way to lure them into solidarity by creating a common European production base and market rather than by appealing to shared ideas. This was a preference that still seems commendable today. The unification of Europe was planned to pursue *economic* interests in the first place.

It is true that, already in 1949, when the Council of Europe was founded, the protection of values such as human dignity, human rights, the priority of law and peacekeeping was appealed to. In later stages these appeals were repeated, including appeals for toleration, non-discrimination, and solidarity. Nonetheless, the founders of the European unification expected Europeans to fight for these values together, eventually reaching a point where they would become economically dependent on one another. Mutual economic dependence was even considered the basis for preventing wars between European nations. Yet, despite this reliance on economic interests, the founders were well aware that they acted on political ideas rather than economic interests when they proposed a common economy for Europe. They believed that once politics had forced common economic interests on the European nations, these interests would form the best basis for further unification.

Thus, on 9 May 1950, the French government declared the following about the Schuman plan:

> Europe cannot be made at one blow, nor by simple roundup. Rather, it will arise by concrete facts which at first create a solidarity of actions ... The French government proposes to put the totality of the French-German production of coal and steel under a common Supreme Authority, in an organization open for accession by other European countries. The integration of the production of coal and steel will immediately secure the creation of common fundaments for economic development, the first stage of the European federation, and will change those branches which for a long time have been used for the production of weapons and became the most secure victims of this production. Thus created, the solidarity of this production will document that any war between France and Germany is not only unthinkable but materially impossible.[1]

[1]*Agence France Presse-Informations et Documentations*, Nr. 291, 13 May 1950. German tr. in *Europa-Archiv* (Folge 11/1950, S. 3091 f.), in: Forschungsinstitut der deutschen Gesellschaft für Auswärtige Politik e. V., Dokumente und Berichte, Bd. 17, Teilband II. Europa-Dokumente zur

The founders of the European unification made a political decision to make economic interests the motor of unification. Today, Europe is being challenged by problems distinct from those that Schuman and his colleagues were responding to, but building solidarity on the basis of shared economic interests is probably still the best policy, although Europe's present problems require new implementations.

Europe's greatest problem today, manifest in the Brexit, is that the EU may fall apart. As the refugee problem illustrates, this danger results from the pressures of economic globalization. Globalization reshuffles the elements of politics and allocates new tasks and chances to politicians and citizens. After World War II, the most urgent task was to prevent another global war from starting in Europe; today, it's to prevent another global war from starting anywhere. European politicians and citizens are challenged to shift their focus from their own navels to a global level and to coordinate their inter-European relations with their international and global relations.

Obviously, it's in the interests of all European nations and citizens to speak with one voice in the global argument about public affairs, such as the use of natural resources and the many other things that require global regulation. It is obvious, too, that the existing mechanisms used to translate the many European voices into one are insufficient. What is worse is that those that exist—the European Parliament, the European Commission and its departments and the European Council—lack the trust of European citizens. There are several reasons for the widespread distrust, but two of them seem to me to have too little attention.

First, irrespective of which societies participate in the common production and market that was the explicit program of the European unification from its outset, there are winners as well as losers. Whether in Europe or elsewhere, common markets reduce employment and increase unemployment. There are certainly chances for new employment created by common markets, but it takes time for them to materialize, and they are subjected to the same imperative of automation that rules the economy everywhere. Firms can survive only if they replace labour power with automation. Automation is accelerated by the establishment of common markets, whether it is the common market within the EU or the international common markets aimed at by TTIP, CETA and the many other projects that contribute to globalization.

The European unification has produced unemployment, too, especially in the middle and eastern European countries that had no time to adapt to the new economic conditions. It will go on producing unemployment because the extension of markets that the European unification makes possible will accelerate automation. Yet, unemployment will be resented as long as it is as humiliating as it is today, not only because it reduces income but because it marks the unemployed as economically superfluous. The European unification will be welcomed by the majority of Europeans only if unemployment is no longer stigmatized but is instead something

Frage der europäischen Einigung, ed., on behalf of the Auswärtiges Amt, Bonn 1962, S. 680 ff. My translation from the German translation.

voluntarily chosen as an opportunity to use one's free time for activities that are more valuable than employment. Unemployment can be voluntarily chosen if a basic income is introduced, along with assisting measures to prevent the basic income from becoming a source of parasitism rather than an opportunity to do things that improve the lives of individuals by promoting their self-esteem (cp. Steinvorth 2014).

Second, the European authorities, Parliament, Commission and Council have prioritized the interests of nations, represented by the Council, over the interests of regions and other local bodies that are closer to the interests of the citizens. Thus, they have blocked one important way for citizens to articulate their interests on a European level and to develop the translation of the various European voices into one that can be better heard in the global argument about the many public affairs in need of global regulation. Such blocking contradicts the principle of subsidiarity recognized in European unification documents. Yet, before elaborating on this point, there will be a remark on the status of nations, as the European nations have violated the subsidiarity principle.

5 An Alternative to Empire Versus Nation

Nation states or national governments have become obsolete today because they can no longer perform the tasks that they once, more or less (rather less), fulfilled: the enforcement of justice and the provision of public goods. Modern technology, by increasing our powers of production and destruction, has made our planet too small for national governance. To prevent more damage to the ecology and more injustice in the distribution and use of the natural resources that belong to mankind (rather than any nation or even individuals), individuals need more effective institutions than nation states. In fact, many tasks in the regulation of trade, traffic, production, education, culture and health, formerly executed by states, are now performed by international institutions, inducing some political theorists to talk of the 'disaggregation' of states along the fault lines of such tasks (Slaughter 2005). Even the most powerful states cannot avoid accepting cuts into their sovereignty by international organizations such as the United Nations. Beyond the intentions of its protagonists, Europe's unification has become a way to cope with the obsolescence of nation states. If the way is well chosen, it may become a model for global governance.

Quite a few theorists find, in the beginnings of global governance, more reasons for fear than hope. They see not only Europe but the world as being at the crossroads of two options: either become a global association ruled by universal liberal principles that enforce not only universal human rights but also the market principles of free trade and unrestricted production or stick with the unrestricted sovereignty of nation states and the principles of the Peace of Westphalia of 1648, which sanctioned an order of national self-determination. Yoram Hazony (2016) has given this view a grand frame by calling the second option empire vs nation and interpreting the Bible as the witness to God's protection of nations and their particularities against the universalism of the empires of Egypt, Babylonia, Assyria, Persia and Rome. They seduce with their power to feed humans but are, nonetheless, houses of bondage and idolatry. Today, the universalism of empire is reincarnated in liberalism and its academic elite and liberal politicians, following the previous incarnations of the Catholic Church, communism and fascism, and possibly followed by the universalism of Islam. Consequently, Hazony interprets Hitler as an adherent of empire rather than a nationalist.

Hazony's understanding of liberalism is widespread. Like Carl Schmitt, he interprets it as the ideology of a class that wants to subject the globe to its interests, which pretend to be universal but are even more particularistic than the interests of nations that don't pretend. Remarkably, Hazony and Schmitt attack liberalism even more principally than Marx. For Marx didn't deny that liberalism is universal; his criticism was that it suits current human interests more poorly than the alternative universalism of communism. However, rather than criticizing the right-wing interpretation of liberalism, I want to show that the world is presently not facing a choice between empire (whether or not associated with liberalism) and nation—there are more choices.

There is, at least, the third option of a global order that splits up the many tasks and competencies of current states and bundles them in international institutions with defined competencies for affairs that current states are obviously not made for global ecology, the distribution of natural resources, laws for international trade, the prevention and punishment of human rights violations by national or local governments and epidemic control. Such institutions would be independent of one another, so would not constitute a global state. In taking over the sovereignty of current states in the affairs they become responsible for, they would radically change the nature and power of current nation states (cp. Caney 2005: 157 ff. with further literature).

We can observe the beginnings of such an order in what Slaughter called the disaggregation of nation states. Yet, Hazony and other theorists subsume them under their concept of liberalism, implying that they will result in a uniform world. This isn't necessary at all. Leaving global ecology, the distribution of natural resources and similar subjects that need global managing to global institutions goes well together with leaving local affairs to local institutions. Benjamin Barber (2013) has argued for the advantages of governance by mayors, showing the many respects in which local politics is superior to national politics. What he cannot show is that even well-governed cities can get into conflicts and will need global institutions to settle them. Rather than opposing local to global governance, we should follow the subsidiarity principle. Subsidiarity recommends combining as much governance on the lowest level as possible, where there is as much contact with the population as possible, with governance on higher levels only where necessary. Subsidiarity is a principle that may well infuse the idea of solidarity with new life.

6 Applying Subsidiarity to Europe

Subsidiarity, as I said, is recognized in European unification documents. The European Charter of Local Self-Government, declared by the Council of Europe in 1985, promulgates the decentralization of public responsibilities (in Article 4, § 3), and the Maastricht Treaty of the EU, declared in 1992, follows the principle of subsidiarity (in Article 3b and two more places). I quote:

> Under the principle of subsidiarity, in areas which do not fall within its exclusive competence, the Union shall act only if and in so far as the objectives of the proposed action cannot be sufficiently achieved by the Member States, either at central level or at regional and local level, but can rather, by reason of the scale or effects of the proposed action, be better achieved at Union level.

National governments prevent subsidiarity from functioning. They draw powers both from the central and the local level. The founders of the European unification and their successors may have seen that national governments are an obstacle. Yet, they established the central European offices as if they were *supranational* rather than *non*-national administrations. They built the EU on the model of a nation state, only bigger, missing the opportunity to create a political association that might become a model for the world: a new order that cures national incompetence through supranational institutions that decide on affairs that nations, but also cities and mayors, are not capable of settling. In such an order, the global institutions would stay independent of one another, lacking the crucial property ascribed to sovereign statehood and the monopoly on deciding on the legitimate use of force (cp. Caney 2005: 163; Archibugi 2008: 96–112). Correspondingly, the supranational European authorities would be independent of one another and not even look like a new super-state, similar to the United States of America.

In contrast, the protagonists of the European unification looked for a capital of Europe rather than distributing the various fields of governance to the many European capitals. They put the new administrations in newly erected towers in Brussels rather than in the many historical buildings there are at the various locations of Europe. They made Europeans feel subjected to rules and regulations coming from Brussels in addition to the laws and taxations coming from their national capitals. Why didn't they split up the tasks of a government into departments located in different places? Just to give some tongue-in-cheek examples, why didn't they establish a foreign office in London, perhaps with a special bureau for relations with Russia in Warsaw? An office for common production in Wallonia or the Ruhr area? An office for a single market in Frankfurt or Milan? An office for art and culture in Paris? An office for agriculture in the Netherlands? A special agency for cheese, wine and oysters in Bordeaux? An office for military coordination in Stockholm? An office for immigration affairs in Berlin or Munich? A bureau for tourism in Athens? An office for sustainable forms of energy in Oslo, to intensify relations with non-members of the EU? An office against tax dodging in Luxembourg?

In the process of European unification, national governments must be the losers in the end; otherwise, citizens will be fleeced and bullied by municipalities, states and the EU. In fact, this is the present state of things, but by behaving like a superstate, the EU, rather than the nation states, has managed to seem like the guilty one. Once we see that national governments are obstacles to progress, it is obvious that European administrations should support the secessionist movements in European nations rather than staying neutral or even disfavouring them. Of course, they should support them under the condition that the new governments cede sovereign rights to central European institutions. Yet if this condition is fulfilled, why should European offices not shift competencies from national governments to European and regional and local offices? Thus, bureaucrats would become politicians, and regions and local communities would become strong motors for the European unification. Many European nation states—regions such as Catalonia, Scotland and Sicily—have been conquered over the course of their histories, and these might flourish with more autonomy. The same applies for cities that can look back on a history of autonomy, such as Venice, Florence, Brussels and even Hamburg. They, too, would be strengthened by a European unification motivated by citizens rather than corporations (cp. Frey 2003, 2012 on citizenship).

Such a strategy presupposes that European administrations become less dependent on the European nation states than the current ones are. This is possible if they are supported by a movement of European citizens that highlights the mutual advantages for citizens, secessionists and the European unification that the subsidiarity principle could bring. Such a movement would also bring back the idea of solidarity to its original form of an idea that regulates interaction between individuals rather than nations.

The current popularity of right-wing movements in Europe that pretend to protect the interests of nations and nation states hides the fact that identification with local areas is more widespread than identification with nations and that identification with mankind as a whole is probably growing. As Archibugi (2008: 78), referring to research by Pippa Norris (2000), states:

> Surveys indicate that about 15 percent of the world's inhabitants perceive the supranational identity as the principal one, compared with 38 percent for the national identity and 47 percent for the local identity . . . considering that the global identity is increasing among young people and those with a higher educational level, it is legitimate to ask: what results will the same survey give us in 20, 50, or 100 years' time?

The trend that Archibugi trusts in, though, depends to a considerable degree on the way representatives of global, national and local institutions act and are commented on by theorists. A lot, therefore, depends on how the European politicians and citizens will act.

References

Archibugi, D. (2008). *The global commonwealth of citizens. Toward a cosmopolitan democracy*. Princeton: Princeton University Press.

Barber, B. (2013). *If Mayors ruled the world: Dysfunctional nations, rising cities*. New Haven: Yale University Press.

Bayertz, K. (Hg.). (1998). *Solidarität*. Frankfurt: Suhrkamp.

Caney, S. (2005). *Justice beyond borders: A global political theory*. New York: Oxford University Press.

Durkheim, E. (1893). *De la division du travail social*. Paris: Alcan.

Engelhardt, H.T., Jr. (1998). Solidarität: Postmoderne Perspektiven. In K. Bayertz (Hg.), *Solidarität* (pp. 430–452). Frankfurt: Suhrkamp.

Frey, B. (2003). Flexible citizenship for a global society. *Politics, Philosophy and Economics, 2*, 93–114.

Frey, B. (2012). Flexible government for a globalized world. In D. Archibugi, M. Koenig-Archibugi, & R. Marchetti (Eds.), *Global democracy* (pp. 150–159). Cambridge: Cambridge University Press.

Hazony, Y. (2016, September 6). Nationalism and the future of western freedom. *Mosaic*.

Metz, K. H. (1998). Solidarität und Geschichte. Institutionen und sozialer Begriff der Solidarität in Westeuropa im 19. Jahrhundert. In K. Bayertz (Hg.), *Solidarität* (pp. 172–194). Frankfurt: Suhrkamp.

Norris, P. (2000). Global governance and cosmopolitan citizens. In J. S. Nye Jr. & J. D. Donahue (Eds.), *Governance in a globalizing world* (pp. 155–177). Washington, DC: Brookings.

Slaughter, A. M. (2005). *A new world order*. Princeton, NJ: Princeton University Press.

Steinvorth, U. (2014). Capitalism, unemployment, and basic income. *Homo Oeconomicus, 31*(1–2), 125–143.

Chapter 3
Solidarity in the EU: A Critique of Solidarity and of the EU

Bengt Beutler

1 Introduction

Solidarity in the European Union (EU) seems at the moment to be a painstaking if not a frustrating topic, faced with the blatant discrepancy between the wording of the treaties and the apparent or at least perceived reality. Whereas in the Treaty on the European Union (TEU) for the first time—beyond its traditional quotation in the preamble—solidarity as an explicit term has been introduced in what seems almost a grand display of firework in the wording of the treaties, in apparent contrast, the discussion of the present state of the Union identifies particularly the lack of solidarity in substantial areas. Solidarity as an explicit term extends from its inclusion in the basic values in Art. 2 TEU covering a multiple reference in Art. 3—phrasing the goals of the Union—to the solidarity clause of Art. 222 of the Treaty on the Functioning of the European Union (TFEU). And that is not to forget the reference for the external and internal politics in Art. 24 and 67 TEU. Last but not the least, the Charta of Fundamental Rights refers to solidarity in a special section including a variety of social rights. In contrast, the lack of solidarity is criticised in ever-growing problem areas, which reach from the Eurozone crisis to the quarrel about refugee quotes. We should also not forget the Brexit, which, as an expression of growing popular opposition or even as the tip of the iceberg, threatens the existence of the Union in its current state.

Being faced with such a finding is reason enough to point at the contrast between facts and norms and the importance of adopting a normative approach (Eriksen 2014), but one has to look also beyond a dogmatic and/or interest-based critical interpretation (Domurath 2012) of the text of the Treaty in order to achieve a

B. Beutler (✉)
University of Bremen, Bremen, Germany

University of Hamburg, Hamburg, Germany
e-mail: bengt.beutler@jura.uni-hamburg.de

A. Grimmel, S.M. Giang (eds.), *Solidarity in the European Union*,
DOI 10.1007/978-3-319-57036-5_3

concept of and a context for solidarity and for the EU and their mutual interdependence, which will allow for a more complex approach to the subject (Sangiovanni 2013). Is the recent creation of 'flexible solidarity' in the context of common actions in the refugee crisis just 'euro poetry' to mask concrete self-interests of certain Member States, especially their governing elites, or does it reflect a multilayered understanding of what real solidarity is in the EU?

Insofar the subject of solidarity in the EU might change to a critique of solidarity and of the European Union—and insofar and in a wider sense allude to Immanuel Kant (1724–1804) and the term critique in his basic works. In this respect, critique means to make conscious under which conditions propositions as judgments could be made. Concerning solidarity in the EU, it would mean to make conscious and shape the conditions necessary to argue about solidarity in the European Union in the adequate conceptual and contextual correlation. Though apparently interests are the driving forces in reality, they are moulded by concepts that cause them to be interpreted according to the context of others (Niżnik 2012).

Such an ambitious goal necessitates at least some preliminary remarks on issues and methods, which will be made in the following section (2). This will be followed by sections on the concept and context of solidarity (3) and of the EU (4) taking into account their mutual interdependence especially under the conditions outlined, before what can only be a preliminary conclusion (5).

2 On Issues and Methods

As perceptions and interpretations of solidarity and the EU are influenced by preconceptions and their premises, which have to be made conscious in order to determine, as far as possible, the substance of both concepts, previous understandings of the notions of solidarity and of the EU shall be briefly outlined. These will be followed by some reflections presented by an adequate methodological approach.

As to solidarity this essay starts with the observation, in which, in the academic writing about solidarity, Emile Durkheim (1858–1917) seems to be the most quoted author. Durkheim's interpretation of solidarity marks a transition from the interpretation of solidarity as a concept based on socially independent reasoning to its insertion into the context of a society that is perpetually growing more complex.

Such a comprehensive approach seems the more appropriate, as our world today seems to be to a large extent construed by men. We live in a very marked sense in a period of Anthropocene, which means that mankind has developed the clue for its own welfare as well as the potential for its destruction and even extinction in its own hands. Insofar solidarity starting from a common perception to its conceptual analysis has to pass the test of whether it is a concept to comprise this literal universal range.

Therefore, the concept of solidarity will be outlined in the following section under the heading of 'Durkheim Revisited' particularly in this evolutionary and universal context. It is evident that in the context of such an essay, this debate has to be limited to some essential features of this development and the reasons why they are preferred concentrating on the elaboration of the concept of solidarity within this specific context.

As to the EU, an exploration of its present perception should probably start with the observation that there is a variety of different approaches. Due to their sheer number, these can hardly be overlooked. Their common feature—whether popular or academic—is that they share a critical assessment of the present conditions of the Union, which could have disintegration as a consequence (e.g. Mak 2012).

Looking for a point of reference in this context, against the background of an updated and reflected version of solidarity, the questions will be, firstly, to which extent does the existence of the EU rely on solidarity and, secondly, is its present shape appropriate and properly applied in the context of solidarity? The title of this chapter will therefore be 'The European Union: Solidarity Revisited'.

It is also evident here that in the context of such an essay, this dispute has to be limited to some essential main features of this development and the reasons for their selection. It has to concentrate elaborating on the concept of the EU in the context of solidarity.

It is apparent that the outlines of such an approach, when featured within the limits of an essay like this one, can only indicate its shape and some select priorities; it cannot describe an elaborate system as a whole. But the form of an essay, in the literary sense, has a long tradition preceding the Age of Enlightenment (Montaigne 1603). Notwithstanding the importance of facts and figures, an essay requires a conceptual framework setting out key concepts and reflecting their historical context. It is not by chance that successful academic contributions focused on contemporary phenomena start with an allusion to key historical notions (Greenblatt 2011; Frankopan 2015) or end after a long day or book's work by a reflection of the impact of social theories on the interpretation of facts and figures (Picketty 2014).

This mutual interdependence of methodologically reflected key notions and their interpretations transcends the limits of academic disciplines (Ellison 2012) as well as the assumption of a scientifically based independent 'objective' position (Rorty 1984). It also contains elements of a hermeneutic circle. But, again, the conscience of such basic principles should not be disqualified as merely philosophical, but instead deemed necessary and appropriate when approaching the universal claim and content of solidarity and its basic importance (Sangiovanni 2012). It should also apply to practice, which concerns in this context the survival of the European Union.

3 Solidarity: Durkheim Revisited

In his work *The Division of Labour in Society* from 1893 (Durkheim 1893/1997), Durkheim develops the concept of solidarity in light of a self-differentiating society. *The Division of Labour in Society* was published between the publication of the two first volumes of *Das Kapital* by Karl Marx, and Durkheim saw the difference between the old and the present and future structure of solidarity in what he called an organic solidarity as emerging in an ever more complex society (as opposed to a mechanical solidarity in older societies) to produce and guarantee the necessary cohesion. As the term 'organic' already indicates Durkheim had something evolutionary in mind, that nonetheless guarantees the cohesion of society by evolving the mutual interdependence between the individual and the society in their proper social context. Notwithstanding the experience and concept of the disruptive stages of developments seen since Durkheim, this section intends to adapt his systematic approach to the present stage of changing societies against a global background. The essay will thus provide a brief survey on the way, in which solidarity in the context of social cohesion has always had a universal claim. Outlined against this background is the necessity of such a claim of universality, which, in the context of our globalised and fragmented world, can only be met by the concept of a distant or remote solidarity and followed by some remarks on the functioning of such concept as real solidarity.

Whereas solidarity, in the everyday language, connotes a moral attitude and a normative understanding, the original Latin term *solidus*, from which the term 'solidarity' is derived, means 'firm ground', which in this context means not only an objective but also a basis for a moral attitude. Independent of the relation between the reality of language and the reality of its object, this normative/basis approach marks the discussion of solidarity, which has explicitly or implicitly been a constant element since the beginning of theoretical thinking about people living together and which has accompanied the evolution of and changes in human development.

Durkheim himself originally referred to Aristotle (384–322 B.C.) albeit in a critical way (Hawkins 2004). Aristotle's statement that the human being is a political one as he has reason indicates a clear connection between the individual and society in terms of social cohesion and the beginning of a debate on the proper relation between the individual case and a general rule under the critical perspective of an open society (Popper 1945). There have been many models and variations of this theme—not at least in the monotheist religious ages (Frühbauer 2007), which continue their mark even in the present post-modern age. On the back of those religious models in modern history, a theory of central importance has been that of the social contract. An important paradigm was established by Hobbes (1588–1697) with his *Leviathan* (Hobbes 1651), which was based on the assumption that without an omnipotent state, there would be civil war between men, notwithstanding their having reason. But Hobbes and his counterpart Locke (1632–1704) relied on the idea of a final precondition outside of this system—Hobbes' reasoning does not imply that the state would abuse his peace guaranteeing the capacity to make people the object of totalitarian arbitrariness. This trace of Enlightenment can be found in Adam Smith (1723–1790) who explains empathy by referring to personal experience and goes on to discuss the proverbial baker who does not bake his bread for others but for his own sake (Smith 1776), albeit while ultimately acting in a context—which Smith previously referred to as a division of labour—of solidarity in the end.

But these examples also reveal the universal claim of solidarity: they all intend to find a clue that is applicable everywhere and at any time to describe and explain human beings as social creatures. But they rely on the other side on universalistic premises, which were mainly founded in religion or the general laws of proper reasoning. With the erosion of the general acceptance of such a universal substructure, solidarity has lost its immediate shape connecting attitudes and actions or its conception as basis and object of social cohesion. The causes and effects in an ever-growing complex society become distant from a concept covering the cohesion of society in an adequate manner, for which, therefore, the arguments quoted above do not suffice and lead to a post-modern dilemma of the non-rationality of a rationally constructed world. From the perspective of solidarity, this necessitates a concept of solidarity that covers the growing distance of interdependencies and ends and means and that is therefore articulated in the concept of distant solitary (Leggewie 2016)—matching to the articulation of distant reading (Moretti 2013), as in both cases the connecting clusters have to be invented out of clouds of incalculable data by using one's own reason and understanding.

The necessity of such a concept of a distant but universal solidarity amending and underlying an ordinary—and, at least, less reflected—understanding of solidarity is reflected by some of the urgent problems that affect us as human beings on a daily basis, be it in reading the newspaper or social media or just feeling and reflecting or, even more, suffering on account of what is happening in the world around us and/or inside of us.

One of the most urgent present aspects in terms of distant solidarity is globalisation. Economically and financially globalisation describes the effect of a self-evolving international order, which is marked by the dynamics of a self-evolving market. But as mentioned above, the market is in itself not an essential structure but a concept that has been based on the idea of solidarity in the sense that it guarantees the freedom of the citizen who has his or her own choice to buy the commodities essential for his or her living (Stehr 2007). However, this idea of solidarity implies rules of fair competition as well as of consumer protection and, as far as raw resources and the concept of nature as a whole are concerned, of the necessary protection of the environment also for further generations. The global market, on the other hand, lacks the framework of a globally binding set of rules. The former protective role of the state has been superseded by a concept of the market that is deemed to be just as essential to the global economic order as the national state. A global state, as the projection of a national one, is neither possible nor desirable. What remains is the necessity of a set of functioning rules that can be used to protect the existing system against an ever-growing imbalance in terms of the distribution of wealth and in the end against self-destruction. The problem is apparent in the project and for the moment failure of the Transatlantic Trade and Investment Partnership (TTIP) agreement.

As said above, the role of the state is indispensable in such an order. But the state itself, like the market, is not an essential body that exists by itself. This is proven by the growing number of failed states. If they are only built on sovereignty, states tend to lack the solidarity necessary for sustainability, which can only be based on the rule of law, which conversely relies on solidarity (Trifunovic 2013)—this is not to be manipulated, but articulated in a protected procedure like the democracy. But democracy itself relies on solidarity, as the rules of its functioning have to be respected, which also means, apart from protecting and respecting of the secrecy of the election, trusting the system and the programmes proclaimed within this context. The scandal of the lack of solidarity evident in the last elections in the United States leads to an election campaign based on the proclaimed distrust in this system itself.

Another important aspect of distant solidarity in democracy is that the people, as citizens, are principally supposed to be capable of making their own deliberated (not manipulated) choices. This necessitates a form of political reflection that needs to be developed by the individual within the proper institutional context of schools/education. And it needs to be supported by the media who without an underlying—albeit distant—sense of solidarity concerning their function will foster a post-factual perception also of solidarity, in which nobody can rely on any party's trustworthiness. This is important in order to escape the growing danger of state-controlled media manipulated and purely superficial democracy.

This also applies to religion, which necessitates the adequate distinction between individual belief and rational argument, as the belief in an order of creation corresponds to a deeply seated desire of man that cannot be replaced by the laws of natural science. *On the Origin of Species* (1859) by Darwin (1809–1882) was directed (albeit in the opposite direction) against such a confusion, but not against the concept of distant solidarity previously outlined, as the survival of the species of mankind relies on such a concept.

Not least of all, these arguments are applicable to the perception and practice of science itself if one deems science as a reflected and, in this sense, developed form of consciousness. When reduced to natural science in the sense of positively verifiable and quantifiable results produced by academic activities, science itself lacks distant solidarity by failing to reflect the conditions of its own organisation, procedure and perception (Chargaff 1994).

In order to avoid the unwelcome results of such loose interpretation and practice of what happens, to revisit Durkheim we should trace the elements and their mutual interdependence in terms of the evolution of a labour-divided society, transferring this understanding to our even more divided society. The elements of such a transfer are emerging individuality (which is dependent on the ever-growing complexity of society) and by the division of activities and their controllable result.

Those elements and their context can be viewed against the background of contemporary keywords in the public discussion as a form of institutionalised liberalism—if liberalism is not connoted too exclusively with its unfettered market version or a purely normative claim, which is neither granted nor guaranteed in practice to every human being.

Despite its name, individuality, from a solidarity perspective, does not imply the sole purpose of satisfying any given human desire and its instant satisfaction or conflating self-interest with selfish interest. Instead it presupposes the liberalisation and protection against external limits to evolve the potential for free choice. Free choice includes the possibility of making a wrong choice, and the individual has to learn to live with this conflict and in conflict with other individuals. This leads to the institutionalised aspect in the sense of a protected set of rules, which do not exist for themselves or insiders, but are individually experienced as a space for one's own freedom in the proverbial sense 'my home is my castle'.

Durkheim referred to the insurance system and the guilds as an example of emerging solidarity, and it is striking that the introduction of obligatory and comprehensive insurance was one of the critical political points towards the end of the nineteenth century in Europe and now in this perspective has only now reached the United States. Projected into the global order, it also means that it is necessary to find adequate institutional systems to balance the risks of an international community divided according to labour and productivity and a growing imbalance in the distribution of wealth.

The main point of reference for real solidarity in both cases is, not accidentally, the state. Instead here we have to look at the Hobbes paradigm and combine it with the basis of solidarity—i.e. a social contract between all people and binding them to the will to pursue the common good. This means that, in the end, the rule of law is a necessary precondition for any protection against arbitrariness and violation of human dignity and human rights. How this can be shaped in an appropriate way is the central question of democracy from a solidarity perspective, which leads to a proper balance between the will of the majority and the protection of a minority (including, for example the wealthy) or the dignity and/or fundamental rights of the individual.

On the other hand, forming a proper distinction between these aspects and interdependencies of solidarity relies on adequate individualisation, i.e. the evolution of the individuals and their capacity to perceive the context and needs of distant solidarity adequately. According to this perspective, it is appropriate to interpret fundamental rights as institutions, which means that they themselves are open to evolution and cooperation, as well as the distribution and protection of property and social participation. The same applies to other institutions as a background for the interpretation of the different structures of society.

To describe and solve the tensions for the individual in this mutual evolution of a civil society, Martha Nussbaum has formulated a theory transforming an originally indispensable anxiety in a proper evolutionary context (Nussbaum 2012). And one could extend a chain of reflection leading to a theory of an observer beyond any observer (Baecker 2014), meaning that any theory is implying and in this sense including some and excluding others. The conscience of this is transcluding though any borderline thus bridging the conscience of any individual and in relation to other individuals. Solidarity in this sense means to be conscious of those interdependencies via distant solidarity. This requires individuals to display what one could phrase as a kind of proverbial self-alienation, for which neither the (capitalist) relations of production nor any other external factor is exclusively the cause—instead, responsibility lies with the human condition itself. This self-alienation, in the sense of being capable and prepared to take a position different from one's immediate desire, is the basis for empathy as well as culture. It is a feature not just of a period of time or particular people but of mankind itself.

Therefore, the development of an institutional context to enable the common development of such different perspectives is the basis of survival in an increasingly complex world. Otherwise, this world is more endangered by an implosion of culture than a clash of cultures. The Thirty Years' War is a terrible historical example—as is the present war in the Near East—not to speak of the two world wars and not to forget the devastating effects of the other wars before and since, including the nightmare of an Earth-destroying nuclear war.

4 The European Union: Solidarity Revisited

The emergence of the European Union exemplifies the necessity and possibility of cultivating real solidarity to protect against such an implosion of culture and its catastrophic consequences. The failure of this in the shape of the failure of the European Union would be due to the lack of real solidarity. This will become clearer when based on a briefly outlined background of a European narrative, in relation to which the unique structure of European integration after the Second World War should become more distinct with its foundation being the basis of real solidarity. As this basis has faded away, it has to be rediscovered in the concept and practice of a revisited real solidarity and its proper institutions.

It is hard to find a link between the catastrophe of the Second World War—which, as was the case with the First World War, started in the centre of Europe—and the myth surrounding the origin of Europe, which is well known to have started with a rape. Europa was the beautiful daughter of a king in the Near East kidnapped by Zeus, who had fallen in love with her. She was taken to a Mediterranean island, which was henceforth called Europe. Zeus changed himself into a bull to seduce her and was helped by one of his sons, Hermes, who drove a cattle herd close to Europa while she was playing at the beach. Though this is a good example of solidarity in terms of the collaboration between Zeus and Hermes—who was the messenger between the gods and the people and to whom the art and method of hermeneutics still refers—it is a less good one in terms of the relation between the genders as well as that between Orient and Occident.

As to relations between the genders, it might be more appropriate to quote an early poetic narrative by Sappho from the island of Lesbos, known today in a less poetical context, who characterised love as 'bittersweet', thus describing the conscience of the human condition from its beginning. But it should not be forgotten that this feeling is complemented for the entrance of the bridegroom, as well as by the proclamation, also by Sappho, 'Raise high the roof beam, carpenters', which found its way not only into contemporary American literature (Salinger 1955/1963) but also into Christian Christmas hymns (Hopkins 1887: 70).

As to the implications for Orient and Occident, one could choose though to pass through the gateway of King David (approx. 1000 B.C.) and the transformation and reception of reason and revelation in terms of its reception and transfer by Islamic thinking in the transition from medieval to modern times, just to mention the names of Avicenna (980–1037) and Averroes (1126–1198) as the most prominent exponents (Bloch 1952/2012).

In this broader context, the Declaration of Human and Citizens' Rights after the French Revolution 1789 has a more convincing reference to solidarity. Those rights reflect a secular context of solidarity against the background of the Enlightenment—though not only of its enlightened aspects (Joas 2013), for which it should suffice to mention the problematic spread of colonisation and the two previously mentioned world wars. But the original context of highlighting the individuals and their social cohesion under the heading of human rights based on solidarity and uniting the then-old and then-new world has laid the groundwork for the phrasing of *the* West and its so-called values (Chargaff 1994).

Notwithstanding the multiple references to solidarity since the nineteenth century (Stjerno 2009), European integration post 1949 started against this background explicitly referring to a new concept of real solidarity, as the preamble of the ECSC and the preceding Schumann Declaration refer explicitly to such a concept. According to the Schumann Declaration (Schumann 1950), 'Europe will not be made all at once, or according to a single plan. It will be built through concrete achievements which first create a *real solidarity* (emphasis by the author)', whereas the third bullet of the preamble states, 'that Europe can be built only by concrete actions which create a *real solidarity* and by the establishment of common bases for economic development'.

The explicit move towards real solidarity based on concrete actions with common bases for economic development, which was the basis for European institutional integration, fell victim to the failed ratification of the Treaty on a European Defence Community. This occurred during the upheaval of the French Fourth Republic, which led to the 'Rélance Européen' of 1955. This was based mainly on the idea of economic integration, so the reference to solidarity was restricted to the preamble, which referred significantly to 'the *solidarity* which binds Europe and the overseas countries'.

Real solidarity, which was to be achieved via concrete actions, as defined in its original European context, was substituted in the academic discussion as well as in practice, with the theory of a spill-over effect on the one side and an ever-growing state-orientated discussion on the other. This discussion could develop under the protective umbrella of the east-west conflict, which itself provided a demarcation of solidarity and a contradiction of its claim to universality. Under the umbrella of this demarcation, real solidarity was emerging in the form of smallest institutional steps and actions. The result of this was that it was not possible to cope with the great changes of 1989, which saw the European Union emerge from this protective umbrella and not prepared to accept the burden of responsibility for solidarity.

Therefore, it is not a coincidence that a new renaissance of solidarity as mentioned already and outlined in detail in the treaties of 2007 can be observed. And these multiple references are, at the same time, a good example of distant solidarity, as they are covering multidimensional aspects of solidarity—centred around the goals of the Union, articulated in Article 3 of the TEU, but beginning with the traditional reference in the preamble, where we find in the fourth bullet point a reference to '*solidarity* between their peoples while respecting their history, their culture and their traditions' reaching up to the solidarity clause in Art. 222 TFEU, according to which, 'the Union and its Member States shall act jointly in a spirit of *solidarity* if a Member State is the object of a terrorist attack or the victim of a natural or man-made disaster'. In Article 2 reference is made to solidarity in the second sentence referring to 'the common basis for values to all Member states in a society in which pluralism, non-discrimination, tolerance, justice, *solidarity* and equality between women and men prevail', whereas according to the second sentence of the third enumerated section (beginning with the common market) of Article 3, 'the Union shall promote *solidarity* between generations'. According to the third section in reference to the context of economic and regional cohesion, '*solidarity* among Member States shall ensure that Europe's cultural heritage is safeguarded and enhanced'. Finally in sentence five, which concerns the external relations, the EU 'shall contribute to peace, security, the sustainable development of the Earth, *solidarity* and mutual respect among peoples'.

Following the impact of explicit solidarity on external relations, Article 24 stipulates in section 2 that 'the Union shall conduct, define and implement a common foreign and security policy, based on the development of mutual political *solidarity* among Member States'. In Article 67, in the context of establishing an area of freedom, security and justice, the TFEU stipulates in Article 67 that by respecting fundamental rights and the different legal systems and traditions of the Member States, the Union shall 'ensure the absence of internal border controls for persons and shall frame a common policy on asylum, immigration and external border control based on *solidarity* between Member States, which is fair towards third-country nationals'. Whereas Chapter IV of the Charter of Fundamental Rights, under the title of 'Solidarity' extends from workers' rights to consumer protection, the preamble articulates the conditions of a comprehensive concept of solidarity, using the following phrasing: 'Conscious of its spiritual and moral heritage, the Union is founded on the indivisible, universal values of human dignity, freedom, equality and *solidarity*; it is based on the principles of democracy and the rule of law. It places the individual at the heart of its activities, by establishing the citizenship of the Union and by creating an area of freedom, security and justice'.

Whereas the other examples quoted refer to solidarity in a different context and sometimes in a rather distant way, the preamble of the Charter presents solidarity as a basis of the EU that is in line with human dignity and fundamental rights, thus representing one of the most articulated concepts of solidarity found in public international law. Though considered and shaped in a more public process, the development of fundamental rights has been influenced decisively by the jurisdiction of the European Court of Justice—thus solidarity has gained an institutional shape through the combination of its distant goals with a real appearance.

As can be seen, European integration was originally explicitly connected to and discussed alongside real solidarity, which was deemed a result of concrete actions together with economic welfare. Those concrete actions as well as real solidarity were not substituted by the undeniable gains of the common market in the meantime, although an institutional setting was shaped already with the beginning of European integration. However, this original institutional setting has changed dramatically from an evolutionary perspective. This concerns the role of the Parliament as well as the decision-making procedure of the Council and the creation of new institutions (viz. the European Central Bank and the emergence of the European Council besides the former Council of Ministers). The cohesion of this system has been based on economic growth as well as the jurisdiction of the European Court of Justice (ECJ), particularly its creation of the former European Community (and now the EU) as a 'new legal order' with the creation of fundamental rights as one important consequence. But the Court's legitimacy is not sufficient to replace the political legitimacy or model the Union as a convincing example of real solidarity.

The critical area in this context remains, in fact, the solidarity of the Member States (both among themselves and towards the EU) and their perception and pursuit of different interests, which sometimes means the EU is perceived as a threat to national identity. The solution to this conflict cannot be achieved through the elimination or dissolution of the states of the Member States in order to pursue the utopia of a European republic (Guérot 2016). It has to take into account the central function of the state in the context of solidarity, as discussed above under section 3. The institutional framework of the EU needs to be more transparent not only in a democratic sense—which, as we have seen, also relies on solidarity (Habermas 2013)—but also by opening the concept of the state to interpretation, as it is an institution operating in a larger context (Hodgson 2006). As the ECJ has stated already at an early stage, the states and their agencies are part of the institutional system not in the sense of being subordinated, but instead in the sense of being coordinated for their mutual benefit, i.e. in solidarity. Thus solidarity is the comprehensive and universal concept used to further the corporate good of all by promoting proper balance and distribution between the Member States (as well as their regions) and the institutional setting of the Union. So, the people have to decide about solidarity in the EU in a normative sense, by using solidarity as the basis of their decision-making, which means they have to be aware of this context. This perspective detaches the perception and pursuit of common goods from the principally as exclusively perceived competence of the state and its notion and shares it with the institutional setting of the Union, if this is more adequate to transform distant solidarity to real solidarity.

From this perspective some of the recent crisis might be interpreted in a more appropriate way. The Brexit did not lack reference to solidarity, but for the majority of those calling for it blamed the Union for the lack of solidarity felt by the losers of a capital-driven globalisation. This reference to solidarity resembles other proclamations in the US presidential election which have not been connected to the EU. On the other hand, many of those calling for Britain to remain in the EU based their arguments on the use of quantitatively based calculations as a benchmark, giving the opponents the argument, or at least the impression, that the EU was an example of a capitalist-driven liberalism. But who cared for the younger generation or the national identity (of which the sovereignty of parliament from the beginning of British membership constituted an important point of contention)—just to mention a few other references to solidarity? On the other hand, one could quote the exit clause in the Treaty as an example of distant solidarity, as, for the first time in a closer state-based cooperation, it opens up the possibility under the rule of law. In contrast, one could ask to which kind of solidarity in this context the partisans of the referendum on the Brexit were attached—not to speak of the participation of the British Parliament itself in this process. On the whole the Brexit remains a sad mixture of justified criticism, ignorance, if not arrogance, on both sides, and lots of selfish personal interests, but in no way of real solidarity.

The appeal to solidarity in the Eurozone crisis (Fernandes and Rubio 2012; Hilpold 2015) should keep in mind that the Euro had a predecessor in the ECU (European Currency Unit) to stabilise the common market. This formed a basis for distant solidarity and allowed all the Member States to agree, through concrete actions, on real solidarity. This did not allow stronger Member States a *carte blanche* to pursue their own interests and invoke the solidarity of the weaker ones in the event of a violation of the commonly agreed stability criteria. On the contrary, it remains necessary for them to find a convincing balance between gains and losses within the Euro system (for which the quarrel about the introduction of Eurobonds is not a convincing example).

As to the quarrel about refugee quotas, the recently invented and proclaimed concept of flexible solidarity has to take into account the wording of Article 67 of the TFEU, which refers to the *spirit of solidarity* between the Member States and how this should be used to achieve common action, as well as the need to combine this with concrete actions. This also includes the global dimension of solidarity, as, for instance, one possible effect of the free-trade agreements established by the EU on the productivity and living conditions in developing countries and emerging nations is a possible deterioration of living conditions and/or raise in the number of emigrants.

And also the reserve of the Walloon Region concerning the EU-Canada Comprehensive Economic and Trade Agreement (CETA) could be discussed more appropriately in the perspective of a distant transformed into a real solidarity—particularly on the back of the failed attempt of the TTIP, which lacked real solidarity not only in terms of transparency (which seems to be a more notorious problem of institutional inclusion also by the European institutions, as the elaboration of the treaty concerning the accession of the EU to the European Convention on Human Rights (ECHR) sadly also exemplifies) but also concerning the right balance between economic needs, purely capitalistic interests and—last but not the least—common good-orientated needs.

Any analysis, in this way, needs a proper methodological approach in the form of an integrated European science, for which it does not suffice to combine the individual branches of science (mainly jurisprudence, politics and economic sciences). European science combines different perspectives, both internal and external, as well as different disciplines to enable a universal, clear and intuitively accessible (though not imperialistic) approach fusing distant and real solidarity. To compete with the growing tendency to simplify the context of solidarity as images of one's own welfare, European science, in the sense of furthering consciousness, needs to reinvent the attractiveness of distant solidarity by shaping it as real solidarity. And the same applies even more to the media.

'Europe is a political body—can you help shape it?' is the text of a poster featured at one of the last Biennales in Venice. The words 'Europe is' and 'can you help shape it?' are printed in bold, whereas 'a political body' is printed in a pale colour, so it can only be read when there is back lighting. This composition somehow reflects the present shape and problems of Europe and perfectly matches Salvatore Settis' proclamation about Venice 'Si Venezia muore' (Settis 2014/2016). Settis describes Venice as *the* human biotope. It embodies the cultural heritage of mankind and is threatened by a purely quantitative, finance-based thinking, which he positions in contrast to the right of every citizen to national culture (which is upheld in the post-war Italian constitution). This appeal is an example of distant solidarity becoming real solidarity through concrete actions that are based on solidarity and have the objective of achieving solidarity, which could also apply to the EU.

5 A Critique of Solidarity and of the European Union

A critique of solidarity and of the European Union that involves interpreting and applying both concepts by going beyond a dogmatic interpretation (*lege artis)* or focusing on a purely instrumental way of realising interests or expectations without reflecting their basis and context reveals a striking similarity between both concepts—or better still a mutual dependence.

Whereas solidarity develops its content through the inherent elements of individualisation and socialisation—as well as, at the same time, its interdependence with society and its differentiation, thus implying a universal claim, whose distant shape needs to be translated into real solidarity—the EU is the first functioning institutional action system based on real solidarity embodied by actions that go beyond the self-interest-based cooperation of states claiming their own exclusive sovereignty. But to function under the conditions of the real world, the EU needs to take the concrete actions necessary to use the historically unique opportunities made available by its basic institutional structure. The mere reference to the values of the Union does not suffice without concrete actions to illustrate their importance to the citizens particularly in the member states. Regardless of the dark sides of the Enlightenment, and even on the contrary conscious of the possible risks of purely instrumental and one-dimensional rationality, the text of the poster mentioned above seems not to be the worst way to interpret *The Issue of Solidarity in the European Union* (Raspotnik et al. 2012) in the perspective of *Enlightenment—The European Project* (Geier 2012). The notion of a critique of solidarity and of the EU is not just a statement of one crisis more, but also an encouraging invitation calling for man's emergence from his self-imposed immaturity—this is not just directed towards the people and citizens of Europe but even more towards those who are responsible for translating and communicating distant reality into real solidarity through concrete actions. Naturally this conclusion cannot substitute those concrete actions necessary to be taken by all concerned but should pave their way by a better understanding—and hence realisation—of the necessity of such concrete actions.

References

Baecker, D. (2014). *Beobachter unter sich – Eine Kulturtheorie* [Observers amongst themselves – A theory of culture]. Berlin: Suhrkamp.

Bloch, E. (1952/2012). *Avicenna und die aristotelische Linke*, Berlin; *Avicenna and the Aristotelian Left* [translated into Arabic by M. Turki]. Tunis: The Tunisian Academy of Sciences Letters and Art, Beit al-Hikma.

Chargaff, E. (1994). *Armes Amerika – Arme Welt.* Stuttgart: Klett-Cotta.

Darwin, C. (1859). *The origin of species.* London: John Murray.

de Montaigne, M. (1603). Essais, S. Milange, Bordeaux (1580). *The essays* (by John Florio), E. Blount, London.

Domurath, I. (2012). The three dimensions of solidarity in the EU legal order: Limits of the judicial and legal approach. *Journal of European Integration, 35*(4), 459–475.

Durkheim, E. (1893/1997). *De la division du travail social: Étude sur l'organisation des sociétés supérieures.* Paris: Félix Alcan; *The division of labour in society*, New York.

Ellison, M. (2012). *Reinventing social solidarity across Europe.* Bristol: Policy Press.

Eriksen, E. O. (2014). *Die Normativität der Europäischen Union.* Freiburg: Karl Aber.

Fernandes, S., & Rubio, E. (2012). Solidarity within the Eurozone: How much, what for, for how long? *Notre Europe.* Accessed May, 2012, from http://www.notreeurope.eu/uploads/tx_publication/SolidarityEMU_S.Fernandes-E.Rubio_NE_Feb2012.pdf

Frankopan, P. (2015). *The silk roads – A new history of the world.* London: Bloomsbury.

Frühbauer, J. (2007). *Solidarität in Islam, Buddhismus und Konfuzianismus. Bausteine für eine interreligiöse Sozialethik, Jahrbuch für christliche Sozialwissenschaften* (pp. 105–120). Münster: Institut für chirstliche Sozialwissenschaften.

Geier, M. (2012). *Aufklärung. Das europäische Projekt (Enlightenment. The European project).* Reinbek bei Hamburg: Rowohlt

Greenblatt, S. (2011). *The swerve – How the world became modern.* New York: W.W. Norton.

Guérot, U. (2016). *Warum Europa eine Republik werden muss.* Bonn: J.H.W. Dietz Nachf.

Habermas, J. (2013, March). *Democracy, solidarity and the European crisis, lecture* held at the University of Leuven. https://www.kuleuven.be/euroforum/docs/pdf/click.php?id=14

Hawkins, M. (2004). Why begin with Aristotle? Durkheim on solidarity and social morphology. *Durkheimian Studies/Études Durkheimiennes, (New Series), 10*(2), 21–37.

Hilpold, P. (2015). Understanding solidarity within EU law: An analysis of the 'islands of solidarity' with particular regard to Monetary Union. *Yearbook of European Law 2015, 34*(1), 257–285.

Hobbes, T. (1651). *Leviathan.* London: Adrew Crooke.

Hodgson, G. M. (2006). What are institutions? *Journal of Economic Issues, XL*(1), 1–25.

Hopkins, J. H. (Ed.). (1887). *Great hymns of the church compiled by the late right reverend John Freeman Young*. New York: James Pott & Company.
Joas, H. (2013). *The sacredness of the person, a new genealogy of human rights*. Georgetown: Georgetown University Press.
Leggewie, C. (2016). *Anti-Europäer, – Breivik, Dugin, al-Suri & Co* [Anti-Europeans – Breivik, Dugin, al-Suri & Co]. Berlin: Suhrkamp.
Mak, G. (2012). *Wat als Europa klapt*. Amsterdam: Uitgeverij Atlas; Was, wenn Europa scheitert (by G. Seferens). München: Panteon Verlag.
Moretti, F. (2013). *Distant reading*. London: Verso.
Niżnik, N. (2012). The concept of solidarity in the European integration discourse. In M. Ellison (Ed.), *Reinventing social solidarity across Europe*. Bristol: University Press.
Nussbaum, M. (2012). *The new religious intolerance. Overcoming the politics of fear in an anxious age*. Harvard: Belknap Press.
Picketty, T. (2014). *Capital in the twenty-first century*. Harvard: Belknap Press.
Popper, K. (1945). *The open society and its enemies*. London: Routledge.
Raspotnik, A., Jacobs, M., & Ventura, L. (2012, August 8). The issue of solidarity in the European Union. *TEPSA BRIEF*.
Rorty, R. (1984). Solidarity or objectivity? In J. Rajchman & C. West (Eds.), *Post-analytic philosophy*. New York: Columbia University Press.
Salinger, J. D. (1955/1963). *Raise high the roof beams, carpenters*. New York; first published in *The New Yorker*, 19 November 1955, p. 51.
Sangiovanni, A. (2012). Solidarity in the European Union: Problems and prospects. In J. Dickson & P. Eleftheriadis (Eds.), *The philosophical foundations of European Union law* (pp. 384–411). Oxford: Oxford University Press.
Sangiovanni, A. (2013). Solidarity in the European Union. *Oxford Journal of Legal Studies, 33*(2), 213–241.
Schumann, R. (1950). *EUROPA – The Schuman Declaration* – 9 May 1950, third paragraph, first sentence. https://europa.eu/european-union/about-eu/
Settis, S. (2014/2016). *Se Venezia muore*. Turin: Einaudi, 2014. If Venice dies. New York: New Vessel Press.
Smith, A. (1776). *An inquiry into the nature and causes of the wealth of nations*. London: Methuen.
Stehr, N. (2007). *Moral markets: How knowledge and affluence change consumers and products*. London: Routledge.
Stjerno, S. (2009). *Solidarity in Europe: The history of an idea*. Cambridge: Cambridge University Press.
Trifunovic, M. (2013). *The principle of solidarity: A restatement of John Rawls' law of peoples*, Dissertation. Humboldt-University Berlin.

Chapter 4
Solidarity as a Legal Concept

Markus Kotzur

1 Introduction

The narrative of "ever-deepening integration" in an "ever closer Union" expressed for quite a long time the European polity's integrationist creed and was shared by many Euro-optimist, if not idealist Union citizens.[1] This, however, does not seem to be the case anymore. Along with the recent crises-driven eurosceptic challenges of this narrative, the fundamental principles and values it is based upon are challenged, too—if not called into question in general.[2] In particular solidarity[3] is at stake, when the financial crisis divides rescue policy supporters from Grexit advocates, or the refugee crisis provokes strong tendencies of re-nationalization in sovereignty-centred "splendid isolation".[4] Is the willingness or reluctance towards burden-sharing the litmus test for European integration in times of solidarity crises?[5] Since solidarity itself is both a contentious and contested[6] idea, the conflicts

[1]See, e.g., Giegerich et al. (2014), Häberle and Kotzur (2016, pp. 939).

[2]As to the Union's value orientation *R. Geiger*, in: id./D.-E. Khan/M. Kotzur, European Union Treaties. A Commentary, 2015, Art. 2 TEU para 1 et subsequent.

[3]The following reflections on solidarity are partly based upon Kotzur and Schmalenbach (2014, pp. 68).

[4]See *Theresa May's* Brexit-Speech on Jan. 17, 2017: "A little over six months ago, the British people voted for change. They voted to shape a brighter future for our country. They voted to leave the European Union and embrace the world" (http://www.independent.co.uk/news/uk/home-news/full-text-theresa-may-brexit-speech-global-britain-eu-european-union-latest-a7531361.html, last visit on Jan. 19, 2017).

[5]Christopoulos and Souvlis (2016).

[6]Wiener (2014).

M. Kotzur (✉)
University of Hamburg, Hamburg, Germany

Europa-Kolleg Hamburg, Hamburg, Germany
e-mail: markus.kotzur@jura.uni-hamburg.de

A. Grimmel, S.M. Giang (eds.), *Solidarity in the European Union*,
DOI 10.1007/978-3-319-57036-5_4

might reach even further and ground even deeper. Keeping all these uncertainties, ambiguities and complexities in mind, the numerous references to solidarity in the Lisbon treaty leave the lawyer with somewhat uneasy feelings[7] and raise some decisive questions: which overall expectations, moral obligations, political assumptions and normative force can be attributed to what the Union's primary law calls "solidarity"?

2 The Concept of Solidarity

The concept of solidarity, even though dating back to the French Revolution's programmatic leitmotif "Liberté, Égalité, Fraternité"[8] and already being enshrined in the 1804 "Code Civil", is rather young—at least compared to other *grand* ideas/ideals in philosophy or social history: It was the French Sociologist *Émile Durkheim* who, based on sociological facts, provided a first comprehensive scientific elaboration.[9] Many other scholars followed, so in modern sociology *Talcott Parsons*, in the field of law in general *Leon Duguit* and in the field of public international law in particular *Georges Scelle*.[10] These scientists not only tried to "translate" the all-too-often neglected revolutionary ideal of "fraternité"—*Anthony Giddens* by the way found it amazing how little scholarly attention has been paid to establishing a precise meaning for solidarity[11]—into modern-day language[12] but also focused on conceptualizing solidarity as a *mode of organizing* a *polity* and, where such a polity transcends the nation state, as a mode of *fostering transnational cooperation*. So conceived, solidarity reaches far beyond certain moral obligations the individual might have towards the other members of her or his polity in cases of necessity/emergency[13]—even though prevailing tendencies to restrain solidarity to the private sphere (the family, friends, the workplace with its semi-private social bonds, etc.), smaller political entities (such as the neighbourhood, municipalities, etc.) or the national "Schicksalsgemeinschaft"[14] should not be underestimated. Not only has the refugee crisis taught the lesson that belonging has a strong emotional impact on

[7]Schmalenbach, et al. (2016) and below footnote 16.

[8]Häberle (1990, pp. 35).

[9]*É. Durkheim*, De la division du travail social, 1893; see *A. v. Bogdandy*, Opening Address, in: R. Wolfrum/Ch. Kojima (eds.), Solidarity: A Structural Principle of International Law, 2010, pp. 1 at 1.

[10]For reference see ibidem.

[11]Giddens (2007, p. 112).

[12]Krüger (1971, pp. 249).

[13]*U. Haltern*, Finalität, in: v. Bogdandy/Bast, Europäisches Verfassungsrecht, 2nd ed. 2009, pp. 279 at 323 (with reference to ICJ, case C-184/99—*Grzelczyk*, ibidem para 44).

[14]*D. Senghaas*, Weltinnenpolitik—Ansätze für ein Konzept, in: Europaarchiv 1992, pp. 643 speaks of a global "Schicksalsgemeinschaft" (p. 646 and subsequent).

solidarity,[15] it also has shown that many would disagree to describe a European demos as a "People composed of Others" (*J. Weiler*).[16] Does solidarity nevertheless have the potential to be or to become a new constitutional paradigm for the EU (*M. Ross*)[17]?

Constitutional law and theory have established some tradition to conceive solidarity as programme and/or principle. They paved the way for shifting the solidarity paradigm from the domestic to the regional (European) and to the global plane.[18] Notwithstanding this transnational progress of *ideas* as well as *ideals*, *Kirsten Schmalenbach, Sonja Puntscher Riekmann* and *Doris Wydra* rightfully outline in a research proposal for the "Salzburg Centre of European Union Studies" that the notion "solidarity"—rather "lavishly if not inflationary" used in the Lisbon Treaty—is ambiguous in its content: solidarity can simply be a "moral orientation" of pre-legal nature or amount to a "legal duty".[19] It can be used in a purely *descriptive* or decisively *prescriptive*, thus *normative* way. Solidarity can draw a real-world picture or call for a better world. Going even further, it can programmatically and purposefully be used as a means of *policy making, constitution building* and *social engineering*.[20] Different *concepts of society* might go hand in hand with different *notions of solidarity*: e.g. the Christian ideal of charity or, in the Islamic world, the principle of "Zakat", both demanding to give a fair share of one's wealth to the poor and the needy.[21] After 1789, as already stated, solidarity's predecessor "fraternité" was conceived as political, philosophical and legal concept within post-revolutionary France.[22] In the age of constitutionalism, many other European legal and political idea(l)s followed the French example. Public international law stepped in later but it did so consequently.

In his influential studies on solidarity, *K. Wellens* refers to the conceptual foundation of solidarity in public international law as some 40 years earlier laid down by *Michel Virally*: solidarity has first been a simple notion, then a political

---

[15]Mavelli and Wilson (2016).

[16]Weiler (2000).

[17]Ross (2010, p. 23).

[18]Wellens and R. St. J. Macdonald (2005); Wellens (2010); for further orientation: Volkmann (1998); aus der (europarechtlichen) Literatur *A. v. Bogdandy*, Europäische Prinzipienlehre, in: ders. (ed.), Europäisches Verfassungsrecht, Berlin u. a. 2003, 149 ff., 182 ff.; vorher bereits *Ch. Tomuschat*, Solidarität in Europa, in: Capotorti u. a. (ed.), Liber Amicorum P. Pescatore, Baden-Baden 1987, S. 729 ff.; *R. Bieber*, Solidarität als Verfassungsprinzip, in: v. Bogdandy/ Kadelbach (ed.), Solidarität und Europäische Integration, München 2002, 38 ff.

[19]http://www.uni-salzburg.at/portal/page?_pageid=465,1835853&_dad=portal&_schema=PORTAL (last visit May 15, 2016).

[20]A term introduced by *K. Popper* in his famous 1945 work on "The Open Society and its Enemies".

[21]*D. Campanelli*, Solidarity, Principle of, in: MPEIL 2012 para 5; in general *U. Volkmann*, Solidarität—Programm und Prinzip der Verfassung, 1998, pp. 52.

[22]Ibidem.

and finally a legal principle in public international law.[23] The principle, having, as *A. Peters* points out, a "strung ethical underpinning", is for sure "value driven".[24] This, however, is true for many, if not all legal principles—human dignity first and foremost—and does not establish a verdict against (binding) legal quality. Another feature which solidarity shares with many public international law principles is its multi-functionality and its multi-layered character (*M. Ross*),[25] not allowing any essentialist definition but requiring context-sensitive interpretations.[26] *Malcom Ross* convincingly argues that solidarity has a "persistent but diverse presence" in EU Law.[27]

Solidarity is perceived as a prerequisite for integration; it is contextualized with democracy, subsidiarity, loyalty, sustainability and citizenship. It is concretized in the human rights context as social right to something. It is interpreted as a means to reconcile competition-based market integration and social welfare orientation. More generally, solidarity as a *legal principle* has to be distinguished in a *negative* and a *positive* component. Negative solidarity is seen as mere response to certain dangers or events, whereas positive solidarity creates, consequent upon the previous negative notion, joint rights and obligations.[28] Solidarity operates as a principle to achieve common goals; sometimes it imposes common, sometimes it imposes differentiated obligations or responsibilities: it encompasses procedural and operational, substantive and normative elements, values and legal obligations (respectively entitlements).[29]

3 Legal Substantiations of Solidarity Within the EU and Beyond

This becomes very clear when focusing on the law of the EU as a form of regional public international law with a specific constitutional quality. Art. 2 TEU, addressing the Union's basic values, declares that these values derive from a society upholding, among others, the principle of solidarity.[30] Besides plain economic

[23]Wellens (2010, pp. 3 at 4); *M. Virally*, Le rôle des "principes" dans le développement du droit international, in: Recueil d'études de droit international en hommage à Paul Guggenheim, 1968, pp. 531 at 542/543; more generally *J. E. Viñuales*, 'The Secret of Tomorrow': International Organization through the Eyes of Michel Virally, in: he European Journal of International Law Vol. 23 (2012), pp. 543.

[24]Peters (2006, pp. 579 at 601).

[25]Ross (2010, pp. 23).

[26]Wolfrum, (2006, pp. 1087).

[27]Ross (2010, pp. 23).

[28]Wellens (2010, pp. 3 at 4).

[29]Wolfrum (2006, pp. 1087), Wellens (2010, pp. 3 at 13).

[30]*R. Geiger*, in: id./D.-E. Khan/M. Kotzur, European Union Treaties. A Commentary, 2015, Art. 2 TEU para 4; *Ch. Calliess*, Europa als Wertegemeinschaft—Integration und Identität durch

interdependence, a political community needs a more demanding "bonum commune" orientation which not only reflects the different national notions of *their* "common good" but also has a clear focus on a *common European* "bonum commune".[31] Beyond that, the "bonum commune" ideal might—in today's globalized world more so than ever before—even require a *Kantian* focus on humankind as such.[32] Consequently, Art. 3 TEU ranks the "bonum commune"-relevant solidarity among the Union's aims and purposes, promoting cooperative solidarity among the Member States (para 3) and in the global realm (para 5).[33] In the still intergovernmental field of the common foreign and security policy,[34] "mutual political solidarity" is a prerequisite for being capable of acting at all; see Art. 24 (2) and 24 (3) TEU. Not surprisingly, solidarity and loyalty are of (and stem from) the same spirit as Art. 24 (3) TEU, which refers to a "spirit of loyalty and mutual solidarity"[35]—re-emphasized when it comes to the voting procedure (Art. 31 TEU). In a field where unanimous decision-making is required, the risk of a blockade or obstructive actions of the Member States, refraining from a vote, would otherwise be too high.[36]

The mutual defence clause enshrined in Art. 42 (7) TEU can—like the collective self-defence option in Art. 51 UN Charter—also be seen as an expression of solidarity ("mutual aid and assistance") but is, of course, much more narrowly shaped.[37] In a broader sense, all policies in the area of freedom, security and justice are based upon the principle of solidarity which thus becomes a *constitutional element* within the European Union's cooperative architecture [Art. 67 (2), 80 TFEU].[38] Not only within times of crisis, economic integration—beyond the

europäisches Verfassungsrecht?, JZ 2004, pp. 1033; *Ch. Mandry*, Europa als Wertegemeinschaft, 2009.

[31]On the current debate, see the examples discussed in: A. Héritier (ed.), Common Goods: Reinventing European and International Governance, 2002.

[32]On the humankind orientation of Kantian legal theory: *I. Kant*, Metaphysik der Sitten, 1797, Einleitung in die Metaphysik der Sitten. For *Kant* it is the quality of being part of humankind that gives the individual his or her inalienable freedom. However, already for *Kant* the personal freedom of the individual was in practical need for an "allgemeines Gesetz" that could harmonize the spheres of freedom of the various individuals: "Tritt in einen Zustand, worin Jedermann das Seine gegen jeden Anderen gesichert sein kann", the so-called "Lex iustitiae", ibid. Eintheilung der Rechtslehre, lit. A.

[33]von Bogdandy (2009, pp. 13 at 69–71); furthermore Lais (2007).

[34]Smith (2008).

[35]Regelsberger and Kugelmann (2012). It is this very interdependence of solidarity and loyalty that make the Union a "Solidargemeinschaft", see Häberle and Kotzur (2016, pp. 82).

[36]*E. Regelsberger/D. Kugelmann*, in: R. Streinz (ed.), EUV/AEUV, 2nd ed. 2012, Art. 31 TEU para 6.

[37]Myrdal and Rhinard (2010); J. *Wouters/S. Bijlmakers/K. Meuwissen*, The EU as a Multilateral Security Actor after Lisbon: Constitutional and Institutional Aspects, Leuven Centre for Global Governance Studies, Working Paper no. 80, February 2012, pp. 9; in general *S. v. Kielmannsegg*, Die Verteidigungspolitik der Europäischen Union, 2005.

[38]Kotzur (2015).

Monetary Union, too—requires solidarity when grave difficulties arise (Art. 122 TFEU and 143 TFEU).[39] A "spirit of solidarity" is present in the field of energy policies as well.[40] Most obviously, terrorist attacks and natural or man-made disasters require "solidarity" which is literally made explicit by Title VII, Art. 222 TFEU, using the phrase "Solidarity Clause" as headline.

When 196 (1) TFEU obliges the Union to "encourage cooperation between Member States in order to improve the effectiveness of systems for preventing and protecting against natural or man-made disasters", it *implicitly* presupposes a "spirit of solidarity" between the cooperating entities.[41] In that regard, Art. 222 (1) TFEU is more outspoken. Stating that "the Union and its Member States act jointly in a spirit of solidarity", the wording discloses a "supranational intent" of the solidarity clause, clearly going beyond merely intergovernmental obligations.[42] The Union's legal architecture corresponds with this "supranational intent". It displays a multi-layered structure of overlapping "constitutional regimes" often referred to as "multi-level constitutionalism"[43] or "constitutional pluralism".[44] The so-described multi-layered structure sees human relationships (as well as order building mechanisms necessary for human relationships in freedom, peace and security) no longer dependent on just one legal system but on a *mixed texture* of multiple legal orders. This order has to take into account, that different (and differentiated) sets of norms do exist on the subnational, the national and the regional plane—overall framed by public international law or other relevant transnational regimes. In parallel, EU law has a strong effect on domestic regulation (in decentralized political systems on all subnational levels as well).[45] From all these observations, it becomes clear that EU membership implies "reciprocal intrusiveness", which might at the end of the day cause "a powerful sense of solidarity"[46]—a sense however of *multi-level solidarity*.

In European Union Law as well as in public international law, finding out the relevant meaning and normative relevance of solidarity might become easier if one focuses on the *nexus* between solidarity and other paradigmatic (or even constitutional) principles of the relevant legal orders. One example that holds true in particular for the law of international or supranational organizations might be the following: loyalty has to be clearly distinguished from solidarity,[47] but without a

[39]See, e.g., *U. Häde*, Die Wirtschafts- und Währungsunion im Vertrag von Lissabon, EuR 2009, pp. 200; *id.*, Haushaltsdisziplin und Solidarität im Zeichen der Finanzkrise, EuZW 2009, pp. 399.

[40]*J. F. Braun*, EU Energy Policy under the Treaty of Lisbon Rules: Between a new policy and business as usual, in: Politics and Institutions, EPIN Working Papers, No. 31/2011.

[41]For the general scope of EU disaster preparedness, disaster response and civil protection, see also the Statements of the Commission, e.g. COM (2010) 600 final.

[42]Myrdal and Rhinard (2010, p. 6).

[43]Pernice (1999, 2009).

[44]Walker (2002, pp. 317), Maduro (2001, p. 21).

[45]Lüder (2009, pp. 251).

[46]Biscop (2005, p. 124).

[47]Hatje (2001, pp. 16).

minimum degree of solidarity, loyalty would theoretically be inconceivable and practically be impossible. Even more inseparably intertwined are solidarity and legitimacy. The successful integration of any polity, national, regional or global depends on what *J. H. H. Weiler* in his famous essay on "The Transformation of Europe" has called "social legitimacy": "What becomes crucial for the success of the integration process is the social legitimacy of the new integrated polity despite the loss of total control over the integrated policy areas by each polity."[48]

Another *nexus* or *systematic context* is quite obvious: solidarity has a human rights basis not only with reference to "solidarity rights" but also when focusing on the human rights-based "responsibility to protect".[49] In that regard, the European Union wanting to promote human rights, democracy and the rule of laws in its external policies can learn from the international community. UN-General Assembly Resolution 59/193 on the "Promotion of a democratic and equitable international order" states under number 4 lit. f: "Solidarity, as a fundamental value, by virtue of which global challenges must be managed in a way that distributes costs and burdens fairly, in accordance with basic principles of equity and social justice, and ensures that those who suffer or benefit the least receive help from those who benefit the most." The Declaration expressly contextualizes solidarity with equity and social justice. Last but not least, solidarity can be seen as "a way of rationalizing collective responses towards a range of new threats"[50]—and of old threats, too, the maintenance of peace and security gives, as stated above, to most striking example.[51]

4 Solidarity as a Constitutional Paradigm

The way EU law uses solidarity qualifies the concept as *constitutional paradigm.* It frames, contextualized with citizenship and loyalty, duties of membership, and it displays, contextualized with human rights, universal tendencies. In its most extensive—and most idealistic—reading, solidarity addresses the needs and aspirations of humankind as such[52] and requires "a humanization of International Law" in general. In a more limited that is to say integration-oriented reading, solidarity is—even if that may sound paradoxical—both a prerequisite for and a means of integration. Solidarity for sure is not a European "deus ex machina", but it is much more than altruistic

[48]Weiler (1991).

[49]Report of the International Law Commission on Intervention and State Sovereignty (ICISS) (2001), UN Doc. GA/Res. 60/1 (2005), Stahn (2007, pp. 99), von Arnauld (2009, pp. 11).

[50]Konstantinides (2011, p. 7).

[51]Slaughter (2005, pp. 619).

[52]Already a classic is *C.W. Jenks*, The Common Law of Mankind, London, 1958; more recently *Antônio A. Cançado Trindade*, International Law for Humankind: Towards a New Jus Gentium, 2010.

semantics about economic re-distribution. As shown above, solidarity found manifold legal substantiations in EU primary law which can be made effective in court proceedings. Being a constitutional paradigm, solidarity displays a reasonably selfish motivation of how to build a politically stable integrated order. As the great European Jacques Delors said: "Solidarity mechanisms are not based on pure generosity but on enlightened self-interest".[53] Whenever we hear the voices of irresponsible populists, trying to destroy the European project, we should never forget that we live in - and have to fight for an age of enlightenment.

References

Biscop, S. (2005). *The European security strategy: A global agenda for positive power* (p. 124). Aldershot: Ashgate.

Christopoulos, D., & Souvlis, G. (2016). *Europe's solidarity crisis: A perspective from Greece*. Last visit January 19, 2017, from https://roarmag.org/essays/europe-refugee-solidarity-crisis-greece/

Delors, J. (2012). In S. Fernandes & E. Rubio (Eds.), *Solidarity within the Eurozone: How much, what for, for how long?* Report by Notre Europe. Retrieved May 16, 2012, from http://www.notre-europe.eu/uploads/tx_publication/SolidarityEMU_S.Fernandes-E.Rubio_NE_Feb2012.pdf

Giddens, A. (2007). *Europe in the global age* (p. 112). Cambridge: Polity.

Giegerich, T., Gstrein, O. J., & Zeitman, S. (Eds.). (2014). *The EU between "an ever closer union" and inalienable policy domains of member states*. Baden-Baden: Nomos.

Häberle, P. (1990). 1789 als Teil der Geschichte, Gegenwart und Zukunft des Verfassungsstaates. *JöR, 37*, 35.

Häberle, P., & Kotzur, M. (2016). *Europäische Verfassungslehre* (8th ed., pp. 939). Baden-Baden: Nomos.

Hatje, A. (2001). *Loyalität als Rechtsprinzip der EU* (pp. 16).

Konstantinides, Th. (2011). *Civil protection in Europe and the Lisbon "solidarity clause". A genuine legal concept or a paper exercise* (Uppsala Faculty of Law Working Paper no. 3, p. 7).

Kotzur, M. (2015). In R. Geiger, D.-E. Khan, & M. Kotzur (Eds.), *European Union treaties. A commentary* (Art. 80 TFEU para 1).

Kotzur, M., & Schmalenbach, K. (2014). Solidarity among Nations. *Archiv des Völkerrechts, 52* (2014), 68.

Krüger, H. (1971). Brüderlichkeit—das dritte, fast vergessene Ideal der Demokratie. In *Festschrift Maunz* (pp. 249).

Lais, M. (2007). *Das Solidaritätsprinzip im europäischen Verfassungsverbund*. Baden-Baden: Nomos.

Lüder, S. R. (2009). Katastrophenschutz in der Europäischen Union und seine Auswirkungen auf das nordrhein-westfälische Recht. In *NWVBl* (pp. 251).

Maduro, M. (2001). Contrapunctual Law: Europe's constitutional pluralism in action. In N. Walker (Ed.), *Sovereignty in transition* (p. 21). Portland: Hart Publishing.

Mavelli, L., & Wilson, E. (Eds.). (2016). *The refugee crisis and religion. Secularism, security, and hospitality in question*. London: Rowman & Littlefield.

Myrdal, S., & Rhinard, M. (2010). *The European Union's solidarity clause: Empty letter or effective tool?* (UI Occasional Papers no. 2, p. 6).

[53] *Delors* (2012).

Pernice, I. (1999). Multilevel constitutionalism and the treaty of Amsterdam: European constitution-making revisited. *Common Market Law Review, 36*, 703.

Pernice, I. (2009). The treaty of Lisbon: Multilevel constitutionalism in action, Columbia. *Journal of European Law, 15*, 349.

Peters, A. (2006). Compensatory constitutionalism: The function and potential of fundamental international norms and structures. *Leiden Journal of International Law, 19*, 579 at 601.

Regelsberger, E., & Kugelmann, D. (2012). In R. Streinz (Ed.), *EUV/AEUV* (2nd ed. Art. 31 TEU para 6).

Report of the International Law Commission on Intervention and State Sovereignty (ICISS) (2001) *The Responsibility to Protect.*

Ross, M. (2010). Solidarity—A new constitutional paradigm for the EU. In M. Ross & Y. - Borgmann-Prebil (Eds.), *Promoting solidarity in the European Union* (pp. 23). Oxford: Oxford University Press.

Schmalenbach, K., Puntscher Riekmann, S., & Wydra, D. Last visit May 15, 2016., from http://www.uni-salzburg.at/portal/page?_pageid=465,1835853&_dad=portal&_schema=PORTAL

Slaughter, A.-M. (2005). Security, solidarity and sovereignty: The grand themes of UN reform. *The American Journal of International Law, 99*, 619.

Smith, K. (2008). *European Union foreign policy in a changing world* (2nd ed.). Cambridge: Polity Press.

Stahn, C. (2007). Responsibility to Protect. Political Rhetoric or Emerging Legal Norm. *The American Journal of International Law, 101*, 99.

UN Doc. GA/Res. 60/1 (2005 world Summit and Outcome)

Volkmann, U. (1998). *Solidarität—Programm und Prinzip der Verfassung*. Tübingen: Mohr Siebeck.

von Arnauld, A. (2009). Souveränität und die responsibility to protect. *Die Friedenswarte, 84*, 11.

von Bogdandy, A. (2009). Grundprinzipien. In: A. von Bogdandy & J. Bast (Eds.), *Europäisches Verfassungsrecht* (2nd ed., pp. 13 at 69–71). Berlin: Springer.

Walker, N. (2002). The idea of constitutional pluralism. *Modern Law Review, 65*, 317.

Weiler, J. H. H. (1991). The transformation of Europe. *Yale Law Journal, 100*, S. 2403 ff., at 2471.

Weiler, J. (2000). *Federalism and constitutionalism: Europe's Sonderweg* (Jean Monnet Working Paper 10/00, p. 14).

Wellens, K. (2010). Revisiting solidarity as a (re-)emerging constitutional principle: Some further reflections. In R. Wolfrum & C. Kojima (Eds.), *Solidarity: A structural principle of international law* (pp. 3 at 4). Berlin: Springer.

Wellens, K. (2005). Solidarity as a Constitutional Principle: Its Expanding Role and Inherent Limitations. In Ronald St. J. Macdonald & D. M. Johnston (Eds.), *Towards world constitutionalism: Issues in the Legal Ordering of the World Community* (p. 775). Leiden: Martinus Nijhoff Publishers.

Wiener, A. (2014). *A theory of contestation*. Berlin: Springer.

Wolfrum, R. (2006). Solidarity amongst states: An emerging structural principle of public international law. In P.-M. Dupuy (Ed.), *Völkerrecht als Weltordnung. Festschrift für Christian Tomuschat* (pp. 1087).

Chapter 5
European Solidarity and Its Limits: Insights from Current Political Challenges

Michèle Knodt and Anne Tews

1 Introduction

Solidarity has served as a fundamental norm or motive for peaceful integration since the beginning of European integration after the Second World War (Menéndez 2003, p. 374). Already, the Preamble to the European Community of Steal and Coal Treaty of 1951 started from the assumption that the Community would "first of all create real solidarity" (Sangiovanni 2013, p. 213). All following treaties have included the term "solidarity". The Preamble of the Maastricht Treaty listed the desire "to deepen solidarity between the peoples while respecting their history, their culture and traditions".

The Lisbon Treaty strengthened the principle of solidarity and brought it to the attention of European citizens as well as social scientists. The Lisbon Treaty not only mentions solidarity in the Preamble in the same formulation as the Maastricht Treaty but also links the principle to policy areas in more than 20 cases. At the same time, recent debates about the financial and migration crises demand profound analysis of the notion of solidarity. This is not an easy task as the term is neither unambiguous nor precisely defined in EU law.

This contribution addresses the significance, reality and limits of solidarity in the European multi-level system. What are requirements for solidarity? What role does solidarity play in European multi-level governance? What are the boundaries of solidarity within the European multi-level system?

To answer those questions, we first endeavour to conceptualise solidarity in the European multi-level system and to develop a typology of forms of solidarity. In the

M. Knodt (✉) • A. Tews (✉)
Technische Universität Darmstadt, Darmstadt, Germany
e-mail: knodt@pg.tu-darmstadt.de; tews@wissensordnung.tu-darmstadt.de

A. Grimmel, S.M. Giang (eds.), *Solidarity in the European Union*,
DOI 10.1007/978-3-319-57036-5_5

following section, we explore the limits of solidarity in the EU and illustrate conceptual considerations drawing on insights from two different EU policy fields: energy and migration policy.

2 Conceptualising Solidarity in the European Multi-Level System

Conceptualising solidarity within the multi-level system of the EU is not an easy task and has been attempted by many scholars. The EU itself does not lend a helping hand, as it makes heterogeneous use of the term within the primary law of the EU itself. Consider article 3,3 of the Treaty on European Union (TEU):

> The Union shall establish an internal market. It shall work for the sustainable development of Europe based on balanced economic growth and price stability, a highly competitive social market economy, aiming at full employment and social progress, and a high level of protection and improvement of the quality of the environment. It shall promote scientific and technological advance.
>
> It shall combat social exclusion and discrimination, and shall promote social justice and protection, equality between women and men, solidarity between generations and protection of the rights of the child.
>
> It shall promote economic, social and territorial cohesion, and solidarity among Member States.
>
> It shall respect its rich cultural and linguistic diversity, and shall ensure that Europe's cultural heritage is safeguarded and enhanced.

Obviously, article 3,3 TEU reveals different understandings of solidarity, from solidarity among citizens to solidarity among member states. To systematise the different uses, terms and conceptions, as well as to define its limits, we will first explore different approaches to the concept of solidarity and possibilities to transfer it to the multi-level system.

Some scholars already question whether solidarity can occur within the EU system at all (see, among others, Faist 2000; Offe 2001; Münch 2001), some see the possibility for solidarity at the EU level (Sangiovanni 2013; Habermas 2013), and others are already working on solidary solutions to current political problems in the EU (see Bast 2014; Heinemann 2012). To determine whether it is possible to transfer the concept of solidarity to the European system, we will first examine classical conceptions of solidarity.

Classical conceptions of solidarity are limiting the possibility to transfer the concept of solidarity to the European multi-level system in two ways. Firstly, classical approaches to solidarity are most often limited to smaller communities or national contexts. Secondly, they mostly address solidarity among the individual members of a group. To transfer classical solidarity conceptions to the European multi-level system, we have to overcome these two limits. In multi-level contexts, we have to construct solidarity at different levels at the same time and among individuals and member states, as implied by article 3,3 TEU. This adaptation will be the main challenge of this contribution.

Bayertz offers a first indication and a broad definition of solidarity. According to him, solidarity is first and foremost an "idea of a reciprocal relationship between members of a group" (translation MK, Bayertz 1998, p. 11). Within this general form, it seems possible to transfer the concept to the multi-level system. The crucial detail, which might disturb such a transfer, lies in the construction of the group and the glue that holds its members together. Could a sense of community or a common identity be a prerequisite for solidarity? Could solidarity be based on a common agreement, on shared values and norms? Could it be built on a contractual agreement on those norms or merely on the reference frame of reciprocity?

Bayertz states more precisely that we understand solidarity as the willingness to vouch for each other within a group of persons linked to each other by specific commonalities (1998, p. 21). A linkage among the persons within the group as an attribute of solidarity does not seem to be the difficult part of the definition. It seems far more difficult to define the specific commonalities, which should exist even in the absence of a corporate feeling or identity.

Within the debate, many scholars argue that European identity is a prerequisite for European solidarity (see Faist 2000; Offe 2001; Münch 2001; Kleger and Mehlhausen 2013). Some even confirm that European identity can exist parallel or in addition to other identities at such a level that it could serve as the basis for solidarity (Risse 2013). We argue that, first, we do not need the identity argument to construct solidarity within the European multi-level system and, second, that the multiple individual-level identities of European citizens do not help us understand solidarity between member states.

We can link this argument to the work of Durkheim (1988), who elaborates on solidarity to explain a stable social order. He starts from the historical development of simple, segmented societies up to complex, modern societies. The latter are characterised by functional differentiation. In Durkheim's concept, these two types of societies are linked to two different forms of solidarity: mechanic and organic solidarity. The less differentiated, archaic and, thus, less developed societies are based on a high degree of resemblance and a low degree of division of labour. Common traditions, conventions and morals, as well as rules with repressive sanctions and the prevalence of penal law and coercion, play important roles. Those societies are also characterised by segmented societies, which are mostly clan or territory based, with a low degree of interdependence. This kind of social order is based on mechanical solidarity. In contrast, Durkheim identifies societies that are highly developed and have a high degree of labour division as highly differentiated, modern industrial societies. Such societies are characterised by the paradox of being highly interdependent while displaying a strong ideology of individualism. According to Durkheim, those societies are dominated by organic solidarity, which is created by contractual structures. The argument is put forward that within highly functionally interdependent societies, self-interest in social goods can only be satisfied by cooperation. Thus, self-interest and solidarity are not mutually exclusive. Some authors, such as Mau, speak of "self-interest solidarity" (Mau 2009).

Communities are constructed as instruments for maximising benefits (Bayertz 1998, p. 51, referring to Hare 1992).

Preuß also notes that solidarity as a modern concept has exceeded the borders of a community based on personal contacts (1998, p. 402). Thus, this concept develops into an inherent element of society. If we talk about the narrative of solidarity within the EU, we automatically refer to Durkheim's organic solidarity. Durkheim identifies the category of "the other" as an important element of organic solidarity. The individual has to think of and calculate with "the other" when acting self-interestedly (Durkheim 1988, p. 468). Durkheim's organic solidarity conception was criticised because of the lack of normative and moral motivations and the strong focus on macro-structural conditions for solidarity. However, these criticised aspects make the concept suitable for the EU context. Only if we eliminate pre-solidarity (sine qua non) conditions, such as community feelings or a sense of a shared identity, as the basis for the connectedness of the individuals can we interpret solidarity as a window of opportunity for a mode of action, which promotes integration in the European multi-level context. Thus, although Durkheim obviously did not construct his concept of organic solidarity with the European Union in mind, it can be used in this context because it does not need the prerequisites of mechanical solidarity and is not explicitly restricted to nation states—even if it is always de facto used in this sense.

Thus, we follow the construction of organic solidarity in Durkheim's sense. Our definition constitutes solidarity as unity, which is based on or creates a community of interests, objectives and standards (Preuß 1998, p. 399 citing Webster's dictionary). With this assumption, the definition overcomes the essential requirement of a common identity or feeling and, thus, rejects the notion that mechanical solidarity is the only form of solidarity existing in the European Union. The highly differentiated multi-level system is characterised by a division of labour, interdependence and cooperative law, as described by Durkheim's concept of organic solidarity. A common identity or feeling is conceptualised here as a possible aspect, not a requirement for solidarity in the EU. Following Durkheim's conception of organic solidarity, it is possible to apply the concept of solidarity to the European multi-level system.

Nevertheless, the complexity and differentiation within the European multi-level system are defined not only by functional differences in societies based on the division of labour but also by differences across government levels and actor categories. While Durkheim's concept is based on individuals as the means of solidarity, European solidarity can occur across different levels and with regard to different actor categories, i.e. individual as well as collective actors, such as member states. The conception of organic solidarity implies the possibility to overcome the boundaries of a community in the sense of Tönnies. It is possible to conceptualise solidarity based on collective actors as well. This extension of the concept is essential if we want to apply it to the EU multi-level system. It also forms the base for our attempt to categorise different forms of European solidarity.

Table 5.1 Forms of European solidarity

	Horizontal	Vertical
Individual actors	Transnational solidarity	Supranational solidarity
Collective actors	International solidarity	Intergovernmental solidarity

To describe different forms of European solidarity, we have to take into account that solidarity can occur within or across government levels as well as between different actor categories: Within multi-level systems, political structures and processes are organised as political entities that are constructed along territorial boundaries and government levels (Benz 2004). The organisation can be analysed in a vertical and horizontal dimension. The horizontal dimension refers to solidarity within one government level, be it supranational, national or subnational. Vertical solidarity spans different levels. Addressees and carriers of solidarity can be individuals as well as collective actors, such as member states, within the EU. When we combine these two dimensions, we can identify four types of solidarity (see Table 5.1).

Transnational Solidarity

Transnational solidarity can be found in the horizontal dimension between individual actors. It is based on similar living conditions of the individuals (similar to national systems) who unite to reach a common goal. Individuals cooperate to represent their interests together. The literature refers to the examples of the French Revolution and the social movements of the nineteenth and twentieth centuries, which used the solidarity norm to form workers', women's or ecological movements. Within those movements, the aim of a group is the common representation of interests and the demarcation of competing interests. Besides the aspect of conflict with outsiders, this form of solidarity is characterised by the elements of commonality and the identity shared among the group members.

Within the European multi-level system, horizontally organised interest groups must always aim to organise across national borders when addressing European policy. Transnational solidarity is based on ideas and values that transcend national boundaries, such as the slogans of the international workers movement. However, transnational solidarity also goes beyond these ideas and norms and can encompass different forms, such as the European Trade Union Confederation and the European Works Council, as well as transnational social movements and civic organisations, such as ATTAC and the "Occupy" movement.

Supranational Solidarity

Supranational solidarity also focuses on individuals but refers to the vertical dimension of the European multi-level system. It directly creates solidarity between European citizens. It is not based on the notion of an existing community but on the sense of belonging as European citizens to a political community with specific rights and duties (Mau 2009). Supranational solidarity aims at the creation of comparable, in the sense of converging, living conditions. This may be achieved by regulations, as well as distributive or redistributive European policies. It can be witnessed in policy areas where the EU shows its supranational character of deepened integration, i.e. when European law overrides national law (Preuß 1998, p. 404). Here, we can witness Durkheim's organic solidarity in highly differentiated societies within the European Union. The vertical character of supranational solidarity implies that it is not exclusively focused on the European level but on complementing or overarching solidarity at the national or subnational levels. The EU grants additional rights to its citizens, which are also citizens of member states with national rights. This concerns areas in which economic integration and the completion of the European internal market are supposed to be complemented by compensation measures and a strengthened social dimension. It also addresses all rights linked to European citizenship.

Intergovernmental Solidarity: Member State Solidarity

Intergovernmental solidarity addresses national member states as collective actors within the multi-level system of the European Union and the vertical dimension without taking into account individual citizens. It creates a kind of membership solidarity. Facing problems and negative externalities that transcend national boundaries, collective action in numerous policy fields is necessary because unilateral action would not succeed.

This form of European solidarity oscillates between the fundamental principles of the EU: the protection of autonomy and the promotion of the community (Scharpf 1996, pp. 129–131), as well as subsidiarity, which shape decision-making processes at the EU level. To evaluate policy instruments from a solidary or integration-supporting viewpoint, one has to always keep the principle of the protection of national autonomy in mind. In addition, the subsidiarity principle influences the distribution of competencies within the EU and serves as a source for legitimacy (Callies 1999). Subsidiarity thus determines the potential content and intensity of solidary acts in the EU (Pernice 2013, p. 19).

International Solidarity

International solidarity involves collective actors on the horizontal dimension as it is carried out beyond European borders into the international sphere. It encompasses solidarity with societies and nation states in the international arena. Article 3,5 TEU specifically mentions this international dimension:

> In its relations with the wider world, the Union shall uphold and promote its values and interests and contribute to the protection of its citizens. It shall contribute to peace, security, the sustainable development of the Earth, solidarity and mutual respect among peoples, free and fair trade, eradication of poverty and the protection of human rights (...). (Art. 3,5 TEU)

In accordance with the concept of an inside-outside analogy, the article indicates that the EU is applying the norms and values it has agreed on within the Union on its external relations.

The conceptualisation of European solidarity first draws our attention to the fact that there is not one form of solidarity within the EU but several. This is neither trivial nor common sense. Most authors who discuss European solidarity and the solutions they provide for a lack thereof refer mostly to supranational solidarity. In his "plea for European solidarity" Jürgen Habermas (2013) called for more supranational solidarity, which is intrinsically connected to deeper integration in the EU. If the EU is shifting more competences to the European level and broadening supranational integration, especially in social policies, the expectation is that national solidarity is transferred to the supranational level. This might be a development in the future. However, it does not help us analyse the current challenges, as it disregards the multi-level context of the EU in the conceptualisation of solidarity. We argue, first, that European solidarity has to be defined more clearly and categorised into different forms, as shown above. Second, it has to be acknowledged that solidarity can exist at several government levels at the same time: within member (nation) states, between member states and at the European level with addressees at the different levels.

However, incidences of transnational, international and supranational solidarity are rare within the EU. To isolate the special characteristics and analyse the state and limits of European solidarity, we focus on intergovernmental, or member state, solidarity. This form of solidarity combines the vertical, or multi-level, aspect with the collective actor category and thus takes into account the specific characteristics of the EU multi-level system. Furthermore, intergovernmental solidarity plays a role in most policy fields of European governance, at least according to the Lisbon Treaty.

To answer the question of what exactly intergovernmental solidarity within the EU multi-level system is and what its limits are, we have to put some more thought into the question of how to model intergovernmental solidarity.

First, we stress the fact that intergovernmental solidarity is overarching and does not replace solidarity within member states. Solidarity within national societies and state systems remains largely untouched. European member states, as modern social welfare states, aim to balance material inequalities to produce sufficiently equal opportunities for all citizens. Even if some hesitate to attribute this objective with the term solidarity because of its anonymous and abstract transfer mechanisms, which no longer operate with any kind of sense of community, this realisation of the principle of solidarity and social justice through redistributive mechanisms only exists at the national level. This is what citizens expect of the welfare state. This is the security of a social community everybody needs in order to live a good life (Hartmann 2013). We cannot expect the same from European intergovernmental solidarity. In fact, we have to ask how member states generally calculate costs and benefits when acting within the European Union. Sangiovanni identifies the main collective benefits that member states obtain from European integration:

> The EU secures a range of collective goods including a stable and predictable legal system (which forms the background for all other goods provided by the EU), a single market

> (comprising a customs union, competition law, elimination of tariff and non-tariff barriers and so on), and regional stabilization both internally among members and on the EU's periphery. (Sangiovanni 2013, p. 225)

Thus, on the one hand, the EU tries to enhance growth, regional stability, global standing and internal problem-solving capacity (Sangiovanni 2013, p. 228). We could add many detailed goals referring to common norms, principles and objectives in different issue areas, including fundamental rights such as the right to asylum, energy security and sustainability.

On the other hand, member states have to calculate the possible costs of European actions such as the integrated single market, challenging member states' social protection measures, their "services of general interest", the rise of tax competition with negative externalities and growing intra-regional welfare disparities and inequalities (Sangiovanni 2013, pp. 225–228).

Every decision and cost-benefit calculation member states make within the EU is taken under uncertainty concerning their costs in the remote and less remote future. They have to calculate the possible costs and benefits of reciprocity, particularly with regard to their potential need for help from the community of European states in the future. Thus, a decision is made partly because states trust in future reciprocity. This trust in future reciprocity has to span medium- or long-term horizons because in a medium- to long-term calculation, it will help fulfil member states' interests. It is a calculation of the fair return member states owe one another. Here, we come back to the category of "the other" in Durkheim's organic solidarity, which has to be taken into account when calculating the costs and benefits of solidarity action.

Sangiovanni frames this kind of calculation as risk insurance that the member states obtain within the integration project. He models European integration as a "project in which states collaborate to achieve aims that they otherwise would have been unable to achieve, but where their capacity to benefit comes with significant risks" (2013, p. 230). The risk and insurance perspective allows us to make assumptions about the limits of the risk (or in other words, of the costs and disadvantages that other member states might cause) a member state is willing to bear. A state that does not want to insure against future risks is less likely to engage in solidary acts based on a reciprocity perspective.

Other limitations of solidarity within the EU can be assumed to come from member states performing calculations relating to the EU not from a medium- or long-term perspective but from a short-term perspective. This is especially true for decisions made in crisis mode, as short-term horizons seem to be preferred during financial or migration crises.

Furthermore, calculations have to include more than one policy issue. If states fail to take into account the costs and benefits of developments in other policy fields, or even in other areas of the same policy field, they will be less likely to show solidarity. Cross-issue calculation is necessary to ensure reciprocity within European solidarity as a whole. Without it, competing principles and issues within one policy field or across policy fields will cause member states to have different interpretations of and calculations regarding the situation. They select certain principles or issues to plea for solidarity, ignoring others.

In addition, we have to be aware that European-level decisions by member state governments are influenced by their national contexts. These can be national interest groups pressing for a special decision at the European level, as is modelled in two-level games by Putnam (1988) and by Moravcsik (1998). However, decisions can also be affected by calculations about the future voting behaviour of national citizens. The closer to an important national (or even subnational) election, the more important the goal of maximising votes will become when government officials decide on solidarity issues at the European level.

In the following sections, we will examine two policy fields in order to gather evidence of the empirical reality of solidarity in the EU multi-level system.

3 Limits of Solidarity in EU Energy and Migration Policy

3.1 Selective Solidarity in Energy Policy

Since the Treaty of Lisbon, energy policy has been part of EU primary law. According to article 194 of the Treaty on the Functioning of the EU (TFEU), EU energy policy shall be guided by "a spirit of solidarity between Member States". It aims to "ensure the functioning of the energy market, ensure security of energy supply in the Union, promote energy efficiency and energy saving and the development of new and renewable forms of energy, and to promote the interconnection of energy networks" (Art. 194, 1 TFEU). Article 194, 2 states, however, that decisions concerning the energy mix of member states are not affected. Member states continue to determine the conditions for exploiting their energy resources, their mix of different energy sources and the energy supply structure. The development and implementation of solidary energy policy within the EU is shaped by three fundamental frames: (1) competitiveness, (2) energy security and (3) sustainability/climate protection. To explore solidary acts among EU member states, we will focus on the energy security and sustainability frames, as they have been closely linked to the concept of solidarity among member states (see Knodt and Piefer 2014).

Discussions of the energy security frame date back to the perceived international energy threats of the late 1960s and 1970s (McGowan 2011). Oil shortages due to international threats pushed energy security to the top of the agenda. In 1968, energy security became an issue within the European Community for the first time as a direct result of the 6-day war in the Middle East, which affected the oil supply (Fischer 2011, p. 112). The Community agreed upon a directive, which imposed an obligation on member states to maintain minimum stocks of crude oil and/or petroleum products (Council of the European Community 1968).

By 2000, the focus had shifted to growing dependence on external energy. Up to 50% of the EU's energy need was met through imports. The European Commission released a green paper on energy security (European Commission 2000) and initiated a discussion of the security frame. The Commission's 2002 proposal to increase obligatory stocks of oil and gas was met with criticism from the Council of the EU and the European Parliament. The counter-argument was that the risk of supply disruption at that moment was very low (see Herranz-Surrallés 2015, p. 10).

However, only a few years later, that perception changed, and the linkage between energy security and solidarity became relevant. The Eastern enlargement of the EU and disputes over gas deliveries between Ukraine and Russia (2006) as well as Belarus and Russia (2007) led to an urgent discussion of the energy security of and solidarity with more vulnerable member states in Eastern Europe. Poland played an especially important role in this debate. The Polish supply of energy is highly dependent on Russian gas and oil; thus, the conflicts of Ukraine and Belarus with Russia threatened Poland's supply as well. During negotiations prior to the Lisbon Treaty, the Polish government demanded more solidarity from EU member states in case of supply disruption to ensure energy security for its citizens (Knodt and Piefer 2014).

The Commission reacted to this development in its Communication on "An energy policy for Europe" (European Commission 2007). The Communication reflects on the EU's dependence on external fossil fuels and, in accordance with the Polish government, demands more solidarity:

> Europe is becoming increasingly dependent on imported hydrocarbons. With 'business as usual' the EU's energy import dependence will jump from 50% of total EU energy consumption today to 65% in 2030. (...) This carries political and economic risks. (...) In addition, the mechanisms to ensure solidarity between Member States in the event of an energy crisis are not yet in place and several Member States are largely or completely dependent on one single gas supplier. (European Commission 2007, p. 4)

The Commission noted that "it remains important for the EU to promote diversity with regard to source, supplier, transport route and transport method" and called for the creation of effective mechanisms to "ensure solidarity between Member States in the event of an energy crisis" (European Commission 2007, p. 10; Knodt and Piefer 2014, pp. 228–229).

The member states discussed the means to reach these goals, especially the diversification of energy supplies. The discussion focused on the advantages and disadvantages of different pipeline projects rather than on the need to show solidarity (see, e.g. Herranz-Surrallés 2015, p. 11; Spiegel international online, 01/29/2009[1]).

This evaluation changes when we examine the sustainability or climate protection frame. In this frame, energy policy aims to reduce greenhouse gas emissions, improve energy efficiency and expand renewable energy sources. The sustainability frame

[1]http://www.spiegel.de/international/europe/europe-split-over-energy-security-merkel-calls-on-eu-to-support-baltic-gas-pipeline-a-604277.html (access: 03/06/2016).

was developed particularly in the Commission's 2006 Green Paper on energy issues. The "European Strategy for Sustainable, Competitive and Secure Energy" (European Commission 2006) stated that European energy policies should fulfil three main objectives (Knodt et al. 2015, pp. 64–65): (1) sustainability with regard to renewable sources of energy and other low-carbon energy sources to combat climate change and improve air quality; (2) competitiveness to open the energy market, which should ensure benefits for consumers; and (3) security of supply, which should tackle the EU's rising dependence on imported energy (European Commission 2006, pp. 17–18). In 2007, the European Council decided to "develop a sustainable integrated European climate and energy policy" (European Council 2007, p. 1) in order to link energy policy closely to climate policy and focus on emissions reduction, expansion of renewable energies and energy efficiency. The targets for these three objectives were described by the slogan "20–20–20 by 2020": a reduction of at least 20% in greenhouse gas emissions by 2020 compared to the year 1990, a 20% share of renewable energy in EU energy consumption by 2020 and the reduction of primary energy use by 20% in comparison with projected levels—to be achieved through energy efficiency (European Council 2007).

To implement the European Council decision from March 2007, the Commission prepared a set of legislative proposals, the "climate and energy package", in 2008. It includes measures to promote renewable energy, regulations for the EU emissions trading system and development of low-carbon technologies, as well as those for carbon capture and storage. In addition, binding targets for member states were agreed upon. All member states were obligated to take part in emissions reduction according to their potential. Both the Council of the EU and the European Parliament approved the package on a very short notice. The remaining controversial issues—especially CO_2 reduction—were to be decided at the EU summit in December 2008. Discussions at this summit illustrate the beginning of Central and Eastern European member state opposition to solidarity within the sustainability frame.

French president Nicolas Sarkozy, then head of the presidency of the Council, negotiated lower CO_2 reduction targets and exceptions for affected industries in order to reach an agreement. In addition to opposition from Central and Eastern European member states, the German government did not support these ambitions. Chancellor Merkel argued for exceptions for German industry.

In 2011, the Commission published the Energy Roadmap 2050 as an addendum to the Climate Roadmap that had been published earlier (European Commission 2011b). The Energy Roadmap focuses on climate policy, as well as energy security and the competitiveness of the EU, and promotes a transition to a low-carbon and climate friendly economy (Knodt and Piefer 2014, p. 235f). The Energy Roadmap highlighted the economic benefits of EU regulation and solidarity:

> The Roadmap does not replace national, regional and local efforts to modernize energy supply, but seeks to develop a long-term European technology-neutral framework in which

> these policies will be more effective. It argues that a European approach to the energy challenge will increase security and solidarity and lower costs compared to parallel national schemes by providing a wider and flexible market for new products and services. (European Commission 2011b, p. 4f)

The EU climate policy goals were opposed by Central and Eastern European member states, including the Polish government, which argued that binding emissions reduction goals would have adverse effects on its national economy. Poland is the largest producer of coal in the EU and is highly dependent on fossil fuels. Consequently, Poland spoke against solidary approaches to these issues. Its criticism focused on binding reduction goals, the idea of a common European approach and the projected speed of the process of transition to renewable energy (Knodt and Piefer 2014, p. 236). Poland was joined in this opposition by other Eastern European countries, i.e. Czech Republic, Slovakia, Hungary, Bulgaria and Romania (Geden and Fischer 2014, p. 11; Fischer 2014, pp. 2–3). These member states insisted on maintaining their sovereignty with regard to their national energy mix and tried to limit the role of the EU while arguing for solidarity and European regulation in the field of energy security (Fischer 2014, pp. 2–3).

The debate about new climate protection targets for 2030 was shaped by the same conflict between Northern and Western sustainability-oriented member states and Central and Eastern European member states asking for solidarity to ensure energy supply. Hence, the targets remained rather ambiguous: "at least" 40% reduction of greenhouse gas emissions compared to 1990, "at least" 27% share of renewable energy consumption and "at least" 27% energy savings compared with the business-as-usual scenario. Additionally, the extent to which the decision can be revised was framed in an ambiguous way. The European Council conclusions included a review of the framework after the climate conference in Paris in December 2015. Both camps interpreted this differently. Whereas the Northern and Western member states hoped for higher percentages of greenhouse gas reduction, the Central and Eastern member states expected unsuccessful international negotiations. Thus, both sides were willing to agree. In addition, the European Council addressed the concerns of the Eastern camp and stated, "these targets will be achieved while fully respecting the Member States' freedom to determine their energy mix. Targets will not be translated into nationally binding targets" (European Council 2014, p. 5). In addition, extensive concessions were made to the governments of Central and Eastern Europe in terms of financial compensation and exemptions from the regulations (Fischer 2014, pp. 3–5). Nevertheless, the current efforts of the Commission to build an Energy Union have been met with the same divide and selective pleas for solidarity.

The field of energy policy illustrates some of the limits of intergovernmental solidarity. The Eastern member states demanded solidarity with regard to energy security because their own interests were at stake. However, they did not link their demands to the discussion of energy policy in the sustainability frame and refused to show solidarity on this issue. Again, this can be explained by their national interests. However, they do not seem to have a reciprocity perspective in mind when demanding or refusing solidarity between member states.

3.2 Lack of Solidarity in Migration Policy

Solidarity or solidary burden sharing is an important pillar of EU migration policy, which covers asylum, immigration and border controls (Art. 67, 2 and Art. 80 TFEU; Bast 2014, pp. 145–146). The Treaty obliges the Union legislature to ensure fair sharing of the financial and administrative burdens of immigration. These burdens are dispersed unevenly due to differences in geographical context and economic power among member states (ibid., p. 147).

However, the specific mechanisms of burden sharing are highly contested. This can be illustrated by the debate on the reform of the Dublin system, a central element of EU migration policy. Currently, the Dublin III Regulation (No. 604/2013) defines a common asylum space that consists of the EU member states, as well as the EFTA states, Iceland, Liechtenstein, Norway and Switzerland. Within this asylum space, the first country a refugee enters is responsible for evaluating asylum applications and granting asylum and protection if the claims are valid. If a refugee applies for asylum in a second Dublin country, they can be transferred back to the country of their first application.

Due to established migration routes and varying populations and economic power of the Dublin states, this arrangement leads to disproportionate burdens for some countries. Southern and Eastern European countries are more often the first countries entered due to their geographic locations. They also face higher costs of examining applications and integrating recognised refugees relative to their populations or economic power. Northern and Western European countries have a much smaller burden to bear. Bast concludes that the Dublin system does not ensure solidary burden sharing but rather reinforces existing differences. Thus, the Union legislature failed to comply with its treaty obligations (Bast 2014, pp. 148–151).

The lack of solidary mechanisms is a main reason for the escalation of the migration crisis since 2014. This can be illustrated by example of Greece. As a Dublin country, Greece was not able to comply with its obligations to ensure fair asylum procedures for all applicants due to an enormous increase in the number of refugees. As early as 2011, returning refugees to Greece, their first country of entry, could no longer be justified, as a fair procedure and humane treatment could not be guaranteed by Greek authorities (ibid., pp. 150–151).

Numerous proposals to reform the Dublin system to include solidary mechanisms and significant burden sharing have been discussed but not implemented due to opposition from some member states (see European Commission 2011a; Bast 2014, p. 152ff). One reform proposal, discussed in 2011, included a mechanism to distribute refugees among EU member states (European Commission 2011a, p. 8ff; Bast 2014, pp. 154–155). As only some Southern member states have been negatively affected and had to cope with the high costs of such an unequal distribution, all the other member states considered only the short-term perspective and decided against solidary action. Member states such as Germany, Austria and Slovenia ignored possible long-term changes, such as new refugee routes, and decided against future needs and reciprocity.

In light of the escalation of the migration crisis, this 2011 proposal was on the Commission agenda again in 2015. However, the aim was not to reform the Dublin system but to react to the dire situations in Greece and Italy with preliminary measures in accordance with article 78, 3 TFEU (Council of the European Union 2015). The debate revolved around a mechanism for distributing a certain number of refugees from Italy, Greece and Hungary to the other member states. One option was the establishment of an automatic mechanism. Based on criteria such as economic power and population size, a certain number of refugees would automatically be allotted to each member state. This mechanism could be used for future crisis situations as well. Without such a mechanism, the number of refugees for each receiving country would have to be renegotiated among the member states for each new crisis situation (European Commission 2011a, pp. 9–10; Lang 2015; Becker 2015).

Lang shows that the Visegrád group in particular opposed an EU-wide automatic mechanism for refugees (Lang 2015, p. 2). He states that opposition was mainly fuelled by domestic concerns. For example, the Polish government under Ewa Kopacz was facing growing conservative and nationalistic opposition and wanted to demonstrate determination and power in light of the upcoming parliamentary election in 2015. Hungarian head of government Victor Orbán followed his tough approach in reaction to growing right-wing extremism. Furthermore, government opposition reflected the growing reluctance of citizens to receive refugees in their countries (ibid., p. 2f). These brief examples show how decisions against solidarity measures can be influenced by national governmental calculations of costs related to the future voting behaviour of their citizens.

In September 2015, the Justice and Home Affairs Council convened to vote on relief measures for Italy, Greece and Hungary. The issue at hand was the distribution of 120,000 refugees among the member states. Due to firm opposition from the Visegrád group, the issue of an automatic distribution mechanism was not even on the agenda (Council of the European Union 2015). Nevertheless, the decision about the distribution of these 120,000 refugees and the fixed quotas that had been assigned to each member state was highly contested. Poland was the only Visegrád country that approved the Council decision to distribute these 120,000 refugees based on fixed quotas for each state.[2] Slovakia, Czech Republic and Hungary rejected the concept of fixed quotas and, together with Romania, voted against the decision. It must be mentioned that at least Hungary would have benefited from the decision, as a number of refugees from Hungary were to be distributed. This would have meant relief for Hungary. Despite this benefit, Hungary voted against the plan. Instead, earlier this year, Hungary refused to take back refugees that had entered the Dublin asylum area in Hungary first and had moved on to other Dublin countries (Becker 2015; Lang 2015, p. 4; Than and Nasralla 2015).

[2]However, this does not mean that Poland contributed to the implementation of this decision.

Lang explains Poland's deviating voting behaviour mainly based on the Polish government's fear of losing political influence in Europe. A continuing blockade would have had serious political costs in terms of influence and negotiating power (Lang 2015, p. 4). At least in this case, the shadow of the future was calculated by the Polish government, although whether it was considered with respect to influence, negotiating power or future solidarity is difficult to determine.

Overall, the opposing Eastern European member states, especially the Visegrád group, could not block solidary relief mechanisms for the most affected member states. However, they prevented the establishment of an automatic EU-wide distribution mechanism. Consequently, member states will be forced to negotiate new quotas for each crisis situation in the future. Based on the complicated and tedious negotiation processes for quotas in the past, the lack of consensus on quotas in general and the lack of implementation of the decisions, it is safe to assume that this will not lead to solidary and effective burden sharing in the future. Thus, member states will have to resort to individual solidary acts. For example, Germany invoked the "sovereignty clause" of the Dublin regulation and refrained from sending Syrian refugees back to the country of their first entry in 2015. However, this unilateral approach was criticised by the Visegrád group as well (Lang 2015, p. 3).

The Visegrád group and other Eastern European countries were criticised for their opposing behaviour and were accused of showing a lack of solidarity with other member states. Interestingly, the accused countries replied with a link to the field of energy policy: Poland and Slovakia criticised the EU's "unsolidary" support for the Nord Stream 2 pipeline project, calling it the result of "national egoism" and "betrayal" within the EU (translation AT, Lang 2015, p. 3).

Discussions of solidarity in migration policy illustrate the limits of intergovernmental solidarity as well. Member states tend to calculate costs and benefits from a short-term perspective and do not take future risks into account. Furthermore, national constraints, i.e. domestic opposition or citizen voting behaviour, play important roles. Again, there is no evidence of a sense of reciprocity or linking of current solidary demands with possible future needs, or vice versa.

4 Conclusion

Within the Lisbon Treaty, a fireworks display of solidarity claims is presented in quite diverse policy fields. However, is solidarity within the EU even possible? What are the requirements and limits of solidarity in European multi-level governance? In modelling solidarity within this context, we built on Durkheim's concept of organic solidarity and adapted it to the multi-level system of the EU. To do so, we assumed that addressees or carriers of solidarity can be individuals and collective actors, such as member states. In addition, with explicit regard to Durkheim's organic solidarity, we do not assume that a prerequisite, such as a European identity, is necessary for solidarity within the European Union. Further, we took the vertical dimension of the multi-level system seriously in constructing solidarity within the EU. The latter is neglected by most approaches aiming to construct solidarity at the European level. Hence, they are not adequate and leave an important dimension of solidarity in the European multi-level system untouched.

To conceptualise European solidarity, we combined the horizontal and vertical dimensions of the multi-level system with the individual and collective actor categories, producing a four-by-four matrix. Based on the matrix, our first conclusion is that there is not one form of European solidarity but several: transnational, international, supranational and intergovernmental or member state solidarity. We examined the intergovernmental form of solidarity more closely and analysed discussions of EU member state solidarity in two fields, energy and migration policy.

The analysis showed that when deciding whether to show solidarity, member states calculate their costs and benefits. To positively evaluate solidary decisions that include higher costs than benefits from a short-term perspective, member states would have to consider medium- to long-term time horizons. They should consider a decision to show solidarity insurance for future reciprocity within the multi-level system. However, the case of migration policy shows that especially in crisis situations, short-term calculations predominate. Thus, one of the limits of European solidarity is the lack of medium- to long-term reciprocity calculations among EU member states.

Closely linked to the time horizon, the examples showed that the calculation of reciprocity is also very much focused on one issue, whereas most decision-making processes within the EU include diverse issues in order to allow for log rolling and similar processes. To ensure reciprocity, member states should calculate the costs and benefits of solidarity across issue areas, but they do not. For example, the Visegrád group demands solidarity in energy security policy but denies solidarity in the sustainability frame of energy policy and in migration policy. Across or within policy fields, different principles are taken up for solidarity claims, while others are ignored. Member states select the issues for which they demand or refuse solidarity and do not consider that others might not agree with their picky claims, as they do not see reciprocity promises within or across policy fields become reality.

Finally, this analysis demonstrated that European intergovernmental solidarity is overarching and that national solidarity has to be provided by member states, which makes national contexts important. The example of migration policy showed that national election horizons are significant constraints in solidarity calculations and are closely tied to short time horizons, another limit of European intergovernmental solidarity.

References

Bast, J. (2014). Solidarität im europäischen Einwanderungs- und Asylrecht. In M. Knodt & A. Tews (Eds.), *Solidarität in der Europäischen Union* (pp. 143–161). Baden-Baden: Nomos.

Bayertz, K. (1998). Begriff und Problem der Solidarität. In K. Bayertz (Ed.), *Solidarität. Begriff und Problem* (pp. 11–53). Frankfurt a.M.: Suhrkamp.

Becker, M. (2015, September 9). Blockade in Brüssel. Verteilung von Flüchtlingen. *Spiegel-Online*.

Benz, A. (2004). Multilevel governance – Governance in Mehrebenensystemen. In A. Benz (Ed.), *Governance – Regieren in komplexen Regelsystemen* (pp. 125–146). Wiesbaden: Verlag für sozialwissenschaften.

Callies, C. (1999). *Subsidiaritäts- und Solidaritätsprinzip in der Europäischen Union* (2nd ed.). Baden-Baden: Nomos.

Council of the European Community. (1968). Council Directive imposing an obligation on member states to maintain minimum stocks of crude oil and/or petroleum products, 20 December 1968, (68/414/EEC), No. L308/14, 23.12.1968, Brussels.

Council of the European Union. (2015, September 22). *Justice and home affairs council. Background information.* Brussels: Press office – General Secretariat of the Council.

Durkheim, E. (1988). *Über soziale Arbeitsteilung: Studie über die Organisation höherer Gesellschaften.* Frankfurt a.M.: Suhrkamp.

European Commission. (2000, November 29). *Green paper – Towards a European strategy for the security of energy supply.* COM(2000) 769 final. Brussels.

European Commission. (2006, March 8). *A European strategy for sustainable, competitive and secure energy.* COM(2006) 105 final. Brussels.

European Commission. (2007, January 10). *An energy policy for Europe, communication from the commission to the European council and the European parliament.* COM(2007) 1 final. Brussels.

European Commission. (2011a, December 2). *Mitteilung der Kommission an das Europäische Parlament, den Rat, den Europäischen Wirtschafts- und Sozialausschuss und den Ausschuss der Regionen über verstärkte EU-interne Solidarität im Asylbereich. Eine EU-Agenda für weitergehende Teilung der Verantwortung und mehr gegenseitiges Vertrauen.* KOM(2011) 835 final. Brussels.

European Commission. (2011b, December 15). *Energy roadmap 2050.* KOM(2011) 885 final. Brussels.

European Council. (2007, March 9). *Presidency conclusions, 7334/1/07, REV 1, CONCL 1.* Brussels.

European Council. (2014, October 24). *Presidency conclusions, EUCO 169/14, Co EUR 13, CONCL 5.* Brussels.

Faist, T. (2000). Soziale Bürgerschaft in der Europäischen Union. Verschachtelte Mitgliedschaft. In M. Bach (Ed.), *Die Europäisierung nationaler Gesellschaften, Kölner Zeitschrift für Soziologie und Sozialpsychologie* (pp. 229–250), Special edition No. 40. Opladen: Leske und Budrich.

Fischer, S. (2011). *Auf dem Weg zur gemeinsamen Energiepolitik. Strategien, Instrumente und Politikgestaltung in der Europäischen Union.* Baden-Baden: Nomos.

Fischer, S. (2014). *The EU's new energy and climate policy framework for 2030*, SWP Comments 55. Berlin.

Geden, O., & Fischer, S. (2014). Moving targets. Die Verhandlungen über die Energie- und Klimapolitik-Ziele der EU nach 2020. *SWP Studie* 2014(1).

Habermas, J. (2013). *Im Sog der Technokratie. Kleine Politische Schriften* (Vol. XII). Berlin: Suhrkamp.

Hare, R. M. (1992). *Moralisches Denken: Seine Ebenen, seine Methode, sein Witz.* Frankfurt a.M.: Suhrkamp.

Hartmann, J. (2013). *Solidarität als Ideologie* (APuZ Grundwerte 34–36/2013). Accessed May 18, 2016, from http://www.bpb.de/apuz/166659/solidaritaet-als-ideologie?p=all

Heinemann, F. (2012). Die Europäische Schuldenkrise: Ursachen und Lösungsstrategien. *Jahrbuch für Wirtschaftswissenschaften, 63*(1), 18–41.

Herranz-Surrallés, A. (2015). An emerging EU energy diplomacy? Discursive shifts, enduring practices. *Journal of European Public Policy, 17.* doi:10.1080/13501763.2015.1083044.

Kleger, H., & Mehlhausen, T. (2013). Unstrittig und doch umstritten – europäische Solidarität in der Eurokrise. *Politische Vierteljahresschrift, 54*(1), 50–74.

Knodt, M., & Piefer, N. (2014). Energiesolidarität im Normdreieck aus Sicherheit, Wettbewerb und Nachhaltigkeit. In M. Knodt & A. Tews (Eds.), *Solidarität in der Europäischen Union* (pp. 219–240). Baden-Baden: Nomos.

Knodt, M., Müller, F., & Piefer, N. (2015). Explaining European Union Energy Governance with emerging powers. In M. Knodt, N. Piefer, & F. Müller (Eds.), *Challenges of European External Energy Governance with emerging powers. Meeting Tiger, Dragon, Lion and Jaguar* (pp. 57–74). Farnham: Ashgate.

Lang, O. (2015). Rückzug aus der Solidarität? Die Visegrád-Länder und ihre Reserviertheit in der Flüchtlingspolitik. *SWP-Aktuell, 84*.

Mau, S. (2009). Europäische Solidarität. Erkundung eines schwierigen Geländes. In S. Harnisch, H. W. Maull, & S. Schieder (Eds.), *Solidarität und internationale Gemeinschaftsbildung* (pp. 63–87). Frankfurt a.M.: Suhrkamp.

McGowan, F. (2011). Putting energy insecurity into historical context: European responses to the energy crises of the 1970s and 2000s. *Geopolitics, 16*(3), 486–511.

Menéndez, A. J. (2003). The sinews of peace: Rights to solidarity in the charter of fundamental rights of the European Union. *Ratio Juris, 16*(3), 374–398.

Moravcsik, A. (1998). *The choice for Europe: Social purpose and state power from Messina to Maastricht*. Ithaca, NY: Cornell University Press.

Münch, R. (2001). *Offene Räume. Soziale Integration diesseits und jenseits des Nationalstaates*. Frankfurt a.M.: Suhrkamp.

Offe, C. (2001). Gibt es eine europäische Gesellschaft? Kann es sie geben? *Blätter für deutsche und internationale Politik, 4*, 423–435.

Pernice, I. (2013). *Solidarität in Europa* (WHI-Paper 01/2013). Berlin.

Preuß, U. K. (1998). Nationale, supranationale und internationale Solidarität. In K. Bayertz (Ed.), *Solidarität. Begriff und Problem* (pp. 399–410). Frankfurt a.M.: Suhrkamp.

Putnam, R. D. (1988). Diplomacy and domestic politics: The logic of tow-level games. *International Organisation, 42*, 427–460.

Risse, T. (2013, May). *Solidarität unter Fremden? Europäische Identität im Härtetest* (KFG Working Paper Series No. 50), Kolleg-Forschergruppe (KFG) "The Transformative Power of Europe" Freie Universität Berlin.

Sangiovanni, A. (2013). Solidarity in the European Union. *Oxford Journal of Legal Studies, 33*(2), 213–241.

Scharpf, F. W. (1996). Politische Optionen im vollendeten Binnenmarkt. In M. Jachtenfuchs & B. Kohler-Koch (Eds.), *Europäische integration* (pp. 109–140). Opladen: Leske und Budrich.

Than, K., & Nasralla, S. (2015). Defying EU, Hungary suspends rules on asylum seekers. *Reuters Online*. Accessed May 20, 2016, from http://uk.reuters.com/article/uk-europe-migrants-austria-hungary-idUKKBN0P31ZB20150623

Part II
The Crisis of Solidarity

Chapter 6
Actual Patterns of Migration Flows: The Challenge of Migration and Asylum in Contemporary Europe

Catherine Wihtol de Wenden

1 Introduction

At the beginning of the twenty-first century, international migration reached 244 million people (i.e. 3.5% of the world population), with roughly the same number of flows going to the north (south–north and north–north: 120 million) as to the south (south–south and north–south: 130 million), which is a new development. No region or country in the world is left out of the migration process, and all countries are involved in either emigration, immigration or transit flows. Most are involved in all three trends simultaneously, which blurs the categories of migrants between people seeking family reunification, foreign workers and asylum seekers. New groups—such as isolated women, unaccompanied children, circulating elites and experts—have entered into international mobility. However, the right to move is among the least shared in the world: global mobility is severely segmented based on nationality, class, gender, race, etc. In Europe, the end of the Cold War and the fall of the Berlin Wall in 1989 brought about a generalisation of the right to exit, with easy access to a passport permitted even in southern countries—along with more restricted rights to enter OECD (Organisation for Economic Cooperation and Development) countries.

In this chapter, we will deal with:

- Actual patterns of international migration flows. These can be divided into four migration patterns: south–north, north–north, south–south and north–south. These correspond to various migration profiles, some of which are recent or emerging.
- The social mechanisms that have underpinned this process (Wihtol de Wenden 2013b, 2016). The border regime will be explored according to the country of

C. Wihtol de Wenden (✉)
Centre d'Études et des Recherches Internationales (CERI), Sciences Po, Paris, France

Le Centre National de la Recherche Scientifique (CNRS), Paris, France
e-mail: catherine.wihtoldewenden@sciencespo.fr

A. Grimmel, S.M. Giang (eds.), *Solidarity in the European Union*,
DOI 10.1007/978-3-319-57036-5_6

departure and the country of destination, as well as the mechanisms of closed or open borders. This may lead to trafficking, which is becoming a pull factor. There are also push factors linked to political crisis and unemployment.

- The different and conflicting ways in which states and European Union (EU) institutions are responding to the influx of migrants. We have observed a fracture line between Eastern and Western Europe in terms of the refugee crisis, as well as a situation where northern European states are displaying a lack of trust towards the southern states that are confronted with new migrant flows on a daily basis. There is weak follow-up of the measures implemented (such as quotas of burden sharing, hotspots and other mechanisms) and a *fuite en avant* with the agreement between Europe and Turkey due to the inability of Europe to find an agreement between the 28 states when it comes to the treatment of refugees.
- The crisis of Schengen, a crisis of Dublin 2 and crisis of Frontex made of 'path dependency' towards the institutions already created without viewing other horizons of management of the migration flows. These institutions seem to preserve themselves in a context where states appear to be obstacles to solidarity.

2 Actual Patterns of Migration Flow

The world is moving. During the last 40 years, international migration has multiplied by a factor of four, rising from 77 million in 1975 to now; this is as well as internal migration (740 million). China itself has 240 million internal migrants, and half of them are illegal. This globalisation of migration, which is defined by the involvement of almost all countries in a process of departure, arrival and transit, is, paradoxically, accompanied by a regionalisation process (Castles and Miller 2014; Rosenau 1990). In all the regions of the world, there are more migrants coming from the same regions than there are migrants coming from other parts of the world. This trend is due to the emerging presence of new groups such as women, unaccompanied minors, environmentally displaced migrants and internally displaced people, who rarely go far. There are now 60 million refugees who have found themselves in a situation of forced migration (with or without this status). This figure includes internal refugees migrating across their own countries and those displaced for climate change and environmental crises (who number 42 million, out of which 17 million are international climate change refugees). This regionalisation of migration can be seen in all regions in the world (Euro-Mediterranean, North America, South America, Russia, Turkey, the Gulf countries, sub-Saharan Africa, Southeast Asia, Australia). In the past, Europeans constituted many of the migrants in some of these regions.

The reasons for this entrance into mobility are structural, being linked to unequal development, demographic structures, gaps between rich and poor, information about better opportunities when crossing borders (due to new information and communication technologies), offers of mobility due to trafficking and political crises creating refugees. Europe is in the middle of these shifting trends. It is the first destination in the world for flows of migrants, followed by the United States (USA), the Gulf region and Russia. But, regarding settled population demographics, the United States comes first with 46 million foreign-born residents. Europe is second with 42 million settled migrants. During 2014–2015, Europe was confronted with the unforeseen arrival of asylum seekers from the Middle East: 625,000 asylum seekers in 2014 and 1.2 million in 2015 (mainly Syrians).

2.1 Four New Migration Trends

We can divide the world into four parts, according to the directions followed by migrations and the types of migrants involved: from south to north (70 million), there is a long tradition of flows of workers, people seeking family reunification and refugees due to geographical proximities, colonial and linguistic links and transnational migrant networks (one nationality being present in high numbers in one country, such as Algerians in France or Mexicans in the United States, or quasi diasporas such as the Turkish or Moroccan communities in Europe, occurs in several countries, resulting in high transnational networking). These flows are still growing, though the numbers of workers have decreased compared with the numbers of those seeking family reunifications, students and highly qualified elites travelling from south to north, as well as asylum seekers and other forced migrants. Restrictive immigration policies have responded to these trends and have been challenged by illegal newcomers. The rights of departure have become easily accessible in most countries of origin, whereas rights of entry have become increasingly difficult to obtain due to securitised border controls. But if the migrant enters legally, he may have progressive access to the rights of other citizens, including access to citizenship in most cases where jus soli and access to naturalisation are open, as well as freedom of association and local voting rights.

From north to north, there are still numerous migrants (50 million). These are mostly qualified young people who have the same rights when leaving and arriving. Some of them are commuters, crossing easily across the borders as a way of life. These new profiles have settled into mobility as a way of life (*circulation migratoire*), being able to leave their country as easily as they can enter another country. The European experience of the free circulation of Europeans from east to west after the opening of the Iron Curtain in 1989, as well as the newcomers travelling from southern European to northern European countries, has shown many examples of people settling into mobility as a way of life. This unique space of internal free circulation in Europe is the most advanced there is at the international level.

From south to south, the movements approach the number of those going from south to north (70 million, but we must remember to add a lot of illegal migrants) due to the new categories that have recently emerged: women (now 50% of international migrants), unaccompanied children and environmentally displaced people. There are also south–south movements of the labour force towards Gulf countries and other emerging countries. Departure from southern countries has been possible since the 1990s due to the generalisation of passport access, and entrance is easier than it is in northern countries. But these people's rights are as poor on departure as they are on arrival, involving difficulty accessing social rights (especially family reunification), citizenship and asylum protection (there are a number of non-affluent southern countries among the 50 countries that were not signatories to the Geneva Convention on refugees of 1951).

When it comes to those travelling from north to south, we find those who consider international mobility a way of life: senior citizens seeking the sun upon retirement as they look for more individual care and young, newly qualified unemployed people travelling south in search of job opportunities. These migrants have freedom of departure and few requirements of entrance. They preserve their social rights (as expatriates), but their access to citizenship, land and property may be limited because many southern countries are ruled by *jus sanguinis*. Their number is not very high, but it is increasing (20 million).

2.2 Conflicting EU and National Migration Policies

Some myths and paradoxes are featured within European migration policy; these are driving anti-immigration discourses and anti-immigration effects. Many of them are treated as answers to short-term political and electoral concerns in member states: one could suggest military dissuasion as a means to stop migration, consider migration a security issue to be managed by repression, conflate irregular migration with terrorism and criminality, call for regularisation of the pull factors leading to new flows, deem a potential brain drain an obstacle to development, perceive immigrant labour as competition in European labour markets (Hollifield 1998–1999; Portes 2003), call for development as an alternative to migration, generalise return migration as a generational dynamic or present environmentally displaced people as the main risk to Europe.

In this broad context, Europe is the first destination for immigration flows (the United States is first in terms of the number of foreign-born residents), but European and national policy makers, along with a sector of the public that hardly accepts this reality, seem to ignore the long-term dimension of this phenomenon. They give answers in emergency contexts, meaning there is a gap between the immigration flows of the present and future and the short-term management policies controlling rights to entrance and residence. For a long time (until 1974, the date of the suspension of the migration of labour forces in most European immigration countries), immigration was viewed as a provisional solution to labour force shortages during a period of high economic growth.

A striking feature of migration politics in the increasingly integrated EU is that European nations and public opinion, as well as governments, have failed to adapt to the change in their status from countries of emigration to countries of immigration from the 1960s onwards. Historically, Europe was a continent of intense emigration, sending millions of its natives all over the world through labour emigration, colonisation, trade, missions, wars and cooperation. Europe clearly became a land of immigration in the 1960s, but both migration and political debates on migration seem to lag behind the statistical and demographic facts.

In Europe, various trends of migration policies and politics in the region have led to the harmonisation of migration policies according to the external dimension of European border controls through the 1985 Schengen visa system, as well as bilateral and multilateral agreements with countries of origin. This led to weakening entrance conditions and the strengthening of military forms of control and closure. The focus on closure in a world on the move can appear paradoxical (Weiner 1995; Sassen 1996). In the meantime, what were once countries of emigration have been transformed into countries of immigration and transit by Europe.

Some recent events, such as the murders in Paris committed by Islamic terrorists in November 2015, which followed a debate on sharing the burden of refugees from Syria, Iraq and the Horn of Africa, have led to many contradictory opinions and debates on whether to open or close national borders in France and Europe, as well as ethical positions concerning the attitude towards Islam as a form of otherness in European countries.

2.3 The Mediterranean as a Crucial Migration Space, System and Regime

Another crucial debate has focused on the Mediterranean, although in terms of migration it can be divided into three different spaces: Maghreb/Europe, the Balkans and the Near East, which corresponds to various forms of migration (immigration of workers and those seeking family reunification, people fleeing ethnic and religious conflict, refugees). This region is a place of intersecting civilisations and ways of life, which are nurtured by transborder networks due to the intensity of the region's shared story of conflict and dialogue, as well as its demographic diversity towards the south (although it is in a state of demographic transition today) and the interdependency of its economies. Now, the globalisation of migration is focused on the Mediterranean, the region where almost all the migrant groups in the world—including refugees, illegals and unaccompanied minors—are concentrated. It is characterised by processes of containment and mobility, integration dynamics and security approaches, transnationalism and diaspora, religious identities and the pluralism of the situation shared by the 22 states bordering the sea.

Migration in the Mediterranean is a very heated topic of debate due to the present refugee crisis, the consequences of the Arab revolutions (with the extent and length of the turmoil in Syria being unanticipated), the proximity of countries of emigration and transit, and the involvement of southern European countries in the arrival of newcomers. The logistics of migration movements in the region, the perverse effects of the dissuasion policies used by border controls, and the various forms of transnational networks are spread between countries of departure and arrival.

1. How far can the Mediterranean—as a migration space, system and regime—use a comprehensive approach to analyse specific migration movements and trends in the region?
2. The Mediterranean immigration model is in a time of crisis, having to deal with the perverse effects of border closure, illegal and trafficked migrants, women at borders, black and segmented labour markets and unaccompanied minors. People are questioning the approach to welcoming and integrating migrants across all the European immigration countries.
3. In European countries of settlement, various forms of transnationalism (social, political and religious) have led to strategies of influence over countries of origin (in terms of voting at a distance, religious networks and diaspora).

3 The Challenge of Migration and Asylum for Contemporary Europe

Today, Europe is being faced with an unprecedented flow of refugees because it is surrounded by countries that are in conflict, which have produced large flows of forced migration from a number of countries, even if they did not enter into the Geneva Convention of 1951. Europe counted around 200,000 asylum seekers per year before the 1.2 million of 2015. But we must remember that this crisis is not so new, because after the fall of the Berlin Wall, Europe received around 500,000 asylum seekers from 1989 to 1993. These mostly travelled to Germany, which welcomed three quarters of all the asylum seekers to Europe. Subsequently, the crisis in the former Yugoslavia led most of the refugees from that region to Germany.

The present flow of refugees is mainly coming from Syria (5 million have left their country since 2013, and 7 million are internal refugees in Syria), Iraq and the Horn of Africa, travelling via Libya, Afghanistan and Kosovo. Turkey has welcomed the largest number of them, with 3 million refugees residing in its territory. This situation has led to conflicting approaches from states and EU institutions responding to the influx of migrants.

3.1 Conflicting Approaches Between the EU and States

The first European answer, through the voice of Jean-Claude Juncker, President of the European Commission, was to propose a burden-sharing deal. In May 2015, it was suggested that 40,000 asylum seekers be spread between the countries of the EU according to their wealth and population. This announcement was met with strong resistance, being perceived as an intrusion on internal European policies. During the summer of 2015, many central European countries closed their national borders to newcomers across the Balkan route. Hungary was the first country to oppose welcoming new refugees, followed by the Czech Republic, Slovakia and Poland (all of these countries, incidentally, are threatened by the rise of extreme right parties). In September 2015, Mr. Juncker again asked European countries to welcome 160,000 asylum seekers. Then, on 7 September Angela Merkel of Germany announced that the country was prepared to welcome 800,000 asylum seekers in 2015. Following the wide dispersal in the media of a photograph of the 3-year-old Syrian boy Aylan Kurdi, who died on the shore of Bodrum after the boat carrying him and his parents was wrecked, the western European states accepted, with some reluctance, the figures proposed by Mr. Juncker (e.g. so 30,000 for France over a resettlement period of 2 years). During 2015, according to United Nations High Commissioner for Refugees (UNHCR), Greece welcomed the largest number of newcomers (many of whom have subsequently tried to enter other EU countries). But Italy, who was at the front stage before 2015 and who led the Mare Nostrum operation of 2013, saving 146,000 people in 1 year (from November 2013 to November 2014), is once more highly involved due to the EU/Turkish agreements of March 2016, which stopped most of passages between Greece and Turkey by sea.

According to this agreement, Europe follows a long trend of evading the rules of its common policy thanks to bilateral or multilateral agreements with neighbouring non-European countries. Libya was the most important partner, with several European countries using the country as a filter for Sub-Saharans who want to reach Europe. Libya has been paid with money, infrastructure and recognition of Gaddafi as a legitimate partner in the dirty job of containment and readmission. As Libya is now the land of traffickers to illegal passage, the co-contractor has been Turkey. This country has been recognised as a safe country for asylum seekers, and it proposed to EU a real bargain: 6 billion Euros, fresh negotiations of Turkey's application to the EU and the removal of visa requirements for Turkish people seeking to travel to Europe. This country does not actually represent a migration risk to Europe, although Turkish people constitute the most important population of non-Europeans in the EU (4.5 million), because there are now fewer Turkish people travelling to Europe than there are Turkish people returning from Europe. The legitimacy of President Erdoğan, who has been somewhat criticised for his authoritarian and Islamic governance, has been restored in the EU. One year, Europe also strangely asked to exchange 72,000 Syrians refugees with people refused asylum by the EU.

3.2 The Factors of Failure and the Implications for States and EU Institutions

Among the main reasons for these bad responses is European immigration and asylum policy. Since 1990, most instruments of dissuasion, repression and confinement have used European immigration and asylum policy as a security approach. The Schengen system reinforcing external border controls led to the deaths of 30,000 people in the Mediterranean between 2000 and 2015 (40,000 since 1990). In 2015, 3000 people died in the Mediterranean Sea; a further 1400 died in 2016 from January until June. Trafficking is the main answer to closed borders, with there being a lot of money to win and few opportunities to locate those responsible. But this endeavour usually leads to lots of people dying at sea. The Frontex mechanism of a common border police (launched in 2004 as a common European police force concerned with the external borders of the EU) has been subsidised with a budget multiplied by four since its creation, and we can perceive some dependency on the institutions created to control illegal migration flows—their efficiency is not being questioned. The Dublin agreements on asylum can also be criticised: the Dublin I (1990) agreement tried to define a common European asylum policy that would reduce the chances of individuals achieving refugee status by aiming for harmonisation between all European countries. But the greatest burden of responsibility can be assigned to the Dublin II agreement of 2003, which has been highly criticised but never refuted. According to this, an asylum seeker entering an EU country is required to ask for asylum in that country (in a 'one stop, one shop' system). This does not work in practice because newcomers are able to choose the country they want to apply to, and Greece is rarely chosen.

The most important failure was the solidarity crisis between EU countries. In years past, burden sharing was the line proposed by the countries most affected by the arrival of asylum seekers, like Germany and Austria, after the fall of the Berlin Wall. Then, the Dublin II regime passed the task to southern European countries positioned along the Mediterranean, mostly Italy and Greece, which lacked the appropriate infrastructure to cope, especially in the case of the Mediterranean islands. In 2015, a gap also appeared between Eastern and Western European countries in terms of the resettlements proposed by the EU: most of the countries belonging to the Visegrád Group (Poland, Hungary, the Czech Republic, Slovakia) refused newcomers and closed their national borders, basing their arguments on the challenges presented to their homogenous identities and the context of terrorism. Solidarity is, however, one of the values of the EU, being defined in several articles of the EU's Treaty of Lisbon and being one of the founding values of Europe, along with democracy, human rights, liberalism, secularisation of the state and diversity. We have seen a lack of trust between EU states regarding refugees, as well as situations where states have been the main obstacles to European solidarity, due to the strength of the emerging nationalist ideologies that are arising all over Europe. The desire to restore national borders and symbols of the sovereignty of the state has often been cited by countries during the refugee crisis.

Other outcomes would be possible but were not debated, such as a 2001 proposal to implement a European directive on temporary protection for newcomers not fitting into the criteria of the Geneva Convention. One could also reopen some other legal channels of immigration in employment, which would weaken the explosion of so-called mixed flows of job seekers trying to get refugee status. Declaring war on migration, as was debated at the EU level in 2014 or dissuading migration with repression through militarised borders, is not a suitable solution for Europe. The weakness of the Euro-Mediterranean dialogue and going back to old, failed solutions such as return policies (as decided in the Valletta Euro-African summit of autumn 2015) are also parts of the crisis, which is more about a lack of solidarity between EU countries and confronting with the EU and a failure of EU dissuasion than refugees, who strongly affect few EU countries except for Germany.

4 Could International Governance of Migration Policies be an Answer?

Governance has recently been applied to migration management in a context of great disorder and human rights violations, with migration progressively becoming an international issue. Most southern countries have no immigration policy, and few of them are signatories to the international conventions on refugees (1951), statelessness (1954), equality of rights at work with nationals (ILO) (International Labour Organisation) and children's rights (1989). New groups—isolated women, unaccompanied children, elites and experts—have entered into international mobility. But the categories of migrants between workers, refugees and family members are now confused due to more similar profiles between themselves than in the past, along with the categories of states (of immigration, emigration and transit), also in turmoil. This confusion, the discrepancies between objectives and results, and the perverse effects of some national policies plead for a form of world governance.

4.1 Historical Background

The gaps between the objectives and the failing practices have led to the idea that migration would be better managed at a larger level than that of the national state. In the meantime, transnationalism has spread as a new approach to migration, suggesting that borders should not be closed for certain kinds of flows (e.g. social, economic, cultural, media). In addition, the experimental use of mechanisms of global governance for dealing with global issues (environment, population, women's rights, climate) has suggested that this idea could be extended to cover migration.

4.2 A Term of Reference: The United Nations Convention of 1990

At the international level, there are some universal declarations covering migration: the Universal Declaration of Human Rights of 1948 says that every man has the right to leave a country, including his own. The ILO also aims to protect social rights for migrant workers. However, while refugees have a universal text, the Geneva Convention of 1951 on refugees, which was first focused on European states before being extended in 1967 and 1969 to cover the entire world, migrants lack general and universal rights because they are ruled by the laws of immigration states that define the rights of entrance, work and settlement at the national level. In 1990, after 10 years of work, the United Nations (UN) proposed to the signatories of all states (193) the UN Convention of 1990 on the Protection of the Rights of All Migrant Workers and Members of their Families. This Convention does not innovate nor open up new rights—instead, it simply refers to all the rights that exist in the world for migrant workers and gives some minimum rights to illegal migrants. For this reason, no northern country of immigration has signed the Convention, which has slowly been signed by 48 countries, all of them belonging to the south as emigration countries. These countries intended to protect their nationals abroad but often encounter difficulties when they are themselves confronted with immigrants (as new immigration countries) claiming the rights they mainly wanted to be recognised for the sake of their nationals (cf. Wihtol de Wenden 2013a; Schmoll et al. 2015; de Gutcheneire et al. 2009).

4.3 Global Governance

The global governance of migration was launched by Kofi Annan, General Secretary of the UN, in 2006. He was interested in a process started by several international organisations and NGOs (non-governmental organisations) in Geneva in 2003 to propose a broader reflection on migration than that led by the states. As a result, the Global Migration Group (GMG) was launched in 2003, and it rapidly gained 17 partners. The idea of speaking about migration at a global level had been broached at the International Conference on Population and Development led in Cairo in 1994, but there has never been a global conference on migration such as those focused on population (Cairo), women (Beijing), discrimination (Durban) or the environment (Copenhagen) under the auspices of the UN. In 2006, Kofi Annan decided to build a high-level dialogue at the UN headquarters in New York, followed by annual meetings of the Global Forum on Migration and Development in Brussels (2007), Manila (2008), Athens (2009), Puerto Vallarta (2010), Geneva (2011), Mauritius (2012) and Stockholm (2014). The UN organised a second high-level dialogue in New York in 2013.

The main idea, starting from the many perverse effects of some national policies of immigration or from the absence of decision making, is to draw from a larger base of expertise than those of the nation states in order to avoid the most unexpected effects: illegal migrants being settled for a long time in countries of arrival without any long-term plan, dead people being washed up along the borders, inequality between men and women being evident in daily life and work, children being required to work, the development of a black market of passage (Ambrosini 2013), as well as the arrival of unaccompanied minors, isolated women and repatriated persons (Ambrosini 2013). The lack of efficiency of efforts to control national borders, in spite of security discourses and practices that come close to military action and human rights violations in almost every operation, has progressively led to the idea that a supranational level of decision making would take into account more contradictory factors and ethical principles than nation states, which are preoccupied with public opinion and security concerns. The Forum is presently a work in progress, and a basis for reflection is the UN Convention of 1990 on the Protection of the Rights of All Migrant Workers and Members of their Families. But the Forum has weak legitimacy on the international scene because the high-level dialogue itself does not belong to the sphere of international diplomacy but to parallel practices. The topic of migration is never dealt with at G8 or G20 meetings. The reason for the slow settlement of the global governance of migration (despite being overseen by the General Secretary, Peter Sutherland, and the willingness of the International Organization for Migrations (IOM) to head the system) is a lack of transnational mobilisation for such a cause. The actors pleading for more open borders are, ironically, uniting the immigration states, nationalist public opinions and political parties and some defenders of the welfare state who feel threatened by new social consumers. Those who are in favour of opening the borders are, on the contrary, emigration states (mostly signatories of the UN Convention of 1990), associations of migrants involved in the development of their countries of origin, human rights associations and enterprises lacking a sufficient labour force. They have no tradition of fighting together, which inhibits the progress of the call for global governance of migration. Although the immigration nation states are losing control of their borders due to the way the world is in motion, they try to resist human globalisation, including migration. But the mechanisms have been introduced, and it will be difficult to stop the movement for global governance of migration, especially due to the support of many NGOs such as the International Catholic Migration Commission (ICMC).

4.4 Regional Governance

In parallel, in order to better reconcile security with a liberal economy of trade and work and facilitate the opening of the borders, which is the last facilitator of mobility lacking in the areas of capital and trade, some regions have organised systems for the free market, freedom of movement, work and settlement. The EU is the most sophisticated system for Europeans (with a severe counterpart for the non-Europeans wanting to cross the external borders of Europe) and the Nordic states that are not members of the EU, but there are other spaces that enable the mobility of the labour force: the Union of South American Nations (UNASUR) in Latin America, the Southeast Asian Network (SEANET) system (which includes countries with freedom of circulation and work towards immigration states in the region), the Trans-Tasman Travel Agreement (TTTA) between Australia and New Zealand and the Economic Community of West African States (ECOWAS) between 15 countries in Western Africa. Other practices are more informal: the CIS (former USSR) has suppressed short-term work visas for people from Central Asia and the South Caucasus seeking work in Russia, while Turkey has arranged for its citizens to have free access to 45 countries, including those in the EU, to encourage trade, tourism and work. We count around 22 regional systems of free circulation in the world, but very few of them are working well due to political conflicts in the regions (cf. Cohen 2008; Massey et al. 1995).

4.5 The Emerging States and New Questions

Global governance is on the move because southern countries are now part of the debate. Some of them are emerging immigration states—such as Brazil, Russia, India, China, South Africa (BRICS) and countries like Algeria, Libya, the Gulf States, Angola and Venezuela—while others are former emigration countries that are becoming immigration and transit countries (e.g. Turkey, Morocco, Mexico). They are trying to enter the scene thanks to diaspora policies aimed at their emigrants, requiring rights for them in their negotiations with immigration states (in exchange for repatriation agreements). As a result of this, they have begun to have a voice in world social forums, as well in the World Forum for Migration and Development (FMMD) annual meetings and the high-level dialogue of the UN.

Another factor implying more global governance is the persistence of unresolved questions: statelessness is one of them, with 13 million of people around the world affected, particularly in Bangladesh, Myanmar and some sub-Saharan countries in the Great Lakes region. Another group is environmentally displaced persons; we currently count 42 million of them across the world, but climate experts are foreseeing that there will be between 150 and 200 million of them by the end of this century. The Nansen Initiative was started in Geneva in 2011 to give a status for environmentally displaced people, but the UNHCR does not recognise environmentally displaced people as refugees. Another unresolved question that could be more easily debated at the world level is the unexpected consequence of decisions that have consequences for migration flows, such as the price of cotton, the development of coffee plants in new emerging countries like Vietnam, extensive fishing in Africa by Chinese or Japanese fishermen and the opening of new markets for raw materials. World governance of migration could provide answers to such questions. But it is still a tentative and fragile area of diplomacy, due to the way in which the long-term illegitimacy of international migration brings disorder to nation states.

5 Conclusion

The issues of asylum and immigration have become high on the European agenda, as well as in national European policies, but the recent increase of refugees since the Arab revolutions of 2011, particularly with the Syrian crisis, has attracted more debates, along with some morally grey situations such as that of the town of Calais in France. This situation has highlighted the limitations of European immigration and asylum policy and the Dublin agreements on a common asylum policy and the strength of the divergent interests of national governments. Most of these policies, at the state level, are not necessarily enacted to build a good policy but instead to satisfy public opinion by appealing to the extreme right, leading to the theatralisation of European and national policies and a situation where all forms of walls, closure and controls have gained considerable political clout. But immigration also interferes with other European and national issues, such as demographic decrease, attracting segmented jobs while avoiding competition with the European labour markets, and concerns about Islamist radicalisation distrust towards all forms of agencies led by migrants such as double citizenship. All these trends are contradicting the values of Europe—solidarity, harmonisation, humanitarian protection and inclusion—which are being challenged by the present crisis.

References

Ambrosini, M. (2013). *Irregular migration and invisible welfare*. New York: Palgrave.

Castles, S., & Miller, M. (2014). *The age of migration* (4th ed.). London: Macmillan.

Cohen, R. (2008). *Global diasporas: An introduction*. London: Routledge.

de Gutcheneire, P., Pecoud, A., & Cholewski, R. (2009). *Migration and human rights: The UN convention of migrants*. Paris/Cambridge: UNESCO/Cambridge University.

Hollifield, J. (1998–1999). Migration, trade and the nation state: The myth of globalization. *UCLA Journal of International Law and Foreign Affairs, 3*, 585–636.

Massey, D., Arango, J., & Taylor, E. (1995). *Words in motion*. Oxford: Oxford University.

Portes, A. (2003). Theoretical convergences and empirical evidence in the study of immigrant transnationalism. *International Migration Review, 37*, 814–892.

Rosenau, J. (1990). *Turbulence in world politics*. Princeton: Princeton University.

Sassen, S. (1996). *Losing control? Sovereignty in an age of globalization*. New York: Columbia University.

Schmoll, C., Thiollet, H., & Wihtol de Wenden, C. (Eds.). (2015). *Migrations en Méditerranée*. Paris: CNRS Editions.

Weiner, M. (1995). *The global migration crisis: Challenges to states and to human rights*. New York: Harper Collins.

Wihtol de Wenden, C. (2013a). *La question migratoire au XXIème siècle*. Paris: Presses de Sciences Po.

Wihtol de Wenden, C. (2013b). *Les nouvelles migrations: Hommes, lieux, politiques*. Paris: Ellipses.

Wihtol de Wenden, C. (2016). *Atlas des migrations: Un équilibre mondial à inventer* (4th ed.). Paris: Autrement.

Chapter 7
Solidarity in European Migration Policy: The Perspective of the Visegrád States

Justyna Segeš Frelak

1 Introduction

Negative reactions against refugees can be seen across the whole EU, with anti-refugee and anti-immigrant parties and movements gaining a growing number of supporters in many countries. At the same time, alongside this growing xenophobic sentiment, some member states have replaced European solidarity with the need for national answers. Migration has also influenced the political agenda by bringing issues of immigration, integration and security to the mainstream—for the first time in history, in the case of Central Europe.

The Visegrád Group (V4) response to the crisis and solutions proposed by the European Commission has been particularly striking. Unexpectedly, the migration crisis has reunited countries that are divided on many other subjects. At the same time, with the exception of Hungary in 2015, the region has been unaffected by the crisis, and the number of asylum seekers and recognised refugees remains rather low. It is important, therefore, to understand the factors behind the policy decisions on and the harsh reactions to refugees in Central Europe, which will be briefly presented in the text.

2 The International Dimension of the Refugee Crisis

Initially, the whole Visegrád Group (with the exception of Poland) opposed the adoption of refugees according to the "Juncker plan", thus exposing itself to fierce criticism from the EU side. The group was in favour of maintaining "the voluntary

J. Segeš Frelak (✉)
Institute of Public Affairs, Warsaw, Poland
e-mail: justyna.frelak@isp.org.pl

A. Grimmel, S.M. Giang (eds.), *Solidarity in the European Union*,
DOI 10.1007/978-3-319-57036-5_7

nature of EU solidarity" and the creation of other alternatives to address the migration crisis. Presently, the Visegrád Group continues to be in strong opposition to compulsory refugee relocation under any scheme. The strongest controversies have been aroused by the proposition to introduce a corrective allocation mechanism, with a compensatory solidarity contribution in the case of not taking refugees.

The counterproposal of the V4 was the concept of "flexible solidarity" and its successor, "effective solidarity". According to these concepts, the solutions should take into account the specific situation of each member state.[1] The Slovak concepts envisaged three scenarios depending on the intensity of migration. First of all, the Dublin system should not be changed but only improved. Under normal circumstances, the EU member states should meet the full requirements of registration and prevention of secondary movements. In a crisis situation, all countries would have to engage in collective assistance to those member states which are struggling with the greatest migratory pressures. Member states would decide themselves on what form of aid they could provide: apart from voluntary relocations, it could take the form of financial contributions, increased support for EU agencies, etc.[2]

One of the priorities of the Polish Presidency of the Visegrád Group (1 July 2016–30 June 2017) is coordination of the position of the V4 at the EU forum that "should enhance solutions to address the migration root causes with emphasis on the effective protection of EU external borders. The V4 countries should focus on opposing any changes that would result in the introduction of any permanent and compulsory redistribution mechanism or would significantly reduce Member States' competencies in this area".[3]

Here the question is whether such flexibility and solidarity can go together as a form of burden sharing on a voluntary basis. (Although there is not a precise definition of solidarity in the case of refugee, asylum and migration law, solidarity is defined in a human rights context.) Furthermore, does flexible or effective solidarity support or undermine human rights standards, and to what extent would the voluntary character of such solidarity actually result in real burden sharing?[4] Taking into consideration the rhetoric of the V4 concerning the refugee and migration crisis, the proposal of flexible/effective solidarity was widely understood as a meaningless message, which in practice meant "no" solidarity. The proposals were also criticised as ineffective, as the proposed solutions would not lessen the burden on the frontier states. Some of the actions presented as a sign of solidarity of the V4—like calls for support of refugee camps outside the EU or tackling root

---

[1]Joint Statement of Heads of Governments of the V4 Countries published on September 16, 2016.

[2]https://euobserver.com/migration/135960

[3]Programme of the Polish Presidency of the Visegrád Group, Ministry of Foreign Affairs, Warsaw 2016.

[4]M. Kotzur, "Flexible Solidarity—Effective Solidarity?", 17 December 2016, https://voelkerrechtsblog.org

causes—have practically not been implemented and at the same time do not address the difficult situation of Italy or Greece.[5]

3 Visegrád: Migration Trends

The V4 attitude towards migration fundamentally differs from that of several Western European countries. This is partially connected to the fact that—with the exception of the Czech Republic (4.1%)—Hungary (1.4%), Poland (0.3%) and Slovakia (1.1%) are among the states with the lowest percentages of foreigners in the European Union.[6] Despite the recent increase in the number of economic immigrants in some countries of the region (e.g. Poland), the migrant communities still remain rather small.

Similarly, the refugee phenomenon concerns V4 countries to a much lesser extent than other EU member states, both in terms of the number of applications and people actually residing there. According to Eurostat, in 2015 there were 1,255,640 first-time applicants in the whole of the EU, 1235 in the Czech Republic, 270 in Slovakia, 174,435 in Hungary and 10,255 in Poland.[7]

Interestingly, despite the geographic proximity of the Visegrád Group, the ethnic structure of asylum seekers differs significantly among the states. In the Czech Republic, the three main groups of refugees come from Ukraine, Syria and Cuba and in Poland from Russia, Ukraine and Tajikistan. In the case of Slovakia, the three main groups are as follows: Iraq, Afghanistan and Ukraine. In 2014, the majority of asylum seekers in Hungary came from Syria, Afghanistan and Kosovo. To give a comparison, in the whole of the EU, the main countries of citizenship of asylum seekers in EU member states were Syria, Afghanistan and Iraq.

Visegrád countries also vary in terms of granting international protection, with Poland and Hungary having one of the lowest recognition rates in the EU. For example, in 2014 only 18% of people were granted protection in Poland and 15% in Hungary, whereas the EU average was 52% for first instance decisions in the EU. For final decisions on appeal, the recognition rate was 14%. The situation is better in Slovakia, where 60% of people receive positive decisions, and the Czech Republic, with 34% positive decisions.[8]

[5]Z. Vegh, "Flexible solidarity", 19 December 2016, http://Visegradinsight.eu

[6]http://ec.europa.eu/eurostat/statistics-explained/index.php/File:Non-national_population_by_group_of_citizenship,_1_January_2014_%28%C2%B9%29_YB15.png

[7]Record number of over 1.2 million first-time asylum seekers registered in 2015, Eurostat44/2016–4 March 2016.

[8]Asylum decisions in the EU, Eurostat, 75/2016–20 April 2016.

4 (No) History of Admitting Refugees

Despite the much smaller scale than in other EU member states, all V4 countries have some experience in admitting persons seeking international protection. Hungary had an episode in its history of admitting refugees in the 1990s, during and after the fall of the Ceausescu regime in Romania and during the Balkan Wars. In the case of Poland, over the years, not only the scale but also the nationality of foreigners seeking protection in Poland has changed, reaching its peak in 2013 with 15,253 applicants. The largest group of applicants for refugee status in the early 1990s came from Armenia and the war-torn Balkans. In the late 1990s, Poland accepted many foreigners from Asia and Africa, mainly from Sri Lanka and Afghanistan. Then, due to the escalation of the Chechen-Russian conflict, Poland was mostly granting asylum to citizens of the Russian Federation, the majority of whom came from the Caucasus—they have become the largest group of refugees in Poland today.[9] As a result of the armed conflict in Georgia, the number of applications from this country increased from 71 in 2008 to 4214 in 2009. Nowadays, as the result of conflict in Ukraine, Ukrainians are seeking refuge across the border in Poland. In the case of Slovakia, in recent years, asylum has mainly been granted to people from Afghanistan, Iraq, Iran, Cuba and Somalia, following patterns of international conflicts. Yet, the number of applications has been moderate, reaching less than 500 per year in recent years.[10] By comparison, the Czech Republic used to receive far more applications for asylum—most commonly from Ukrainians—in the years 1998–2006 than nowadays. For example, in 2000 there were 8788 applicants, while in 2001 there were 18,088 applicants in total.[11]

5 Challenges of Transit Countries

The V4 are transit countries for the majority of people seeking international protection. The final destination of refugees entering the V4 is Western Europe, usually Germany or Sweden. This is reflected, among other things, by a high rate of cancelled cases, as asylum seekers leave V4 countries during the procedure. The low attractiveness of V4 countries is connected with issues such as the limited job opportunities and social support, the overall strict asylum procedure and the limited experience of institutions working with migrants. The circumstances mentioned above force migrants to leave the country—even those who are committed to

[9] A. Kosowicz and A. Maciejko, "Integracja uchodźców w Polsce w liczbach (Refugee integration in Poland in numbers)", Polskie Forum Migracyjne (Polish Migration Forum), Warsaw 2007.

[10] http://www.unhcr-centraleurope.org/pdf/resources/statistics/asylum-trends-in-central-europe-2010-2012.html

[11] http://www.mvcr.cz/migrace/clanek/mezinarodni-ochrany.aspx

staying. As a result, the stock of people with refugee status is generally low. For example, in Poland, in 2015 there were only 4863 humanitarian migrants with valid residence cards.[12]

It should be emphasised that—in connection with membership in the EU and obligations under international law—the situation of people seeking protection in the V4 is much better than it was in the 1990s, when the construction of a refugee system took place. In all four analysed countries, persons granted international protection are entitled to integration support, yet, as available data shows, it is generally not effective and does not solve the most crucial problems of refugees, such as the unavailability of (permanent) work and a surplus of jobs below migrants' qualifications. This is linked to their poor command of the local language resulting from, e.g. limited access to or low quality of language lessons.[13] Lack of access to appropriate housing, housing exclusion or homelessness are other important problems.[14]

Hungary, Poland and the Czech Republic have state-funded integration programmes, while Slovakia implements integration programmes co-funded from EU funds. The role of EU funding is increasing, often replacing instead of complementing state integration measures—a tendency that is highly criticised by expert circles as this situation does not ensure stable project implementation. As EU projects are usually implemented by the NGO sector, integration support is very often provided on an ad hoc basis, and significant delays in payments often force organisations to close due to financial problems.

Since 2014, recognised refugees have been allowed to stay in camps for up to 2 months in Hungary. During these 2 months, they are supposed to sign an "integration contract" with a Hungarian city or district, which will be responsible for their integration. As for financial support, they receive a monthly allowance of 90 thousand forints (€300) for 6 months, which is then gradually reduced. Although learning the local language is a condition of successful integration, the state does not offer any free language courses. However, social actors provide help with learning the language as well as with finding accommodation, among other things.[15] Despite some positive changes, such as increased financial support,

[12]UDSC, statistical data, 2016.

[13]K. Wysieńska and Z. Karpiński, "Kapitał ludzki i społeczny uchodźców w Polsce—podsumowanie wyników badania" (Human and social capital of refugees in Poland—summary of results of research), Institute of Public Affairs, Warsaw 2012.

[14]"Access to Employment for Beneficiaries of International Protection in Bulgaria, Poland, Romania and Slovakia", UNHCR, Budapest 2013, V. Antolová, M. Martinkovič, Ľ. Kovács and D. Knošková, "Where is my home? Homelessness and Access to Housing among Asylum-Seekers, Refugees and Persons with International Protection in the Slovak Republic", UNHCR, Bratislava 2013, K. Wysieńska, Gdzie jest mój dom? Bezdomność i dostęp do mieszkań wśród ubiegających się o status uchodźcy, uchodźców i osób z przyznaną ochroną międzynarodową w Polsce (Where is my home? Homelessness and access to housing among asylum seekers, refugees and persons granted international protection in Poland), IPA, UNHCR 2012.

[15]http://ec.europa.eu/dgs/home-affairs/financing/fundings/mapping-funds/countries/hungary/index_en.htm

there are also some challenges concerning the "integration contract": the experience of social workers regarding working with refugees is limited, and the refugees' right to free movement is often violated, since they are obliged to report to the authorities once a week.[16]

The procedure to grant refugee status in Poland can take a year or two, despite the fact that the statutory time limit is defined as 6 months. Most people applying for refugee statuses are placed in a refugee centre in an unfavourable location, often far away from major urban areas, which makes access to health services, schools and NGOs difficult. Moreover, the people staying in the centres may only seek work 6 months after submitting their application, which does not help them to become active in the labour market and gives rise to great frustration among some of them. Such a long period of inactivity during their stay, resulting from a lack of pre-integration policy, hinders immigrants' ability to begin an independent life in Poland. Foreigners can only count on state-funded Polish language lessons, while workshops or professional training courses are conducted by NGOs.

People who have been granted refugee status or subsidiary protection qualify for participation in the annual Individual Integration Program (*Indywidualny Program Integracji—IPI*), while migrants who have obtained permission for so-called tolerated stay are deprived of this assistance, only having the right to assistance in the form of shelter, food, necessary clothing and designated benefits that cover the costs of purchase of food, medicines, household goods, etc. The main goal of programmes coordinated by District Family Assistance Centres (*Powiatowe Centra Pomocy Rodzinie*) is to assist migrants in overcoming the language, material and social barriers that they might come up against in their new homes. Although the establishment of *IPI*s has been considered a positive development, the programmes have been criticised for their limited effectiveness—few participants speak Polish or have actually found stable work or a flat at the end of the programme.[17]

In the case of Slovakia, only basic integration support is provided to asylum seekers—which includes, among other things, counselling, language courses and material support. These types of activities are cofinanced from European Funds. Presently, only one NGO offers integration services across the whole country—the Slovak Catholic Charity. The integration programme lasts 6 months and includes financial support for finding accommodation and other necessary expenditures such as social services, assistance with bureaucracy and administration, Slovak language courses and psychological and labour counselling. The integration programmes are—as in other countries—considered to be far too short to ensure effective integration of forced migrants. Additionally, existing integration tools lack professional coordination, which is manifested in differences in the quality of services provided across the country, fluctuations in numbers of NGOs providing integration

---

[16]http://www.migszol.com/integration-contract.html

[17]J. Frelak, W. Klaus and J. Wiśniewski, (Eds.), Przystanek Polska. Analiza programów integracyjnych dla uchodźców (Next stop Poland. Analysis of refugee integration programmes), Warsaw: Institute of Public Affairs, Warsaw 2008.

and lack of monitoring. Furthermore, many measures often have counterproductive results (e.g. locating refugees in localities with high unemployment rates).[18]

In the Czech Republic, humanitarian migrants are the subjects of special integration measures funded by state integration programmes. Integration support includes obtaining housing and education, learning the Czech language and finding a job. Similar to other Visegrád countries, services are provided on the basis of a contract, placing a number of responsibilities on the migrant, such as attending a compulsory introductory Czech language course. Under the State Integration Programme, recognised refugees have an opportunity to get a rented apartment or obtain a state contribution to rent.[19]

6 Attitudes Towards Refugees

The refugee and migrant crisis has had a significant impact on attitudes towards immigration in Europe. In the case of Central Europe, where knowledge about immigration is limited and stereotypes are widespread, the refugee crisis has contributed to the increase in negative opinions about immigration. As was already noted, due to the relatively small number of foreigners residing in the countries under study, the anti-immigrant sentiment in the region is not based on real experience with non-nationals. Contrarily, in the case of countries overwhelmed by an influx of refugees like Germany or Sweden, attitudes have been much more positive.[20]

In 2015, immigration was seen as the second biggest challenge within the EU. Interestingly, Central European countries tend to be more concerned with immigration. Similarly, while on average 65% of all EU citizens agreed that their countries should support refugees, opposition to the idea was much stronger in Central Europe.[21]

According to the EU Parliament Eurobarometer, citizens of Central and Eastern European states were also sceptical regarding the distribution of refugees (entering the European Union) between member states. This support was by far the lowest among Czechs and Slovaks, who are largely opposed to such actions. Only half of them agreed that the distribution of asylum seekers should be decided on an EU level on the basis of binding quotas, compared to 74% of Hungarians and 70% of Poles.[22]

[18]M. Hlinčíková, M. Sekulová, Integrácia ľudí s medzinárodnou ochranou na Slovensku: Hľadanie východísk, IVO, Bratislava 2015.

[19]http://www.mvcr.cz

[20]B. Junyadi, C. Molnar, Central Europe's Faceless Strangers: The Rise of Xenophobia, Political Capital Institute, Hungary 2016.

[21]European Commission, Standard Eurobarometer 84, December 2015.

[22]European Parliament: Parlemeter 2015. The main challenges for the EU: migration, and the economic and social situation.

A public opinion study showed that not only do Visegrád politicians have a more critical attitude towards refugees, but Visegrád societies also often oppose admitting people seeking international protection. At the beginning of the refugee crisis, the results of the opinion polls showed significant differences in attitudes towards refugees among residents of the Visegrád Group. Hungarians, who experienced an increased influx of refugees, appeared to be most receptive to sheltering refugees from areas affected by war (65% accept welcoming refugees from countries affected by armed conflicts, and 32% are against). Poles were slightly more sceptical: 40% oppose admitting any refugees. At the same time, the majority of Polish society (56%) agreed to admit them temporarily into Poland. Czechs had even more negative opinions—half of the respondents (50%) oppose accepting them by the Czech Republic, while more than two-fifths (44%) approve such actions. Giving shelter to refugees encountered the strongest opposition in Slovakia, where only 33% of respondents accept giving temporary help and nearly two-thirds (62%) express complete disapproval.[23]

Today, negative opinions dominate in the whole region, including Poland: from 2015 to 2016, Poles transformed from moderate supporters to opponents of admitting refugees. According to the most recent CBOS research, more than half of respondents (52%) oppose the admission of refugees. Two out of five respondents (40%) agree to grant them temporary shelter (until they can safely return to the country from which they came). Only less than one in 20 respondents (4%) says we should allow refugees to settle in Poland permanently. The same poll showed a clear difference in attitudes between supporters of the more conservative PiS and the more liberal PO. Among the supporters of PiS, 64% are opponents of reception, and only 32% support such activities. Conversely, support among PO voters clearly outweighs opposition (60% vs. 36%).[24] At the same time, the attitude of Poles towards accepting Ukrainian refugees is much more positive compared to people from the Middle East or Africa. Almost two-thirds of respondents (58%) agree to help their Eastern neighbours, while one in three (37%) is opposed.

According to a more recent survey commissioned by the Slovak Academy of Sciences and conducted by TNS Slovakia in 2016: in the opinion of 52.5% Slovaks, Europeans should help refugees who have already arrived only when absolutely necessary, while 18.7% of people stated that we should not be helping refugees at all. People continued to express fear towards refugees—41.4% of respondents were a little worried, while 29.6% were quite worried. The voters of the far-right Kotleba ĽSNS expressed the greatest concern. The most important reason to fear refugees, according to respondents, was connected with the opinion that refugees would increase crime (36.6%) and that a large proportion of them would not want to adapt to the Slovak way of life (30.6%). About 30% of respondents feared that the

[23]CBOS, Stosunek do uchodźców w krajach Grupy Wyszehradzkiej (Attitudes to refugees in Visegrád Group countries), Warsaw, November 2015.

[24]Stosunek Polaków do przyjmowania uchodźców, CBOS 2016.

arrival of refugees would increase the risk of attacks by Islamic extremists or that acceptance of refugees would cost a lot of money.[25]

Similar opinions are shared by Poles and Hungarians who also believe that the refugee crisis and the threat of terrorism are very much related to one another. According to more than 70% of them, refugees will increase the likelihood of terrorism in their countries. What is more, the majority think that they are a burden on host country because they take jobs and social benefits.[26]

7 The Internal Dimension of the Crisis

In the whole EU, the refugee crisis has become fuel for traditionally anti-immigration forces. Yet, in the case of the Visegrád countries, both populists and mainstream right- or left-wing parties have made use of fears over immigration for their political purposes. In the case of the whole Visegrád region, one may observe the scapegoating of "ghosts"—as refugees from Southern Europe did not reach these countries (with short exception of Hungary). Furthermore, it proved to be a very easy political tactic, with the majority of society unable to ascertain the veracity of the often-xenophobic message. The general trend was also to focus on the security issue connected with migration, which resulted in the perception of refugees as a challenge to the state's internal security.

In the Czech Republic, migration has become one of the dominant political topics of the past 2 years, with President Miloš Zeman saying "Not all Muslims are terrorists, but all terrorists are Muslims" and describing the refugee crisis as "an invasion organised by the Muslim Brotherhood". Here one should mention new extremist initiatives such as IvČRn ("We don't want Islam in the Czech Republic") or anti-immigration movements such as the Party of Direct Democracy, the sixth most successful party in the regional elections in 2016. Public debate on migration has become radicalised due to, among other reasons, linking refugees and terrorism in a country with almost no Muslim community.[27] Despite such a political climate, in the opinion of experts, the policy maintains the same direction as before the start of the crisis.[28]

During the election campaign 2016, Slovak Prime Minister Robert Fico stated that he wants to "prevent the creation of a coherent Muslim community in the country"—again in a country with a very small number of Muslim migrants. The centre-left party SMER-SD has framed a discourse that has been dominated by security and the cultural differences of Muslim migrants and succeeded in

[25]https://www.aktuality.sk

[26]Europeans Fear Wave of Refugees Will Mean More Terrorism, Fewer Jobs, Pew Research Centre, July 2016.

[27]A. Jurečková, Refugees in the Czech Republic? Not a trace—but still a problem, https://www.boell.de

[28]Visegrád and migration: Few prospects for a change in position, http://www.euractiv.com

marginalising pro-EU and pro-refugee voices. Besides the ruling party, far-right forces like Marian Kotleba's L'SNS and the Slovak National Party (SNS) also capitalised on fears over immigration and Islam and successfully entered parliament in 2016. Opinion polls at that time showed a rise in people considering migration as one of the most important issues.[29] At the same time, it should be underlined that all political actors seemed to concentrate on one common element—mandatory quota relocation of refugees between EU member states. Overall, very few parties (a notable exception being MOST-HID) presented definitely positive opinions regarding the reception of migrants or a truly sympathetic voice. As a result, concrete proposals concerning the reception and integration of refugees from political actors were heard only occasionally. The only exception on the political scene was Slovak President Andrej Kiska.[30]

In the case of Hungary, the government's response to the refugee crisis was also inspired by domestic political goals. The political party Fidesz and Prime Minister Viktor Orbán exploited the refugee crisis starting from the beginning of 2015, just a few days after the terrorist attack on the French magazine Charlie Hebdo, in order to regain popularity. The party also wanted to prevent the far-right Jobbik from dominating the topic and started anti-immigration campaigns that induced xenophobic attitudes by, among other things, labelling refugees and migrants and demonising them.[31] Hungary was the first country to create a fence to prevent migrants from entering the country. Prime Minister Viktor Orbán rejected the quota mechanism from the very beginning, lobbying for stronger border protection instead. Public opinion data show that there was a link between the government's anti-immigrant activities and the increased level of xenophobia.[32] In 2016 in order to keep immigration at the top of the political agenda and strengthen his position within the EU, V. Orbán initiated a referendum on the binding EU refugee quotas. Although the referendum was invalid, 98% of the 3.3 million people casting a vote were against refugee relocation quotas.[33] In the case of Hungary, it is also telling that more people are satisfied with the crisis management by the Fidesz government than with any previous measures taken by the cabinet.[34] In this environment, it is very difficult to hold rational public debates: only small opposition parties have been able to challenge the government's agenda.

[29]Security More Important than Migrants' Rights', Spectator.sme.sk, 16 November 2016.

[30]M. Hlinčíková, G. Mesežnikov (ed) Otvorená krajina alebo nedobytná pevnosť? Slovensko, migranti a utečenci, IVO 2016.

[31]A. Juhász, B. Hunyadi, E. Zgut, 'Focus on Hungary: Refugees, Asylum and Migration' (Political Capital, Heinrich-Böll-Stiftung, December 2015), http://www.politicalcapital.hu/wp-content/uploads/pc_boll_hungary_refugees_asylum_and_migration_web.pd

[32]B. Junyadi, C. Molnar, Central Europe's Faceless Strangers: The Rise of Xenophobia, Political Capital Institute, Hungary 2016.

[33]S. Schultheis, B. Hunyadi, The Referendum in Hungary: "A Clear Foreign Policy Debacle and a Temporary Domestic Setback for the Government", 20 October 2016.

[34]http://www.median.hu/object.c38fa2c9-5bc2-40c9-ae38-bab515a5f172.ivy

The refugee crisis started at a very specific moment in the Polish public debate—just before the electoral campaign. The refugee crisis combined with the political campaign caused an unprecedented outburst of xenophobia publicly and on social media. At the peak of the campaign, PiS was warning that Poland was in grave danger of a massive inflow of Muslim immigrants—and only they could prevent this.[35] At the same time, other parties (including left-wing parties) were avoiding taking a concrete position in defence of the decision to accept refugees in Poland. Only some activists in civil society tried (with limited success) to influence the debate with a positive message.

Here it should be underlined that the previous Polish government, after long negotiations, supported the proposed way of distributing refugees and hence agreed to admit approx. 7000 people, which it knew would be difficult to accept domestically. Prime Minister Ewa Kopacz, in support of the decision, stated that taking refugees was Poland's responsibility and a "test of decency".[36] The previous government, by breaking the coalition of countries of the Visegrád Group, was accused by the opposition—mainly PiS—of betraying the country and members of the group.

Initially, the new PiS government announced a continuation of the relocation plan, but, after the March 2016 terrorist attacks in Brussels, the new Prime Minister Beata Szydło announced that Poland would not accept any refugees under the relocation plan. The Polish position, expressed by, among others, Interior Minister Mariusz Błaszczak, emphasises that the redistribution mechanism is "a way to attract more migrants" rather than a solution to the crisis situation. At the same time, Poland has been lobbying for increased assistance in the countries of origin. In the case of the refugee crisis, PiS has been promoting a discourse of conflict by presenting the situation in terms of "us" and "them": "us" and "the opposition", "us" and the "liberal elites" and "us" and "dangerous migrants".[37]

8 The Debate on the Refugee Crisis and the Role of the Media

"Are we ready for a wave of refugees?" and "The invasion of refugees" have been common slogans appearing in Polish newspapers and those of other nations since the beginning of the migration crisis. The migrant crisis in Europe has sparked a heated debate on migration on a previously unknown scale in the V4 countries and shares many common features, despite the fact that the countries have not

[35]Nothing to Fear but Fear Itself? Case study—Poland/Institute of Public Affairs, 2017.

[36]Kopacz: Przyjęcie uchodźców to nasz obowiązek, test na przyzwoitość (accepting refugees is our responsibility, a test of decency), Gazeta Wyborcza, 10 September 2015, http://wyborcza.pl/10,82983,18748772,kopacz-przyjecie-uchodzcow-to-nasz-obowiazek-test-na-przyzwoitosc.html.

[37]Visegrád and migration: Few prospects for a change in position http://www.euractiv.com

experienced an increased influx of refugees. Typical anti-immigration slogans ("immigrants do not assimilate", "they are terrorists", "they are good for nothing", etc.) have become very popular in V4 countries. A side effect of this rhetoric has been a tendency to confuse economic migrants with refugees, which further highlights the lack of knowledge on the subject. The debate has been characterised by emotional narratives, stirring up fears of Muslim refugees, and a systematic disregard for facts and data.[38] Dehumanising terminology used in government campaigns relating to illegal migrants, welfare migrants, etc. has been reproduced in the media.

In the case of all the countries included in the study, TV and the Internet are the most important/main sources of information about refugees. According to a report by Kultura Liberalna's Public Debate Observatory, two motives have dominated in the media: "the clash of civilizations" and the moral obligation to accept refugees. The authors of the study conclude that manifestations of radicalisation of the language used on the issue of immigration can be found in large sections of the monitored media. Reports that are unfavourable or even hostile to refugees can mostly be found in media that are closer to the right end of the political spectrum.[39]

In the case of the Czech Republic, national TV channels are the main source of information for most Czechs, regardless of their age. A report prepared by Masaryk University in Brno showed that most of the news broadcast on two analysed channels concerned the impact of the refugee crisis in the Czech Republic and the impact of the crisis in other countries. At the same time, presenting the causes of the refugee crisis and providing its broader context were of minor significance, giving the impression that refugees were the cause of the crisis. According to the authors of the study, coverage of the refugee crisis may be considered equally unbalanced, with a one-sided accent on security risks related to migration. This may cause anxiety, while limited information on the humanitarian aspect and the critical situation in source countries might result in a lack of compassion for refugees. Similarly, very superficial broadcasts can be observed in the whole region. The fear and lack of understanding was clearly seen in the opinion surveys mentioned above.[40]

Interesting findings can also be seen in a report by the Central European University. This comparative analysis of Hungarian and Austrian media coverage of the refugee crisis revealed significant differences. Although the news media in

---

[38]D. Hall and A. Mikulska-Jolles, *Uprzedzenia, Strach Czy Niewiedza? Młodzi Polacy o powodach niechęci do przyjmowania uchodźców (Prejudice, Fear or Ignorance? Young Poles on reasons for the reluctance to accept refugees)*, Warsaw, Stowarzyszenie Interwencji Prawnej (Association for Legal Intervention), 2016.

[39]Ł. Bertram, M, Jędrzejek, Analiza Specjalna Obserwatorium Debaty Publicznej: Islamskie hordy, azjatycki najazd, socjalny dżihad. Jak polskie media piszą o uchodźcach (Special Analysis by the Public Debate Observatory: Islamic hordes, the Asian invasion, social jihad. How the Polish media write about refugees), "Kultura Liberalna", 14 October 2015.

[40]M. Tkaczyk, P. Pospěch, J. Macek. Analýza mediálního pokrytí uprchlické krize (výzkumná zpráva). Brno: Masarykova univerzita, 2015.

both countries reported intensively about events related to the refugee crisis, Hungarian media showed a strong emphasis on the governmental and political agenda. Additionally, Hungarian media coverage was marked by almost no discourse about the integration of refugees, whereas Austrian media frequently talked about issues of social inclusion.[41]

Additionally, in the case of Hungary and Slovakia, the government and part of the media deliberately avoided using the term "refugees", preferring the expressions "illegal migrants" or "economic migrants" instead, whereas NGOs looked at the crisis from an exclusively humanitarian point of view. In all the analysed countries, the same tendency could be observed—even just by reporting about the actions of governmental actors, the media may have contributed to the dissemination of an anti-refugee agenda. Moreover, in the case of Slovakia, media analysis indicates that a large proportion of news was passively reprinted without any specific contribution of the media. As A. H. Chudžíková notes, the media have the potential and perhaps the social responsibility to provide a broader picture of more complex problems such as the refugee crisis, especially when it has become an instrument of political rivalry, regardless of the social consequences.[42]

9 The Role of Civil Society

As reflected in the aforementioned surveys' results, societies in the V4 are deeply polarised about the refugee crisis. Consequently, while some Poles organise or join rallies under the banner "Refugees Welcome", others join rallies that carry banners like "better repatriated than immigrated". The amount of hate speech on the Internet is also shocking. It has been clear that the majority of the population does not have appropriate information about refugees, and their attitudes are based on fear and stereotypes.

At the same time, academia and the nongovernmental sector supported a policy of "open arms", tolerance and (in Poland's case) admission of an even higher number of refugees than that declared. It is worth mentioning the example of the Polish Day of Solidarity with Refugees, which took place on October 15 and involved 130 institutions (NGOs, theatres, museums, etc.). In another undertaking, more than 40 Polish newspapers initiated a campaign titled "more knowledge—less fear—refugees in Poland" to present the refugee problem fairly and bring it to the attention of Poles.

---

[41]B. Gábor and V. Messing, Infiltration of political meaning-production: security threat or humanitarian crisis? The coverage of the refugee 'crisis' in the Austrian and Hungarian media in early autumn 2015.

[42]A. H. Chudžíková Obraz utečencov v médiách na Slovensku, in: M. Hlinčíková, G. Mesežnikov (ed) Otvorená krajina alebo nedobytná pevnosť? Slovensko, migranti a utečenci, IVO 2016.

At the same time, various grassroots movements and civil society in Slovakia have been demonstrating solidarity and offering practical assistance to partners in countries experiencing a high number of arrivals of asylum seekers. For example, many volunteers from Bratislava contributed to supporting refugees located across the border in Austria. A coalition of religious groups offered housing for 2000 refugees.[43] Concurrently, thousands of Slovaks gathered for an anti-immigration protest in Bratislava in June 2015.[44]

In the case of Hungary, civil society actors have also been active both in the debate and in terms of direct support for refugees. For example, a day before the parliamentary debate on immigration, six NGOs published an open letter protesting against government migration policy and rhetoric. MKKP initiated a very successful "counter-government campaign" and raised €105,000 (compared to projected €9500) for this purpose.[45]

10 Perspectives

Political parties in the Visegrád countries are successfully exploiting anti-immigration fears and sentiments. As the examples of Poland and Hungary show, the governments' strategy is to exploit the topic permanently. This is done, for example, via a referendum against the quota system in Hungary and changes in the asylum and migration legislation in Poland. In this context, changes in the understanding of solidarity in EU migration policy are unlikely. The question is, of course, how long politicians will be able to maintain migration at the top of the agenda, especially since such rhetoric may be counterproductive—for example, when the Polish government combines xenophobic rhetoric with plans to open up the labour market to Ukrainians.

Unfortunately, the public debate surrounding refugees and immigrants has been conducted on a very low level, and a stereotypical approach to this problem seems to dominate the public discourse. The debate's negative emphasis is surprising given that the number of refugees in the V4 is rather small, and those from Southern Europe have never arrived. Moreover, Poland, for example, has accepted thousands of refugees from Chechnya for years, and this has not led to serious concerns comparable to the present ones relating to the refugee crisis and the vague prospect of a significantly smaller number of refugees from the Middle East or North Africa.[46]

---

[43] Milan Nič, Claire Sturm, Are Slovak and V4 societies ignorant and without any empathy for people escaping war?, 25 May 2016, http://Visegradinsight.eu

[44] Anti-immigrant protest organisers seek to unite extremists, 23. Jun 2015 https://spectator.sme.sk/c/20058361/anti-immigrant-protest-organisers-seek-to-unite-extremists.html

[45] Attila Juhász, Bulcsú Hunyadi, Edit Zgut, 'Focus on Hungary: Refugees, Asylum and Migration', Political Capital, Heinrich-Böll-Stiftung, December 2015.

[46] J. Segeš Frelak, Zuwanderer unerwünscht: die Flüchtlingsfrage spaltet die polnische Gesellschaft. Berlin: Friedrich Ebert Stiftung, November 2015.

The civil society engagement shows that solidarity with refugees is not absent in the region. As in many other countries, there is a civil society that expresses solidarity and humanity, but these efforts are overshadowed by the anti-immigration discourse. At the same time—similar to other EU states—civil society organisations, but also religious actors, academics and local authorities, have been trying to reshape the dominant discourse. However, such initiatives continue to be fragmented and have so far not had any serious impact.

Chapter 8
Structural Injustice: The Eurozone Crisis and the Duty of Solidarity

Erik O. Eriksen

1 Introduction

Through the pacification of conflict between states and through establishing democracy between states, the European Union (EU), in many respects, furthers the great European *civilisation process*.[1] It has domesticated international relations in Europe and has protected the individual from the abuse of power and dominance by external forces or their own state. The EU has protected against discrimination based on nationality, gender, sexual orientation, race, disability or age. Martti Koskenniemi (2006) speaks of the *Kantian constitutional mind-set*, i.e. that citizens' political autonomy must be secured through constitutional and representative structures. This is the mind-set of the French Revolution, propelled by social movements and their rallying cry for social justice. Legal orders are orders of peace, and by raising elements of constitutional democracy to the European level, the EU has contributed to the abolition of arbitrary rule. A brutalised Europe was supplanted by a civilised one. The dignity-protecting, juridification and democratisation processes, which have been underway for the last 60 years in Europe, have brought about a *post-humiliation society* (see Eriksen 2015).

However, the manner in which the Eurozone crisis has been tackled has brought humiliation back and not merely in the form of economic and social exclusion. Humiliation also occurs as the preemption of choice and *decisional exclusion*.

[1]This work is part of ARENA's EuroDiv project financed by the Research Council of Norway's research initiative 'Europe in Transition' (EUROPA). A draft version of this paper was read at the conference on 'Solidarity and its Crisis in the European Union', held on 2–3 June 2016 Universität Hamburg. This version has benefited from comments made by Andreas Eriksen and Kjartan Koch-Mikalsen.

E.O. Eriksen (✉)
ARENA—Centre for European Studies, Oslo, Norway
e-mail: e.o.eriksen@arena.uio.no

A. Grimmel, S.M. Giang (eds.), *Solidarity in the European Union*,
DOI 10.1007/978-3-319-57036-5_8

Heads of government who lack a European mandate have agreed to a series of financial, economic, social and wage policies that affect the freedom and wellbeing of many European citizens. According to the Lisbon Treaty,[2] such issues belong to the remit of the Member States. Executive, intergovernmental dominance is abnormal politics according to European democratic standards. The lingering crisis—the many non-decisions, stop-and-go measures and austerity programmes initiated by the European Central Bank (ECB), the Commission and the International Monetary Fund (the Troika)—has brought the European civilising process to a standstill. In some respects, this process has even been reversed. The public autonomy of citizens—their right to participate in making the laws they are subjected to—is being infringed when an unaccountable technocracy is making decisions with severe consequences.

When the crisis struck, it became clear that the Economic and Monetary Union (EMU) was an unfair arrangement in the sense that some fared better than others under the same system of rules. The EMU was not a win-win arrangement but one with uneven distributive effects. The design of the Eurozone and the crisis management create losers and winners. Some lose and some profit from the same arrangement. The Eurozone crisis raises the problem of *structural injustice:* the beneficiaries receive a diverse array of benefits under an enduring social structure. Who is responsible? Some injustices particular actors have directly or indirectly participated in causing, some not. Moreover, some injustices benefit them, some harm them and some do both. Equally, there may be situations where things are wrong but not unjust in the sense that they are the fault of others.

What type of obligations do the winners have towards the losers in the Eurozone? If there are wrongs that benefit the winners, if there is unjust enrichment, it is a question of redress—payback time. But if there is no 'isolatable action or event that has reached a terminus' causing the harm, it is hard to hold individual agents responsible (Young 2006: 121). Then we are confronted with the normative puzzle of *injustices that benefit some*, and no one in particular is liable to pay damages. In that case, what type of duties are involved—those referring to moral responsibility or those referring to solidarity?

In this paper I will deal with the Eurozone crisis and the problem of structural injustice and the types of duties it triggers. First, I make it clear why there is a problem of structural injustice involved in the crisis arrangement of the Eurozone. Then, I raise the problem of unjust enrichment and compensatory obligations in the so-called wrongful-benefits paradigm (WBP). Thereafter, I discuss the concept of political justice and the paradigm of solidarity as opposed to that of the liability model of responsibility and the WBP. The idea is that the type of *structural injustice* generated by the Eurozone arrangement gives rise to duties

[2]The Lisbon Treaty entered into force on 1 December 2009 (Official Journal of the European Union 2007). See also the consolidated versions of the Treaty on the European Union (TEU) and the Treaty on the Functioning of the European Union (TFEU) (Official Journal of the European Union 2012).

that are not in the form of compensatory obligations. Rather, it gives rise to duties of solidarity—to correct wrongs akin to political justice.

2 Structural Injustice

The Greek crisis was never solved. Greece is disconnected from the European banking system and capital control is still in place. This crisis reveals the structural problems of the EMU, which is a product of the Treaty on the European Union (TEU). The Eurozone is not an optimal currency area partly because of the large differences between the economies and partly because there are no efficient mechanisms to provide economic transfers from economies that fare well to those that fare less well—which essentially gives way to procyclical fiscal policies (Tuori and Tuori 2014, 53 ff). The euro area as such lacks the fiscal instruments to redistribute income across different levels of economic development. It also lacks fiscal instruments fit to handle sudden demand shocks. Moreover workers are insufficiently mobile across countries for labour markets to absorb the sudden increase in unemployment. While the Union holds exclusive competencies in monetary policy, the Member States are sovereign in fiscal and economic policy. Counter cyclical (Keynesian) fiscal policies are constrained because of the rules of the Stability and Growth Pact (SGP). The consequence is austerity policies in the crisis-ridden countries.

The SGP commits Eurozone members to balanced budgets (the structural deficit is not to exceed 0.5% of GDP) and to public debts of less than 60% of GDP. There are automatic penalties for noncompliant states, and there is automatic supervision by the European Commission. The EMU has produced new treaties of its own, establishing the European Financial Stability Facility (EFSF), the ESM and the Treaty on Stability, Coordination and Governance (TSCG) also referred to as the Fiscal Compact.[3] The Fiscal Compact and the task-specific de novo EU bodies were introduced as a new (i.e. stricter) version of the previous SGP. They include the European Stability Mechanism (ESM), which has a lending capacity of up to 500 billion euros and a bank resolution fund of, ultimately, 55 billion euros

[3]The European Financial Stability Facility (EFSF) was created as a temporary rescue mechanism by the Eurozone Member States in 2010 to safeguard financial stability in Europe. In October 2010, the EU decided to create a permanent rescue mechanism, the European Stability Mechanism (ESM), which entered into force in October 2012. With the Euro-Plus Pact (adopted in March 2011), some Member States have made concrete commitments to political reforms intended to improve their fiscal strength and competitiveness. The EU economic governance, Sixpack, a set of European legislative measures designed to reform the Stability and Growth Pact (SGP) and to introduce new macroeconomic surveillance, entered into force in December 2011. Finally, the Treaty on Stability, Coordination and Governance in the Economic and Monetary Union, also referred to as TSCG or the Fiscal Compact, is effectively a new, stricter version of the SGP. The TSCG has been signed by all Member States (except the Czech Republic and the UK) and entered into force in January 2013 for the 16 states that completed ratification prior to this date.

(Genschel and Jachtenfuchs 2016: 47). This is in addition to the two other Eurozone 'mechanisms' of banking union: the Single Supervisory Mechanism (SSM) for Eurozone banks and the Single Resolution Mechanism (SRM). The de novo 'European semester' effectively establishes European and national institutions as *a joint fiscal authority* for managing large questions of taxing, borrowing and spending. Its objectives are, in the first instance, to promote differentiated, growth-friendly consolidation and restore normal lending credibility.

The EFSF, the ESM and the Fiscal Compact were established outside of the Lisbon Treaty and the SGP as part of the application of the amended Article 136. They have their own intergovernmental decision-making bodies and operate behind a shield of extensive immunity and confidentiality. Neither treaty provisions based on the principle of transparency nor complementary secondary legislation apply, and hence parliamentary and public control is 'extremely difficult' (Tuori 2012: 47). The purpose of these treaties was to provide *conditional assistance* to Eurozone Member States in financial difficulty due to banking failures, fiscal imprudence or both.[4]

Conditionality is intended to avoid moral hazards—that is, to prevent actors from taking risks when others are liable for the damages—and to help sovereigns to get back on track. Access to aid packages is provided in exchange for domestic reforms. The Fiscal Compact is heavily dependent on the supranational Commission and the ECB. Still it is an intergovernmental treaty and one with an alienating effect on the EU's representative institutions. It is also difficult to invoke the EU's Charter of Fundamental Rights in relation to matters regulated by the Fiscal Compact.

These arrangements for monitoring and ensuring compliance severely restrict the fiscal policy space of the Member States, which have already, by adopting the Euro, given up national control of interest rates and currency exchange rates. Since crisis-ridden states are members of the Euro, they cannot devaluate and have little space for overspending in order to recover from recession. The instruments for national fiscal policy are thus largely abolished for crisis-ridden countries. The crisis-ridden states are left in a 'take it or leave it' position (see Scharpf 2014: 11; Menéndez 2017).

3 Constraining Self-Rule

The debtors are subjected to the imperatives of the financial markets and to the dictates of the largely unaccountable Troika.[5] The members of the creditor club of the EU are privileged by the rules of the Eurozone, which position debtors in a subjected position. The debtors' freedom of choice is limited because their

[4]Treaty establishing the European Stability Mechanism, Article 3 (European Commission 2012)

[5]See, e.g. Schäfer and Streeck (2013), Streeck (2013), Altvater et al. (2013), Varoufakis (2016), Galbraith (2016), Stiglitz (2016) and Blyth (2013).

unbalanced budgets compel them to accept conditions imposed by creditor countries—the creditor club. Loans and credit are conditional on reforms, which are not initiated by citizens' representatives or justified to the affected citizens. There is a preemption of choice, as debtors must obey the rules and the instructions if they are to be seen as reliable borrowers and trusted members of the Eurozone. There is also decisional exclusion. Technocratic bodies, not citizens' representatives, make vital decisions. There are infringements of both European law and democratic principles.[6]

> Today, the 'general' laws and policies of the Union cause highly diverse effects and impact the different member states with the result of producing the feeling of more and more people in more and more countries that they are ruled by 'others' not themselves or the likes of them. (Offe and Preuss 2016: 13)

The present Euro arrangement interferes with the interests and preferences of the states and citizens of Europe—it creates winners and losers, it benefits and threatens, it rewards and punishes, and it transforms identities. Hence, there is a transnational context of justice and democracy beyond the nation state in Europe. There is a circumstance of justice to talk with Hume and Rawls.[7] There are claims to corrective justice, to compensation. However, arbitrary rule, which is in breach of European citizenship rights, also gives rise to a different kind of claims. To be subjected to the arbitrary wielding of power is to be dominated, which is the essence of injustice. Dominance is wrong, but is it also unjust in the sense that it is the responsibility of others? Whose fault is that? Who is guilty? Who is to blame?

What we are dealing with in the Eurozone is not merely episodic or transactional injustices, which can easily be mended as the perpetrators and beneficiaries would then be traceable. Rather, what we are faced with is an instance of *structural injustice*. The politico-legal arrangement grants the members unequal political status. When persons are systematically treated differently due to the way institutions operate, there is a case for structural injustice.

4 Moral Blame

Justice is the first commandment of morality and stems from the person's right to freedom and respect. Justice is a duty of right: of equal freedom for all (Kant 1797/1996). A has an original right to independence from B and vice versa.[8] The right to have one's freedom protected infers obligations on the part of the actors and

---

[6]See also Menéndez (2013), Enderlein (2013) and Kreuder-Sonnen (2016).

[7]'The circumstances of justice obtain whenever mutually disinterested persons put forward conflicting claims to the division of social advantages under conditions of moderate scarcity' (Rawls 1971: 128).

[8]'... my first-person judgment *I have the right to life* entails the judgment *you owe me the duty to respect my right to life,* and vice versa. Furthermore, the reciprocity condition shows that the

institutions inflicting harm and injustice, when there are transgressions of zones of freedom. Actors and institutions are responsible for the consequences of their wilful actions. They are responsible for faults of harm.

Guilt for harm and wrongdoing 'is tied to violations of what we owe to each other' and is the basis for moral blame (Scanlon 1998: 271). An act is wrong when it is in breach of principles that no one could reasonably reject. Guilt constitutes the basis for claims-making and for moral criticism aimed at changing or modifying an actor's behaviour by making him or her aware of the faults and responsibilities involved (ibid. 277). To be morally responsible for an event is for a person to be properly attributable to one. The actor is then open to a certain kind of response in light of the event. What renders the responsibility moral is that the event is within the domain of actions and attitudes implicated in our relations with one another (Scanlon 2008: 131). Guilt and wrongdoing thus give rise to duties. Culprits are obligated to provide assistance or to compensate in other ways for the harms inflicted. An obligation or duty stipulates a rule of action, specifying which actions count as performing the duty. Protest and opposition are indicators of unredeemed moral obligations. When reactions such as resentment, indignation and guilt are triggered, moral criticism hits home. Legal reasoning, for its part, helps us to establish guilt or fault for a harm, i.e. who is liable. Rights and compensation schemes identify legal obligations.

Directed duties should, however, be distinguished from undirected ones: 'while directed duties correlate with another's rights, undirected duties have no such correlate' (Zylberman 2014: 154). Responsibility for wrongdoing presupposes a correlation between directed duties and rights.[9] Thus, 'if you bear a claim-right, then another owes you a relational duty . . . of providing assistance or remuneration. For *A* to be endowed with a claim-right is for *B* to owe a duty to *A*, and vice versa' (Zylberman 2014: 155). Later in this chapter, I introduce the term *forward-directed duties*, which straddles the line between directed and undirected duties. Such duties are oriented towards the political citizenry.

In general, duties are created when one party's acts affects another's rights. The liability model of responsibility underscores the causality dimension.

> Under [the] liability model, one assigns responsibility to a particular agent (or agents) whose actions can be shown to be causally connected to the circumstances for which responsibility is sought. (Young 2006: 116)

In the extension of this, the so-called WBP sees justice as a question of fulfilling compensatory obligations (Butt 2014). The beneficiary should pay when responsible for harm as well as when profiting from wrongs. According to Kant, moral obligations are categorical, and the WBP requires rational consistency between compensatory obligations and actions. Obligations arise in a context when our

---

judgment *I have the right to life* must also entail *you have the right to life*, for you and I are one in original rights' (Zylberman 2014: 167).

[9]'A duty or a legal obligation is that which one ought . . . to do. 'Duty' and 'right' are correlative terms. When a right is invaded, a duty is violated' (Hohfeld 1913: 32).

actions have consequences for others—their rights, freedom and values—but they also arise when we are part of a wrongful regime. The identification of injustice, of benefiting from injustice, including wrongs committed by others, involves a duty to act and to compensate for wrongdoing:

> If our moral condemnation of injustice, our regret that injustice has occurred, is to be taken seriously, it must be matched by action to remedy the effects of injustice, insofar as they persist as the automatic effects of injustice. We are right to feel guilty at benefiting from others' misfortune, precisely because this suggests that we have not fulfilled our compensatory obligations. (Butt 2007: 144–145)

However, when the causal connection is unclear, there is a problem of delineating moral obligation. Blameworthiness requires causality and foreseeability, as well as responsible actors and clear rules of evidence. The wrongful-benefits framework is demanding, as it implies *disgorgement*—that is it requires a party who profits from illegal or wrongful acts to give up any profits he or she made.[10] A full compensatory scheme, in line with the requirement of rational consistency, is demanding when it comes to information. One question is whether there is, in fact, any benefit from the injustice at all. The other is 'the epistemological question of how to determine what benefit, if any, has been thus derived' (Brooks 1989: 40).[11] We need to know who did what, to whom, when and how and whether they were coerced or not, whether the choice situation was open or not, whether consequences could be foreseen, etc. In order to be responsible for harm, one needs to have contributed to causing it. One must have had some control of it and could have prevented its outcome if they had wanted to (Stilz 2009: 188). One's actions must have made a difference. Otherwise, no charge applies: 'If past injustice has shaped present holdings in various ways, some identifiable and some not, what now, if anything, ought to the done to rectify these injustices?' (Nozick 1974: 154).

According to Robert Goodin:

> Full-bore compensation would require us to know all the following things that Nozick lists:
>
> 1. We would have to know (a) who did what (b) to whom.
> 2. We would have to know all of the consequences that followed from that.
> 3. We would have to know all the counterfactuals concerning what would have happened had the wrong not occurred.
> 4. If the principals are no longer alive, we would have to know who (if anyone) in the current generation has inherited (a) the responsibilities and (b) the claims of each of the individuals involved in the original wrongdoing. (Goodin 2013: 485)

[10] 'Agents can be morally blameworthy for failing to disgorge in compensation benefits which they involuntarily receive as a result of wrongdoing which harms other agents' (Butt 2014: 343).

[11] And further, 'a probabilistic distribution curve might be developed so that the closer one is to the injustice, the likelier it is that one has benefited even though there is nothing to prevent someone a good deal further off from benefiting more or someone very close from not benefiting at all' (ibid.). So, 'the general duty to prevent injustice bears more heavily on those who are closest to it' (p. 31). See also Waldron (1996) on Kant's proximity principle.

When applying this to the Eurozone crisis, one is inclined to think that since Germany—Europe's biggest country and largest economy—has profited from the single market and the EMU (which it contributed to the establishment of), it also has specific obligations.[12] Here, there is a circumstance of both benefit and causality, but are the conditions for benefit and causality met?[13]

According to some simplified, stylised facts, Germany has benefited the most from the single currency as a net exporter. It profits from the single market, the abolition of customs and non-tariff barriers and the stable framework of common currency. Germany also benefits from the Eurozone crisis as 'financial investors have been fleeing from investments in risky bonds of the deficit countries, seeking the safe haven of German bonds. As a consequence, German real borrowing costs have been lower (in fact negative) than they would be in 'normal' times. Also, Germany profits from the favourable external value of the Euro, which allows it to remain Europe's export champion' (Offe 2014: 98). Germany is benefiting from the decrease in interest rates for the German government bonds created by the crisis (which are matched by an increase in interest rates for over-indebted, crisis-stricken countries). It is also profiting from the influx of well-trained workers from crisis-ridden countries (see also Habermas 2015: 19; Offe 2013). There may be a case to be made for enrichment at others' expense because the '"bailout for Greece" was nothing more than the rescue of private banks through EU taxpayers' money, only 5% of which went into the Greek economy' (Bantekas and Vivien 2016; see also Huliaras and Petropoulos 2016).

It looks like Germany has benefited from the Euro and Eurozone crisis arrangement, but is it also responsible for creating it? The circumstances of benefit seem to be met, but the circumstances of causality seem more unclear. The effects and injustices of the Eurozone crisis do not add up to a particular directed duty for Germany to compensate for wrongful benefits, because links of causation are diffuse (again, according to some stylised facts):

- The structural problems of the Eurozone were not common knowledge.[14]
- The crisis could be seen as an unintended consequence of the US-instigated financial crisis, first caused by the collapse of Lehman Brothers Holdings Inc.
- Many of the failures in the crisis-ridden countries are due to domestic policies, banking failures and fiscal imprudence.[15]

---

[12]Germany has benefited at the expense of the weaker economies, according to Varoufakis (2016), Galbraith (2016) and Stiglitz (2016). On 28 November 2011, on the occasion of an official visit to Berlin, the Polish foreign minister Radek Sikorski addressed an audience, pointing out that Germany is the biggest beneficiary of the Euro and has 'the biggest obligation to make [it] sustainable' (Offe 2014: 98).

[13]Causality and responsibility are tricky. The circumstances of benefit and causality may, in fact, be interlinked; one may be responsible when benefiting from injustice. In that case, it is a question of inverted or reversed causality.

[14]However, there were warnings. See Yeager (1962).

[15]See, for example, Issing (2014).

- The Eurozone is a cooperative scheme and risks have been distributed and redistributed throughout the integration process. According to some calculations, on average most countries have won. The internal market is expected to have increased GDP considerably.
- Even if Germany profits the most from Eurozone cooperation, the EMU is a collective initiative, and many countries have for a decade profited from the Eurozone due to low borrowing costs.
- The political decision to create a monetary union and to abandon national currencies was taken unanimously by 11 governments and ratified by 11 parliaments, in some cases being accompanied by referendums.

If we compare this to Nozick's list on what makes up a moral obligation—in line with the full compensatory scheme of the liability model—we find that:

1. It is not clear that Germany has particular responsibility because it is unclear who did what to whom in initiating the EMU.
2. It was not clear what the long-term consequences of the EMU would be when it was created.
3. We are not sure what would have happened in Europe in the period after the EMU was introduced had it not been established.
4. Even though states also have legal personality[16] and hence responsibility, it is unclear which responsibilities present principals have for the putative original wrongdoing.

The Eurozone governance structure is the product of many actions and many actors are responsible for its effects. There may be duties to provide assistance, but there are difficulties inherent in measuring liability, probability and proximity.[17] Conditions of causality are not easily met. Hence, there is a case for *structural injustice*: many persons, organisations and policies have contributed to the present state of affairs, but it is not possible to identify specific culprits or track which specific actions of which agents are responsible for particular parts of the structure and their outcomes. It would be hard to bring Germany to court for being part of the decision-making body that established the EMU and gave rise to the present politico-economic structure. It would be hard to establish morally significant responsibility. Structural injustice puts persons under a systematic threat of dominance, but this 'is a kind of moral wrong distinct from the wrongful action of an individual agent or the wilfully repressive policies of a state' (Young 2007: 114). There are structural injustices in the Eurozone, but the processes that produce wrongs are consequences and by-products of many institutional actors and policies.

---

[16]Who, like persons, have legal personality and can sign and terminate contracts

[17]See, e.g. Lastra and Buchheit (2014), Kenadjan et al. (2013), Olivares-Caminal (2009) and Rieffel (2003). See further: Lienau (2014), Esposito et al. (2013) and Wong (2012). On the general problem of measuring liability, probability and proximity, see Feinberg (1968), Brooks (1989), Birks (2005) and Hedley (1997).

It is unclear who is responsible for which harm at a certain point in time. When this is the case, which type of duty is involved?

In order to grasp the normativity of structural injustice, we need to move beyond the strict requirements of causality and clear evidence in the liability model of responsibility. There are obligations regardless of blameworthiness. Some have lost because of the politico-economic arrangement established as a response to the financial and economic crisis. What type of obligations, if any, does this systemic wrong trigger?

5 Corrective Justice

The European context is one of justice in the sense that its cooperative scheme affects interests and gives rise to claims for assistance or remuneration. Someone is guilty, but it is unclear what kind of obligations there are. Benefiting from injustices or inquisitives raises a prima facie obligation of compensation, but when it is unclear who the perpetrators are and what exactly they are responsible for, there is a problem with the WBP. The WBP confronts the beneficiaries as moral debtors, as it entails a *perfect duty of compensation.* However, when it comes to structural injustice, the causality conditions necessary for such duties to apply are not in place. Correcting wrongs through compensation is blocked. Goodin, therefore, suggests an alternative mechanism to that of the information-demanding model of 'full-bore' compensation. Goodin suggests that mere non-compensatory disgorgement—with the return of the benefits to the public purse—is available when we don't know who the victims are or how to help them. Even when one is not able to locate the culprits or the wronged ones in time and space—they may be dead, hard to find or indisposed; the wronged ones may have disappeared; it may be difficult to identify the rightful heirs—*innocent beneficiaries* have an obligation to give up wrongfully possessed goods. Disgorgement refers to requiring a party who profits from illegal or wrongful acts to give up any profits he or she made thereof. The purpose of this remedy is, according to Goodin, to prevent *unjust enrichment*, while not demanding all the information that the liability model of responsibility requires. Disgorgement only requires that the fruits of wrongdoing be relinquished:

> People wrongfully in possession of goods should acknowledge that they have no legitimate claim to them and should be prepared to give them up. … In that limited sense, disgorgement is at least a partial undoing and rectification of the wrongdoing. It is corrective justice. (Goodin 2013: 478)

Non-compensatory disgorgement may capture the problem of historical wrongdoing, which is Goodin's main target, but, as Avery Kolers (2014) underlines, it does not capture the main difficulty of structural injustice. As mentioned, this is a kind of moral wrong distinct from the wrongful action of a particular agent at a particular point in time. Structural injustice raises not only the problem that since wrongdoers are not easily identifiable there is no point in seeking to exact compensation or redress. It also raises the question of what we owe each other in a context of justice. Are we only expected to pay our dues? Is responsibility exhausted by compensatory obligations?

The problem with the WBP, also when it involves disgorgement, is that it individualises responsibility and conceives of it in quantitative, financial terms. It turns the problem of injustice and the severity of the wrongs into a question of personal debt. The WBP simultaneously demands too much and too little of the actors. It demands too much because individual actors are never able to do enough; they will always be in the red. Due to societal cooperation, particular actors continuously incur more duties than they can reciprocate—more debts than they can pay back. In general, we owe much more to society—due to social cooperation—than we may lay a rightful claim to.

The WBP demands too little, because if 'I can somehow pay back my debt in full, I am released from further work against injustice, no matter how onerous or odious that injustice remains' (Kolers 2014: 428). But 'why should the fact that *G* is no longer my biggest personal moral creditor carry any weight in whether I continue to work to end the injustice suffered by *G*? Why is my moral balance of payments so crucial in the face of ongoing structural injustice?' (ibid. 427). If I can pay back, I am off the hook. This view is problematic because there are obligations regardless of guilt or individual consent. Children have obligations towards their unchosen parents, just as citizens have obligations towards their own coercive state. There are natural duties of justice and there are non-voluntary associative obligations stemming from membership in institutions that are necessary or cannot be avoided (Rawls 1971: 114; Dworkin 2011: 320).

The WBP is morally insufficient when it comes to structural injustice because it disregards obligations to correct systemic wrongs. Proper non-compensatory disgorgement would require that structural injustice be abolished. There would be no point in paying back to the public purse when injustice prevails and new wrongs are produced. Duties will be undirected, and payers will not be sure that their payments are reaching the right pockets.

Another question is whether all kinds of injustices should be addressed through the WBP. This necessarily involves a process of identifying the needy, wronged, disadvantaged actors and groups, which may have stigmatising consequences. We see this logic playing out in the Eurozone. Humiliation is brought back in as naming, shaming and blaming take place among groups and states in Europe. This creates stigmatising images of suppliers and spenders, of donors and receivers. Images of guilty debtors flourish.

> The debtor is morally inferior—guilty—because he lacks the self-control necessary to live within the limits of his means; that is to say: *not* because his low income and poor social security forces him to rely on consumer credit, *not* because uniquely cheap credit, facilitated by faulty monetary policy, plus lax conditions have offered him an irresistible opportunity to purchase 'subprime' mortgages, *not* because actors in the financial industry were granting credit frivolously because they could confidently expect to be bailed out according to the 'too big-to-fail' logic in case something 'goes wrong', and *not* because sovereign debtors have incurred debt in order to stimulate investment and employment in the 'real' economy—all these possibilities are being obscured and excluded from consideration through the 'guilt' frame. (Offe 2014: 96–97)

The WBP is not fit to handle the duty to correct structural injustice. We are right to feel guilty about benefiting from others' misfortune, but our responsibility is not exhausted by individualised contributions and compensations. As fellow citizens, we are obligated to contribute to the remediation of an unfair political structure. A move beyond a concept of justice based on a parity of dues, debts and credits is needed to analytically handle the problem of structural injustice.[18]

6 Political Justice

In contemporary political discourse, justice is often thought of as the morally proper distribution of rights, duties, material resources and opportunities understood as public goods or utilities.[19] This focus on the distribution of goods in theories of justice risks blocking out the first question of justice, namely, the political question of how the goods were produced and allocated in the first place. There is a great difference between lacking certain goods and being deprived of them unjustly, and there is also a great difference between allocating goods fairly and identifying injustices.[20] Put otherwise, a distributive understanding of justice, which allocates goods according to some ideal, moral pattern, misses what we owe each other as a matter of justice. In order to establish a distributive pattern in a fair way, an institutional structure that protects basic rights must be in place. The basic structure that determines which are justified claims and who is empowered to ensure justice must itself be just. Only then can a fair distribution of goods come about.

Further, a distributive understanding of justice, which treats political institutions as goods or utilities, as something that can be traded, exchanged and allocated, misses the deontological character of this basic structure. Basic institutions are not merely 'public goods', which can be divided and traded,[21] but conditions and necessary presuppositions for being able to sort out and handle justice claims. They exist prior to distribution and 'the circumstances of justice'. The *goddess Justicia's* task is, then, not to dispense gifts or allocate shares, but first of all to institutionalise a fair system of rule.[22] The political approach to justice is not only needed because rights can be up for grabs but also because a just distribution of goods may be accomplished through the benevolent acts of a hegemon (a dominating agent), hence leading to paternalism and new forms of injustice.

---

[18]The next section draws on Eriksen (2016).

[19]These are so-called end-state approaches to justice (Nozick 1974).

[20]'The goods-fixated view of justice...for the most part ignores the question of injustice, for by concentrating on overcoming deficiencies of goods, it treats someone who suffers a deficiency as a result of natural catastrophe as equivalent to some who suffers the same deficiency as a result of economic or political exploitation' (Forst 2011).

[21]See Young (1990: 25) and Habermas (1996: 418–19).

[22]'The goddess *Justitia* does not come into the world to dispense gifts; her task is instead to banish arbitrary rule, i.e. domination' (Forst 2015).

When there is structural injustice, as the systemic wrongs of the Eurozone attest to, there are obligations according to a political concept of justice. They stem from the responsibilities generated by membership in associations, the acts of which have consequences for others' rights. There are political duties stemming from interdependencies and connectivity that affect the conditions for freedom and wellbeing. Thus, we may ask if not the right framework for addressing these questions is that of solidarity and not that of the wrongful benefits and the liability model of responsibility. Can there be a duty of solidarity?

7 Arbitrary Rule

Solidarity goes to the core of the problem of structural flaws, to the source of injustice and the obligations involved as it ascribes to the addressees the duty to repair unjust orders.[23] Solidarity captures the intuitive force of wrongful harms, but instead of demanding compensation, it demands that we join in collective action for justice.[24] But according to what criterion can there be a duty of solidarity?

There is a need for an alternative to the victim-focused decision criterion that applies when it comes to compensatory justice. In that system, we need to know who suffers, how much and why (with the unhappy side effect of inevitably marking some as downs). When dealing with claims to solidarity, there is a need for a structure-focused criterion. Solidarity is the building block of every democratic community, as it expresses a norm of equal membership. This foundational norm makes it possible for citizens to relate to others as fellows—compatriots and equals—and demands they take on collective responsibilities.

I suggest dominance as a criterion of structural injustice that triggers duties of solidarity. Dominance designates structural oppression, which undercuts democratic self-rule. It undermines compatriots' ability to see themselves as equal members of the polity. Those who suffer from dominance are subjugated and governed without justification. To be dominated is to be subject to arbitrary power or alien control. Citizens' autonomy is respected only when they are included as equal members of a self-governing association (Kant 1785: 85). Hence, dominance does not merely appear as arbitrary interference in zones of (private) freedom (cp Pettit 1997), but as hindrances to co-legislation as well. I understand dominance primarily as a question of *political status*, in terms of barriers to citizens' public autonomy and their ability to politically determine

---

[23]Here, 'The point is not to blame, punish, or seek redress from those who did it, but rather to enjoin those who participate by their actions in the process of collective action to change it' (Young 2006: 122).

[24]See also Jonas (1984).

their destiny. Autonomy or political freedom entails relationships of mutuality and power bound by law[25]:

> In a legal community, no one is free as long as the freedom of one person must be purchased with another's oppression. (Habermas 1996: 418)

The crisis management of the Eurozone and the new fiscal governance provisions in the treaties and austerity policies curtail citizens' social and political rights by making it harder for governments to correct and compensate for unjust market outcomes. This undercuts the fair value of political institutions. *Decisional exclusion* and the *preemption of choice* resulting from the handling of the Eurozone crisis testify to the type of dominance that affects citizens' public autonomy. Because the Eurozone is a context of justice—as there are citizenship rights, associative political rights and interdependencies that generate obligations—there is a moral duty to solidarity. But such a duty is imperfect.

8 The Paradigm of Solidarity

As long as the European integration project could be portrayed as advantageous for everyone, as Pareto improving, the citizens of Europe were not called upon in the name of solidarity. The portrayal of the EMU as a mutually beneficent arrangement, which had been persistent, was definitively erased with the Eurozone crisis. As social protest and political claims-making attest to, the financial crisis has rendered the integration project visibly moral. European integration is not a win-win arrangement, and it is not merely a matter of joint convenience and choice; instead, it is a matter of collective responsibility—of justice and solidarity. Some are structurally suppressed and there are unredeemed moral obligations. However, solidarity is in short supply: social solidarity tends to stop at national borders (see Habermas 2012: 62). At the European level, there is only weak competence and limited resources available for socio-economic justice and for redistribution across the borders. There are structural barriers to socio-economic justice as there is no European liability. As mentioned, the Eurozone lacks the fiscal instruments to redistribute income. Solidarity is, however, not an administrative category.

While justice is required by morality in order to safeguard the autonomy and self-respect of the individual and can be achieved through impartial laws, solidarity, which is also a moral demand, has another basis and logic. According to Kant, justice is formally determined, while solidarity is *material*. While justice raises an unconditional categorical claim, solidarity (like friendship) is conditioned by relationships and aims. Solidarity has to do with experiences of wrongs, felt commitments and a

[25]The legal standing of the individual requires 'a full adequate scheme of equal basic rights and liberties, which scheme is compatible with the same scheme for all; and in this scheme the equal political liberties [. . .] are to be guaranteed their fair value' (Rawls 1993: 5).

common destiny; it has to do with particular goals to be attained—to reduce the misery and enhance the wellbeing of a group. It relates to experiences of rights violations and injustice and the collective 'we' feeling that can be mobilised in a cooperative context. Solidarity is not a legal obligation (i.e. a perfect duty corresponding to a right)—rather, in the tradition from Hegel to Durkheim, it is seen as belonging to the domain of ethics and hence to an imperfect duty of beneficence. Like friendship it commits, but in a different manner. The duty of beneficence, according to Kant, stems from the claims of the deprived ones on the well-off ones to provide help, without which they will succumb (Kant 1795/1996: 328–329).

Solidarity is a question of the will of and the onus on compatriots to pay for each other's misfortune, a will which depends on a common vision—a conception of the common good. Solidarity can neither be bought nor administratively enforced, as it springs from commitments to care for affected parties, from the common interests that can be articulated and from the virtues of cooperation and relief that can be mobilised. Solidarity is the *virtue* that is demanded when there is a shortage of material resources to satisfy pressing needs and legitimate interests (Steinvorth 1998: 69).

However, there is a difference between feeling responsible and being responsible. Solidarity is not an organic phenomenon resting on natural duties. Rather, it is artificially created and has a legal basis (Habermas 2015: 24). Solidarity is a political category revolving around redeeming the unredeemed moral claim of equal citizenship. It refers to righting wrongs and harms through collective action. Acts based on solidarity are, then, not presupposing a pre-political *Sittlichkeit* or primordial values,[26] but a political context of struggle, claims-making and justification. Such a struggle for equality presupposes a basic structure of rights' protection. Solidarity sustains the value of the victims and repudiates injustice. It invites a common struggle against injustice—to end the misery, hardship and disparity created by committed wrongs, dire conditions or natural catastrophes. It involves a specific moral motive of ensuring social cohesion and mutual recognition. In this context, the actor understands his action as help, which he believes he is obligated to provide (Wildt 1998: 212).

> What differentiates both ethical expectations and appeals to solidarity from law and morality is the peculiar reference to 'joint involvement' in a network of social relations. That involvement grounds both another person's demanding expectations, which may even go beyond what law and morality command, and one's own confidence that the other will behave in a similar manner in the future if need be. Whereas 'morality' and 'law' refer to equal freedoms of autonomous individuals, ethical expectations and appeals to solidarity refer to an interest in the integrity of a shared form of life that includes one's own well-being. (Habermas 2015: 23)

[26]See Habermas' self-correction: 'I no longer support the assertion that "Justice conceived deontologically requires solidarity at its reverse side" because it leads to moralization and depoliticization of the concept of solidarity' (Habermas 2015: 158).

In solidarity discourses, actors are called upon in their capacity as fellows—as compatriots, and companions—to do more than can be expected by norms of impartiality. But solidarity is not a question of *supererogation*, viz. action beyond the demand of duty.[27] Solidarity is not merely a question of altruism. Prototypically, actors are called upon to help others in need through the establishment of a more just economic system, a better political regime or a policy that is in the common interest. By helping the ones in need now, you can also be expected to be helped out yourself at a later point in time. There is a dimension of mutuality involved—not only in the sense that actors' extra efforts may be recompensed at a later stage but also in the sense that actors who succeed in establishing a more robust political and economic regime will themselves profit from this in the long run.

9 Forward-Directed Duties

The concept of solidarity has undergone transformation. It is possible to conceive of solidarity from an evolutionary perspective, as it has developed from the classical ethical idea of civic friendship (Aristotle) via the religious idea of a universal element in the self—'equality before God', in the Middle Ages—to the moment where it was politically transformed into *fraternité*—the universal brotherhood, 'equality before the law'—with the French Revolution (see Brunkhorst 2005). Throughout the eighteenth and nineteenth centuries, old forms of solidarity were replaced by new ones in the building of first the nation state and then the welfare state within the parameters of the democratic *Rechtsstaat*. The republic includes all of humankind in a rightful order. Solidarity concerns the struggle for equal citizenship. It aims at realising unredeemed obligations and shared values. The expansion from civic and economic rights to political and social rights is indicative of the struggle to banish dominance and ensure equality—recognition and equal membership in the polity. Solidarity is thus internally related to political justice and equity. Solidarity and justice should, then, not be counterpoised; they are part of the same system of virtues. It is not a question of either justice or solidarity [as Kolers (2014) maintains], because a non-solidaristic society is not a just society. Solidarity and justice belong to the same group of virtues, but differ with regard to towards whom claims should be raised.

Solidarity does not invite us to look after our own interests and our dues, but to instead participate in the struggle for a better future for all. Whether or not we have benefited, or are in debt, we are obligated, as equal citizens, to abolish dominance and repair unjust structures.[28] Political obligations akin to those of solidarity are

[27] For the concept of supererogation, see Eriksen (2015).

[28] Solidarity 'ascribes to me a duty to join in efforts to repair unjust social relations and restore equitable relationships. ... Because solidarity does not trade in the language of quanta of unjust

more limited than moral duties and are more extensive than enforceable legal duties. Political, associative obligations are more restricted than moral (cosmopolitan) ones that apply to all humans as demands on political institutions. Political obligations stem from membership in an organisation that cannot be avoided or is needed.[29] Claims to solidarity, which are directed towards persons (i.e. compatriots), aim to achieve political justice for subjected parties living under a common law. There is thus a close relationship between solidarity and political justice. However, political obligations go beyond legally enforceable rights as they call for new measures, new laws and the repair of the existing legal order. Thus, political obligations may differ from the obligations applying to the members of a 'given' community. There are *forward-directed duties* that apply to interdependent actors and their ways of coping with contingencies and conflicts. In that case they refer to the kind of solidarity that an intended community—a project under construction—requires.

We see this in the reciprocal and offensive character of struggling to discharge the promise of equal citizenship involved in the European unification process. In the protest, in the opposition to prevailing injustices, in the initiatives to establish a rights-based union and deepen integration (i.e. to take on social obligations), an ambition to abolish dominance and build a socially democratic European republic can be discerned. In one interpretation, it is possible to see the European integration project as one struggling to realise the promises of the French Revolution—of equality, freedom and fraternity or *solidarity* (as we would say today)—through solidaric acts of *pre-commitment.*

The preconditions of a European democratic republic are not in place, according to the 'no-demos' thesis, viz. there is no European people, no common culture or common language and no common civic-democratic infrastructure (see Grimm 2004). There is no common identity produced by a nation-like culture. Still, the initiators created institutional arrangements to foster such. This type of undertaking may rest on the thought that one cannot bemoan the lack of civic solidarity as long as the political institutions necessary to bring it about are not in place. What happened at the national level can also happen at the European level, i.e. supranational political institutions precede and create the requisite underlying solidaristic basis. Through the formative role of political institutions, through media and communication, a shared basis for collective action can come about. In other words, there may be no collective European identity, but in order to form it, decision-makers established common institutions. For example, the original common assembly (of the European Coal and Steel Community) decided to create a true

benefit, it does not confront me as a moral debtor. Thus, I am neither required to pay back in full what I owe, nor released from my obligations when I have done so. I am instead required to join the struggle' (Kolers 2014: 428).

[29]Political obligation is a special case of involuntary associational obligations: 'we are related to our fellow citizens in some special way that gives each of us special responsibilities to the others independently of any consent' (Dworkin 2011: 319).

European Parliament by proclaiming it. The European Parliament developed from the body initially labelled the European Assembly as follows:

> In choosing to call itself a 'parliament', the Assembly was not so much pretending to *be* a parliament as clearly pointing out that it *wanted* to become one. The same logic lay behind the name change from European Assembly to European Parliament in the Single European Act: the Member States were not so much declaring that the Assembly *was* a parliament as effectively recognising that it *should become* one. (Westlake 1994: 16)

A popularly elected parliament is intrinsic to the democratic republic, and 'moderns' 'regard the republic as the institutional embodiment of an idea which unites human kind as a whole' (Offe and Preuss 2016: 12). Only parliaments have achieved the competence to speak for the people. The parliamentary principle has become the institutional embodiment of popular sovereignty, which paves the way for committed actors to take on new duties.

Along the same lines: even though the Eurozone is not 'an optimal currency area', authorised decision-makers established the EMU and calculated that it would spill over into a political union with a treasury. Creating the EMU attests to the forward-directed duties of solidarity, as the Eurozone crisis attest to. The economic meltdown makes it clear that a monetary union without political union is futile and undemocratic and makes a country fiscally fragile. The crisis also makes the need for solidarity evident in the functional sense: solidarity is needed to solve the Eurozone crisis. If all stood for one, all would be better off. However, there is no determinacy in the social world. A as the reaction to the Eurozone crisis shows, creating the EMU was a risky undertaking.

10 On Political Duties

The crisis arrangement for the Eurozone does not leave the basic political structure of the European political order—of the Member States—intact. It affects, as is documented, the very basis of political autonomy and raises the question of political justice, i.e. the legitimation of political authority. To paraphrase Kant, one may say that actors whose conduct regularly affects others' rights, and who refuse to abolish an unjust order—the unregulated 'state of nature'—and bring about a rightful political-legal order, are collectively breaking their natural duty of justice (see also Waldron 2002). When people live close by and/or cannot avoid affecting one another's rights, they have a forward-directed duty to establish a rightful order—a state.

Thus, any group of individuals whose acts regularly affect one another's rights and who do not currently have a set of legal and political institutions are obliged to create one (Stilz 2009: 199).

As mentioned, in order to be responsible for harm, one needs to have contributed to causing it. There must be morally significant responsibility. One's actions must have made a difference. With regard to the EMU, no individual member can be held responsible because no one in particular was crucial to its realisation or the consequences of it. The liability model of responsibility is problematic in such cases, because it leaves no one responsible for the wrongs. But the EMU and the harm it created did not come about on their own. Rather, it was created by a set of the Union's members acting together, and the members are responsible even though they could not foresee the consequences. As a collective, they are responsible. Since the decision-makers had some control of arrangements and since their acts have consequences for others' rights, there are responsibilities and hence duties. By consenting to make the EMU, and later the Eurozone crisis arrangement, they have taken on obligations. Simply by joining, 'the members have incurred a liability to the burdens required to meet the collective's obligations' (Stilz 2009: 189). Voluntary membership changes the moral reasons for action—it gives the members new sui generis reasons, as it brings about legitimate expectations in others. There are, so to say, involuntary collective obligations stemming from membership in an organisation, the acts of which have consequences for political and social rights.

11 Conclusion

The economic meltdown of the Eurozone effectively demonstrates the common vulnerabilities and the degrees of affectedness and global interdependence that have been reached. The Eurozone has brought its members into a community of fate, in which all are dependent on all, and where some are profiting and some are suffering from the same economic regime. By creating or consenting to the EMU, the EU's members have taken on obligations. They have created expectations of collective responsibility. There are thus *reasons for solidarity*. European solidarity is not beyond the demand of duty. Mending the Eurozone's flaws has become a matter of justice.

The Eurozone is a redistributive arrangement, and risk is redistributed along with the integration process, which has now brought the background conditions of justice to the fore. There is structural injustice and those that have made the monetary union and gained from it a duty to mend it. They are the addressees of the unredeemed moral obligations generated by the integration process. According to the political concept of justice, which revolves around the duties towards fair background conditions, they have an obligation to put the integration process back on democratic tracks.

References

Altvater, E. et al. (2013). Demokratie oder Kapitalismus? Europa in der Krise. In Blätter für deutsche und internationale Politik. Berlin: Blätter Verlagsgesellschaft mbH.

Bantekas, I., & Vivien, R. (2016). The odiousness of Greek debt in light of the findings of the Greek Debt Truth Committee. *European Law Journal, 22*(4), 539–565.

Birks, P. (2005). *Unjust enrichment*. Oxford: Oxford University Press.

Blyth, M. (2013). *Austerity: The history of a dangerous idea*. Oxford: Oxford University Press.

Brooks, D. (1989). On living in an unjust society. *Journal of Applied Philosophy, 6*(1), 31–42.

Brunkhorst, H. (2005). *Solidarity: From civic friendship to a global legal community*. Cambridge, MA: MIT Press.

Butt, D. (2007). On benefiting from injustice. *Canadian Journal of Philosophy, 37*(1), 129–152.

Butt, D. (2014). "A doctrine quite new and altogether untenable": Defending the beneficiary pays principle. *Journal of Applied Philosophy, 31*(4), 336–348.

Dworkin, R. (2011). *Justice for hedgehogs*. Cambridge, MA: Harvard University Press.

Enderlein, H. (2013). Das erste Opfer der Krise ist die Demokratie: Wirtschaftspolitik und Ihre Legitimation in der Finanzmarktkrise 2008–2013. *Politische Vierteljahresschrift (PVS), 54*(4), 714–739.

Eriksen, E. O. (2014). *Die Normativität der Europäischen Union*. Freiburg: Verlag Karl Alber (English edition (2014). *The normativity of the European Union*. London: Palgrave Macmillan).

Eriksen, A. (2015). Beyond professional duty: Does supererogation belong to the morality of roles? *International Journal of Applied Philosophy, 3*(32), 85–101.

Eriksen, E. O. (2016, November). *Three conceptions of global political justice* (GLOBUS Research Papers 1/2016). Oslo: ARENA.

Esposito, C., Li, Y., & Bohoslavsky, J. P. (Eds.). (2013). *Sovereign financing and international law: The UNCTAD principles on responsible sovereign lending and borrowing*. Oxford: Oxford University Press.

European Commission. (2012). *Treaty establishing the European Stability Mechanisms (ESM)*. Accessed February 2, 2017, from http://europa.eu/rapid/press-release_DOC-12-3_en.htm

Feinberg, J. (1968). Collective responsibility. *Journal of Philosophy, 65*, 674–687.

Forst, R. (2011). *Transnational justice and democracy* (RECON Online Working Paper 2011/12). Oslo: ARENA.

Forst, R. (2015). Transnational justice and non-domination. In B. Buckinx, J. Trejo-Mathys, & T. Waligore (Eds.), *Domination and global political justice*. London: Routledge.

Galbraith, J. (2016). *Welcome to the poisoned chalice: The destruction of Greece and the future of Europe*. New Haven, CT: Yale University Press.

Genschel, P., & Jachtenfuchs, M. (Eds.). (2016). *Beyond the regulatory polity? The European integration of core state powers*. Oxford: Oxford University Press.

Goodin, R. E. (2013). Disgorging the fruits of historical wrongdoing. *American Political Science Review, 107*(3), 478–491.

Grimm, D. (2004). Treaty or constitution? The legal basis of the European Union after Maastricht. In E. O. Eriksen, J. E. Fossum, & A. J. Menéndez (Eds.), *Developing a constitution for Europe*. London: Routledge.

Habermas, J. (1996). *Between facts and norms: Contributions to a discourse theory of law*. Cambridge, MA: MIT Press.

Habermas, J. (2012). *The crisis of the European Union: A response*. Cambridge, MA: Polity Press.

Habermas, J. (2013). *Im Sog der Technokratie*. Berlin: Suhrkamp (Translated: (2015) The lure of technocracy. Cambridge, MA: Polity Press).

Hedley, S. (1997). Ten questions for "unjust enrichment" Theorists. *Web Journal of Current Legal Issues*. Accessed February 2, 2017, from http://www.bailii.org/uk/other/journals/WebJCLI/1997/issue3/hedley3a.html

Hohfeld, W. N. (1913). Some fundamental legal conceptions as applied in judicial reasoning. *The Yale Law Journal, 23*(1), 16–59.
Huliaras, A., & Petropoulos, S. (2016). European money in Greece: In search of the real impact of EU structural funds. *Journal of Common Market Studies, 54*(6), 1332–1349.
Issing, O. (2014, March 25). Get your finances in order and stop blaming Germany. *Financial Times*. Accessed February 2, 2017, from https://www.ft.com/content/9a1636a6-b2c1-11e3-8038-00144feabdc0
Jonas, H. (1984). *The imperative of responsibility*. Chicago: University of Chicago Press.
Kant, I. (1785/1996). Groundwork of the metaphysics of morals. In M. J. Gregor (Ed.), Practical philosophy. Cambridge: Cambridge University Press.
Kant, I. (1795/1996). Toward perpetual peace. In M. J. Gregor (Ed.), Practical philosophy. Cambridge: Cambridge University Press.
Kant, I. (1797/1996). The metaphysics of morals. In M. J. Gregor (Ed.), Practical philosophy. Cambridge: Cambridge University Press.
Kenadjan, P. S., Bauer, K. A., & Cahn, A. (Eds.). (2013). *Collective action clauses and the restructuring of sovereign debt*. Berlin: Walter de Gruyter.
Kolers, A. (2014). The priority of solidarity to justice. *Journal of Applied Philosophy, 31*(4), 420–433.
Koskenniemi, M. (2006). A response. *German Law Journal, 7*(12), 1103–1108.
Kreuder-Sonnen, C. (2016). Beyond integration theory: The (anti-) constitutional dimension of European crisis governance. *Journal of Common Market Studies, 54*(6), 1350–1366.
Lastra, R. M., & Buchheit, L. (Eds.). (2014). *Sovereign debt management*. Oxford: Oxford University Press.
Lienau, O. (2014). *Rethinking sovereign debt: Politics, reputation and legitimacy*. Cambridge, MA: Harvard University Press.
Menéndez, A. (2013). The existential crisis of the European Union. *German Law Journal, 14*(5), 453–525.
Menéndez, A. (2017). The crisis of law and the European crises: From the Social and democratic Rechtsstaat to the consolidating state of (pseudo)-technocratic governance. *Journal of Law and Society, 44*(1), 56–78.
Nozick, R. (1974). *Anarchy, state, and utopia*. Oxford: Basil Blackwell.
Offe, C. (2013). Europe entrapped: Does the EU have the political capacity to overcome its current crisis? *European Law Journal, 19*(5), 595–611.
Offe, C. (2014). *Europe entrapped*. London: Polity Press.
Offe, C., & Preuss, U. K. (2016). *Citizens in Europe. Essays on democracy, constitutionalism and European integration*. Colchester: ECPR Press.
Official Journal of the European Union. (2007). *Treaty of Lisbon*. 2007/C306. Accessed February 2, 2017, from http://eur-lex.europa.eu/legal-content/en/TXT/?uri=CELEX%3A12007L%2FTXT
Official Journal of the European Union. (2012). *The consolidated versions of the Treaty on European Union (TEU) and the Treaty on the Functioning of the European Union (TFEU)*. 2012/C 326. Accessed February 2, 2017, from http://eur-lex.europa.eu/legal-content/en/TXT/?uri=CELEX%3A12012M%2FTXT
Olivares-Caminal, R. (2009). *The legal aspects of sovereign debt restructuring*. London: Sweet & Maxwell.
Pettit, P. (1997). *Republicanism: A theory of freedom and government*. Oxford: Oxford University Press.
Rawls, J. (1971). *A theory of justice*. Oxford: Oxford University Press.
Rawls, J. (1993). *Political liberalism*. New York: Columbia University Press.
Rieffel, A. (2003). *Restructuring sovereign debt: The case for ad hoc machinery*. Washington, DC: Brookings Institution Press.
Scanlon, T. M. (1998). *What we owe to each other*. Cambridge, MA: Harvard University Press.
Scanlon, T. M. (2008). *Moral dimensions: Permissibility, meaning, blame*. Cambridge, MA: Belknap Press of Harvard University Press.

Schäfer, A., & Streeck, W. (Eds.). (2013). *Politics in the age of austerity*. Cambridge, MA: Polity Press.
Scharpf, F. W. (2014). *No exit from the euro-rescuing trap?* (MPIfG Discussion Paper 14/4). Cologne: Max-Planck-Insitut für Gesellschaftsforschung.
Shoemaker, D. (2011). Attributability, answerability, and accountability: Toward a wider theory of moral responsibility. *Ethics, 121*(3), 602–632.
Steinvorth, U. (1998). Kann Solidarität erzwingbar sein? In K. Bayertz (Ed.), *Solidarität–Begriff und Problem*. Frankfurt am Main: Suhrkamp.
Stiglitz, J. E. (2016). *The Euro: How a common currency threatens the future of Europe*. New York: W.W. Norton.
Stilz, A. (2009). *Liberal loyalty*. Princeton: Princeton University Press.
Streeck, W. (2013). *Gekaufte Zeit: Die vertagte Kris edes demokratischen Kapitalismus*. Berlin: Suhrkamp.
Tugenhat, E. (1993). *Vorlesungen über Ethik*. Suhrkamp: Frankfurt am Main.
Tuori, K. (2012). *The European financial crisis—Constitutional aspects and implications* (EUI Working Papers, LAW 2012/28). Florence: European University Institute.
Tuori, K., & Tuori, K. (2014). *The Eurozone crisis: A constitutional analysis*. New York: Cambridge University Press.
Varoufakis, Y. (2016). *And the weak suffer what they must? Europe's crisis and America's economic future*. New York: Nation Books.
Waldron, J. (1996). Kant's legal positivism. *Harvard Law Review, 109*(7), 1535–1566.
Waldron, J. (2002). Redressing historic injustice. *University of Toronto Law Journal, 52*, 135–160.
Westlake, M. (1994). *A modern guide to the European Parliament*. London: Printer.
Wildt, A. (1998). Soldidarität—Besgriffsgeschichte und Definition heute. In K. Bayertz (Ed.), *Solidarität—Begriff und Problem*. Frankfurt am Main: Suhrkamp.
Wong, Y. (2012). *Sovereign finance and the poverty of nations: Odious debt in international law*. Cheltenham: Edward Elgar.
Yeager, L. B. (Ed.). (1962). *In search of a monetary constitution*. Cambridge, MA: Harvard University Press.
Young, I. M. (1990). *Justice and the politics of difference*. Princeton, NJ: Princeton University Press.
Young, I. M. (2006). Responsibility and global justice: A social connection model. *Social Philosophy and Policy, 23*(1), 102–130.
Young, I. M. (2007). *Global challenges: War, self-determination and responsibility for justice*. Cambridge, MA: Polity Press.
Zylberman, A. (2014). The very thought of (wronging) you. *Philosophical Topics, 42*(1), 153–175.

Chapter 9
Disintegration from Within: Independence and Separatist Movements, the EU Response and the Role of Solidarity

Henri de Waele

1 Introduction

At the turn of the last century, the threat posed by independence and separatist movements seemed more imaginary than real. After the numerous upheavals that altered the political and geographical landscape, with effects that persisted until the end of the 1990s, the dust had largely settled. The then existing, duly recognised countries managed to agree on the most appropriate delineations. The remaining nationalist cravings could thus be swiftly relegated to the folkloristic margins (cf. Held 1995; van Creveld 1999). With the benefit of hindsight though, in the post-9/11 era, we can re-label as grossly naive the thought that borders were rendered trivial by the advent of a new cosmopolitan world order. In particular, popular rumours regarding the demise of secessionist sentiments have been greatly exaggerated.

Whilst at present the issue of member state withdrawal is catching most attention, arguably, the most profound 'tearing apart' of the fabric that holds the European Union (EU) together risks to occur from further below: independence and separatist movements that eventually succeed in their crusade, sparking a potential domino effect, and an incremental fragmentation of the EU from the inside. Often still, these scenarios are considered to be of academic interest only and unlikely to actually materialise. Yet, already the Scottish referendum of 18 September 2014 (whereby no less than 44.7% of the voters expressed a preference for Scotland leaving the UK) indicated that the matter is becoming of increasing concern, no longer a figment of the imagination. The spectre of the UK itself leaving the EU has reinvigorated cries for self-determination amongst its constituent nations, now also extending to the

H. de Waele (✉)
Radboud University, Nijmegen, The Netherlands

University of Antwerp, Antwerp, Belgium
e-mail: h.dewaele@jur.ru.nl; henri.dewaele@uantwerp.be

A. Grimmel, S.M. Giang (eds.), *Solidarity in the European Union*,
DOI 10.1007/978-3-319-57036-5_9

Northern Irish hemicycle.[1] In a similar vein, the Catalan saga has not quite reached its terminus, with comparable aspirations on the rise in the Basque country (see Ferreres Comella 2014; Bengoetxea 2015). In Italy, economic stagnation and (perceived) cultural differences have excited calls for independence in the Veneto and South Tyrol regions (Carlà 2016). Related tensions, as well as the linguistic rift between Flanders and Wallonia, continue to raise doubts on the long-term survival of Belgium (Laborderie 2014; Popelier 2015). Beyond these familiar examples, also take France, hiding behind the surface a dazzling variety of subnational peoples and identities—where inter alia the Alsatian, Breton, Occitan and Corsicans cherish their own dreams of going it alone. A recent count suggests that the number of active separatist movements in Europe today may well lie above one hundred (Siroky and Cuffe 2015).

Of course, it is far from realistic to presume that all of these movements will ever succeed in their endeavour, let alone that they will all do so simultaneously. Nevertheless, even when not materialising soon, for the EU a serious danger of 'disintegration from within' does continue to exist. Moreover, the cautious trend that can be observed offers further testimony of the prevailing crisis of solidarity in Europe. After all, if that concept already proves so problematic to implement and maintain at the domestic level in some states, how should it be expected to take root, let alone become entrenched, between different countries?

This chapter succinctly reflects on this *problématique*, not from an empirical but a legal-theoretical perspective. Hereby, the core objective is to evaluate in normative terms the strength of the case for separatism, independence or secessionism, highlighting what the EU response to the phenomenon should look like. To this end, we will discuss the main drivers of the tendencies at play (Sect. 2), as well as the range of possible reactions to a successful secession (Sect. 3), in order to arrive at a sound holistic assessment (Sect. 4). A short final section that draws the threads together, paying oblique attention to the fallout of Brexit, completes the contribution (Sect. 5).

2 Independence and Separatist Movements: Their Continuing Attraction

Across the world, independence and separatist movements have been around for almost as long as developed polities became a fact of life (cf. Belser et al. 2015). In the modern era, their rise and growth is intimately connected with the decline of colonial powers. Against that backdrop, the early 'remedial' trail of thought posited

[1]Even if a majority overall had expressed a preference for the UK remaining in the EU, a breakdown would undoubtedly have revealed that the English and Welsh voted differently from the Scottish and Northern Irish—underscoring the engrained nature of these internal fracture lines, keeping alive the secession potential.

that suppression by an external power legitimised any attempt to sever the (political, geographic, cultural) links with the foreign tyrant (Beran 1987; Philpott 1998). The alternative 'primary right' approach regards the right to secede as something that is inherent and readily invocable: although its actual exercise may well be qualified, its existence does not depend on, or derive from, a prior or ulterior source (Birch 1989; Buchanan 1998). Instead, the former theory perceives secession as principally responsive—a remedy merely coming into play in case of grave and intolerable injustices.

In legal doctrine, the 'remedial' variant is far from accepted (see e.g. Van den Driest 2013). Most authors equally dismiss the 'primary right' view but (at the peril of fudging both approaches) occasionally tolerate such a reliance on self-determination in postcolonial settings (de Waele 2015). Neither are likely to apply in the European context, where an elaborate supranational framework demands that the rights of minorities and indigenous peoples are properly protected. Malfunctioning domestic safeguards or other gross abuses do not easily escape the scrutiny of the EU or the Council of Europe, as far as the matter is left unaddressed by the OSCE or competent UN bodies. It is perhaps especially in this light that the continuing attraction of independence and separatist movements requires an explanation, now that respect for regional identities is more firmly entrenched than ever, and contemporary democratic systems are supposed to give the persons concerned access to all means necessary to guarantee their political, economic and cultural well-being.

We face a bewildering paradox. As known, the European integration project was always meant to rein in nationalist sentiments and the fostering of micro-communities. It was to operate as a means to inculcate a transnational sense of belonging. Whilst the EU ought perforce to embody a shared destiny, in reality, it does not succeed in overcoming nested divisions. Rather, the EU actually appears to trigger and fan destructive 'bottom-up' tendencies in various quarters—being regarded as a paragon of globalisation that does not preserve, but acutely threatens the individual sphere. At the second level of the paradox, for many separatist and independence movements, the existence of the EU simultaneously proves very reassuring, as it presents an attractive lifeline and a future stability in case of a successful rupture. These groups will happily believe that their region stands to gain from seceding, so long as that does not entail forfeiting the membership of the European Union. They presume that EU membership will either not be lost, or quickly re-acquired upon gaining independence. In this calculation, accession to the Union ensures significantly lower 'transaction costs' of turning a region into an independent state, since key state functions may be reassigned to the supranational level. Hence, it should turn out less taxing to cope with globalisation in that safe harbour than if the new entity were to find itself *sans famille*, out in the cold.

The preceding reveals how the EU itself, instead of diminishing the attraction of separatist and independence movements, can be seen to foment the underlying tendencies—both wittingly and unwittingly. Contrary to the earlier impressions of how matters unfolded, fuelled by the conviction that integration would naturally lead to a dilution of the desire to face the world alone, national sovereignty has retained a definite appeal. Furthermore, the benefits of scale associated with EU membership have massively enhanced the viability of mini-states. At the same time, we must not overlook that once admitted to the Union, the tendencies are toned down, with the overarching structures imposing some healthy constraints on the exercise of their (newly) sovereign powers, and the injurious goals they might otherwise want to keep pursuing.

3 Successful Pushes for Secession: Possible Responses from the EU

What then should be the most immediate response from the side of the European Union, if a majority of the people in a region were to succumb to the temptation of 'going solo'? Should the EU indeed behave in welcoming fashion, or rather adopt an evasive, even hostile stance? As will be illustrated below, whilst the law provides no unequivocal answers (cf. de Waele 2014), some inferences are more plausible than others.

For starters, the EU is barred from actively meddling in situations that are wholly internal to a country. This flows from several general, established precepts of public international law, such as sovereign equality, non-intervention and respect for territorial integrity.[2] As a responsible actor on the global scene, despite its alleged *sui generis* character, the Union remains fully subjected to those principles (cf. De Witte 2012). Consequently, whereas the EU might want to dissuade potential breakaway regions from following through their agenda, it must refrain from such actions on pain of being held accountable for its transgressions. Resorting to covert strategies provides no real alternative, since in line with the case law of the International Court of Justice, not even the application of informal pressure or 'soft' methods of coercion is allowed.[3]

Are thus its hands tied entirely? Perhaps the foregoing does not necessarily mean that the Union has to adopt a strictly neutral course either; the legal and the moral dimensions ought not automatically be conflated. Imminently, we shall bring into the equation also the role that is to be attributed to the principle of solidarity. Let us first focus on the practical side, acknowledging that the tearing away of a part of a member state is certain to have ramifications that will reverberate widely. The EU cannot escape being impacted, nor can the country from which the separation is undertaken, nor can the seceding (or seceded) region itself. These ramifications run along three axes.

[2]See e.g. Article 2 of the UN Charter and the so-called 'Friendly Relations Declaration', UN General Assembly Resolution 2625 (XXV) of 24 October 1970.

[3]International Court of Justice, *Military and Paramilitary Activities in and against Nicaragua* (Nicaragua v. United States of America), Merits, Judgment, ICJ Reports 1986, p. 14.

To begin with, let us look at the repercussions for the administrative-political plane, comprising inter alia of the need to reconsider the allocated number of representatives in the European Parliament, alongside reviewing whether all civil servants employed by the institutions, bodies and organs may retain their positions (or should vacate their offices, in case they choose the nationality of the region concerned). Second, there is the legal-institutional axis, throwing into relief the relations between the seceding entity, the EU and the rump state. Public international law dictates that the newly independent country does not eo ipso become party to the agreements and organisations it participated in before the rupture, but tailor-made arrangements, deviating from that outcome, are imaginable.[4] Even when the newly independent country prefers to join the European Free Trade Association, optionally becoming part of the European Economic Area, the Union will need to adjust a host of rules and policies accordingly. Third, the most noxious consequences might lie in the economic-financial sphere. The exit of a region, particularly when it is wealthy, impacts heavily on the Union's overall GDP. If it does not seek (re-)accession, the EU budget and allocation of contributions require an overhaul. More importantly still, in the Belgian, Spanish or Italian scenario, we are dealing with a country that has adopted the Euro—which entails that a successful secessionist venture is bound to have monetary consequences (if only on the stock markets and exchange rates), further exposing the fragility of the EMU. Of course, in this context the newly independent country is likely to want to maintain the common currency, instead of creating its own—yet again, it can in no way be sure it will be permitted to do so.

The magnitude of the repercussions evinces the severity of the threat that separatist movements pose to the manageability as well as the constitutional integrity of the EU (cf. Amtenbrink and van den Berg 2010; de Waele 2017). They equally underpin that the broader coherence and stability of inter-state relations in Europe lies in the balance, especially since a successful separation risks to provoke a bandwagon effect, whereby ever more regions get inspired by the achievements of others. Even assuming that most of them wish to accede to the EU in their own right, the incremental fragmentation holds little appeal—placing additional strain on the Union's integrity and manageability, ushering in the next steps on the road towards disintegration.

Arguably, the best response from the side of the EU is one that is coloured by this knowledge. The principle of solidarity has a genuine role to play here too, supplying an excellent incentive to counter the above-mentioned tendencies and try to stave off the concomitant calamities. All the same, whilst morally, or at least pragmatically justified, the law offers no firm support to obstruct the plans of separatist and

[4]Problems are exacerbated in case of a breakup in equal parts (think Flanders and Wallonia), whereby international law regards both as placing themselves outside existing rules and conventions, thus needing to reapply.

independent movements, since the International Court of Justice confirmed that there exists no absolute ban on secessions.[5] Again, the territorial make-up of a country is in principle to be regarded as non-violable, exuding a preference for continuity of states within the pre-set boundaries. Moreover, throughout time it has proven notoriously difficult to influence, determine or predict the moment when a seceding territory officially comes into being. Real-life experience suggests that, notwithstanding the casual exception, ordinarily it is nigh impossible for a breakaway region to thrive if the permission of the 'parent nation' was not obtained first (Crawford 2006). Use of force forms a complicating factor, which the EU also has to take on board: as the International Court indicated, if an independence movement were to pursue its objectives with violence, that could militate against recognition of the resulting regime. Conversely, any violent activities from the side of the 'parent nation' could provide a solid (but not watertight) justification for the secessionists.[6]

Hence, the EU may cling to the one certainty that independence and separatist movements cannot fulfil their dreams under all circumstances, in spite of the self-determination claim they so frequently peddle.[7] Another potentially helpful element for the EU to take into account is the perspective of domestic legality, for it makes a crucial difference whether or not national law enables a region to withdraw from the larger whole. The Edinburgh Agreement, concluded between the British and the Scottish government in 2012, demonstrated that nothing in the UK impedes the move as such. Remarkably, the constitution of the Soviet Union featured a right to secede. The basic law in Belgium appears agnostic on the issue, whereas its Spanish counterpart (as interpreted by the *Tribunal Constitucional* in Madrid) is averse and the Canadian (as interpreted by the Supreme Court in Ottawa) seemingly only a little bit more permissive. In its *Québec* ruling, the latter rightly underlined that no right to become independent accrues to regions that already enjoy extensive individual and collective liberties, enabling the full vindication of their national and/or cultural identity within their respective states (cf. Haljan 2014). In the eyes of both national and international law, a detailed statute of autonomy suffices to safeguard the groups and peoples' internal self-determination, there being no overriding reason to (at least in law) require or permit a redrawing of the existing boundaries. Therefore, it matters greatly which situation the EU is confronted with.

---

[5]Albeit that technically, its pronouncement pertained not to that act but to Kosovo's declaration of independence, and although it simultaneously expressed that no people or territory enjoys a general entitlement to take their destiny into their own hands either, negating the 'primary right' approach. See International Court of Justice, *Accordance with International Law of the Unilateral Declaration of Independence in Respect of Kosovo* (Advisory Opinion of 22 July 2010), ICJ Reports 2010, p. 403.

[6]Opening the gates for the 'remedial' paradigm, discussed earlier, to take hold.

[7]In this regard, when remembering the rhetorical flourish of the Wilsonian pledge (in his 14 Points speech of 1918, raising hopes to an ecstatic, wholly unrealistic level in the first half of the last century), one rejoices in the wisdom that neither article 1 of the International Covenant on Civil and Political Rights nor article 1 of the International Covenant on Economic, Social and Cultural Rights was designed to privilege modern movements.

Whilst the international law parameters themselves do remain a bit fuzzy (and precisely *because* they remain a bit fuzzy), in some cases the national rules or interpretations of those rules supply decisive guidance. In contrast, if those national rules are ambiguous as well, the argument could go either way. How to assess the separation and respond to it then predominantly hinges on its (perceived) legitimacy, rather than its validity.

4 The Emerging Normative Picture

Let us now proceed to canvas the emerging normative picture, in order to evaluate the strength of the case for secession holistically. For starters, from the foregoing considerations, it seems clear that the EU is perfectly entitled to 'say no' and withhold any assistance from those breakaway regions that aspire to join the Union in their own right—particularly if their genesis is tainted by a violation of national or international rules ab initio. Admittedly, this assertion rests on the premise that the constitutional law of the EU has nothing to add here either. I have argued before that, despite allegations to the contrary, it indeed adds nothing conclusive; a hard and fast rule is simply nowhere to be found (de Waele 2014).

As remarked above, the Union does nevertheless possess a distinct interest here, albeit that it flows not from codes and statutes, but rests partly on a principled and partly on a pragmatist footing. To begin with, the supranational edifice nowadays struggles with a membership of 28. The plight is compounded by a socio-economic situation wherein the burdens are piled more heavily on the shoulders of some countries than on others (Weiler 2012). Notwithstanding these tribulations—and deliberately to help overcome them—there are numerous visible signs of solidarity, e.g. in the form of investment leveraging schemes, financial aid packages or ambitious migrant relocation plans. In this light, and especially from the perspective of the solidarity that gave birth to the European integration project itself, one wonders how anyone can expect the EU to be receptive towards those who are no longer willing to face the ordeals together. At heart, the Catalans show themselves unwilling to take on the role of paymaster for other Spaniards. The Flemish protest that they are fed up with covering the bill for the Walloons. The *Lega Nord* flaunts its contempt for the idle Italians of the south. But, if rancorous independence movements succeed in their quest for disassociation, they must consciously accept that therewith they abandon the common narrative—a narrative which allows no *à la carte* partaking. Principally, no manifestation of solidarity is requested vis-à-vis those who spurn solidarity themselves. After all, the concept functions as a two-way street and presupposes reciprocity. If one agrees to align and support without any guarantee of repayment in kind, we are not talking about solidarity but altruism.[8] Additionally, there is the

[8]Ergo, the idea of 'reciprocal solidarity' (see e.g. Feher 1987; Helie-Lucas 1991) amounts to a pleonastic misnomer.

pragmatic consideration that the EU, were it to take a receptive stand, is liable to trigger a domino effect, inspiring a plethora of regions to consecutively push for independence in the comfortable knowledge that (re-)accession to the Union follows suit.

The preceding lines undergird the contention that, although there is no sound basis for blocking or actively preventing the emergence of a new state that seeks (re-)accession, there is vice versa no requirement for the EU to do the opposite, i.e. deploy all available means to shore up and draw in the region in question (cf. Kochenov and van den Brink 2016).[9] A stand-off approach appears fully justified on ideological grounds, predicated on the community of values the Union strives to be, and the causes that it longs to promote—the overcoming of nationalist, small-minded, neo-tribal tendencies. Its core ethos or founding myth revolves around a transnational solidarity, bluntly negated by most separatist and independence movements. By that token, the EU cannot seriously be requested to hearken to the wishes and demands of such movements, offensive as they are to the Union's own history and spirit.

From a normative perspective, the obvious critique of this position will be that the reasoning exhibits a predominantly utilitarian character. Yet, as remarked earlier, those movements and regions that want to take their fate into their own hands in fact employ similar utilitarian arguments. In tune with the aforementioned verdict of the Canadian Supreme Court however, when they have little left to crave for as a group or people in terms of legal entitlements within the established polity, the ample room for internal self-determination displaces their claim for external self-determination. Of course, it bears reminding that the EU was from its inception designed as an inclusive organisation. The situations of the (post-communist/dictatorial) countries admitted in the past decades must nonetheless not be compared to those of the affluent and complacent secession-minded regions we witness today (Weiler 2012).

Whereas some insist that contemporary minority nationalisms are refreshingly forward-looking, purporting to create their own democratic habitat (Kymlicka 2001; Kochenov and van den Brink 2016), one still fails to see why the lavish existing facilities do not suffice. Moreover, their revolutionary zeal often stems from exaggerated feelings of exploitation, as well as a bloated sense of distinctiveness. The slightest concession that they are free to push their agenda at all times and places (in line with the overly voluntarist 'primary right' vision) pulls the rug away from under the feet of the international legal order. Whilst there is no denying the actual *possibility* to secede, investing that possibility with a general lawfulness remains something else entirely, and such liberal permissiveness easily elicits a virtually endless cascade. On that cue, and as a matter of principle, the EU has been

---

[9]The term 'EU' here primarily refers to the institutions and their specific interests, yet also stretches out the collective of member states (amongst which Spain, Italy, Belgium and the UK), as represented in the Council and the European Council. Undoubtedly, the latter will display a great individual obstinacy as well.

unwilling to go down that route. To the mind of the present author that reticence, *pour encourager les autres*, in the end boils down to not just a defensible but to the least objectionable point of view.

5 Conclusion

This chapter sought to exemplify how the current crisis of solidarity manifests itself through the rise of separatist and independence movements. Thereby, it also attempted to sketch the most credible response. The disquisition culminated in the thesis that the EU need not necessarily be very welcoming towards newly independent regions in search of accession; that it may justifiably adopt a more evasive stance instead; and that, inter alia when weighing up the negative ramifications of a contrary position, it is actually well advised to do so.

There are many different conceptions of solidarity, but various authors recognise the unique status of the EU in this respect, in contrast to other regional integration organisations (Hartwig and Nicolaides 2003). In the founding treaties, we repeatedly stumble upon the term, from the external action provisions to the supranational energy policy. All the same, the concept has nowhere been fixed or quantified. This fuzziness renders it vulnerable to divergent interpretations, far from ensuring unconditional mutual assistance regardless of the context. Quite fittingly, in the present contribution, solidarity was eventually taken to mean that independence and separatist movements should not count on automatic loyalty or support either.

Having said this, qualifications on the normative picture may be due pursuant to the 2016 Brexit referendum. If the eventual fallout were to include a Scottish secession in the wake of a UK withdrawal from the European Union, the argument presented here—somewhat surprisingly perhaps—militates in favour of welcoming Scotland back in.[10] Though there arises no *legal* obligation to reach out even then, solidarity *does* nudge in the direction of a warm reception. After all, the English were first to reject the ideas of sharing and cooperating by voting to leave, whilst the Scottish clearly expressed their desire to stick together, subscribing to the harmonious overarching paradigms embodied by the EU. Consequently, a Scotland breaking away under those circumstances offers testimony of a much more mature secessionism than the maudlin, self-interested rendition that prevailed in 'Little England'.

Finally, the success of the 'take back control' mantra in the run-up to the British referendum should give us pause. The outcome of that plebiscite suggests that the slogan possesses a mesmerising quality, so that separatist movements everywhere are likely to sit up and take notice. Indeed, without much complementary effort, it has shown to catch on and tip the balance harrowingly quickly. The fallaciousness

[10] Leaving aside the complexity of a potential Northern Irish secession, prior to an envisaged reunification with the Republic of Ireland.

of the claim therefore ought to be exposed urgently, as in an interdependent world, sovereignty lost its meaning and content long ago. The EU can use that to its advantage, knowing that nowadays, no newly independent state is able to hold out long on the outside. Driving home that message, coupled with the notification that 'Brussels' will not be forthcoming once the extraction is complete, may be enough to put off the most arduous of secessionists. Naturally, they could accuse the Union of restricting its solidarity to the happy few on the inside. Even so, it is through that posture, and that posture alone, that the member state collective will be able to effectively counter the threat of disintegration from within.

References

Amtenbrink, F., & van den Berg, P. A. J. (Eds.). (2010). *The constitutional integrity of the European Union*. The Hague: TMC Asser Press.

Belser, E. M., Fang-Bär, A., Massüger, N., & Oleschak Pillai, R. (Eds.). (2015). *States falling apart? Secessionist and autonomy movements in Europe*. Bern: Stämpfli Verlag.

Bengoetxea, J. (2015). Federalism and secession. The tension between pact and fact and the Basque *Fueros*. In E. M. Belser, A. Fang-Bär, N. Massüger, & R. Oleschak Pillai (Eds.), *States falling apart? Secessionist and autonomy movements in Europe* (pp. 189–214). Bern: Stämpfli Verlag.

Beran, H. (1987). *The consent theory of political obligation*. London: Croom Helm.

Birch, A. (1989). *Nationalism and national integration*. London: Routledge.

Buchanan, A. (1998). The international institutional dimension of secession. In P. B. Lehning (Ed.), *Theories of secession* (pp. 227–256). London: Routledge.

Carlà, A. (2016). Secessionist parties' approaches to migration: The weight of history on south Tyrolean nationalism. In R. Medda-Windischer & P. Popelier (Eds.), *Pro-independence movements and immigration discourse – Policy and practice* (pp. 58–85). Leiden: Brill Nijhoff.

Crawford, J. (2006). *The creation of states in international law*. Oxford: Oxford University Press.

de Waele, H. (2014). Secession and succession in the EU: Fuzzy logic, granular outcomes?. In C. Brölmann & T. Vandamme (Eds.), *Secession within the union: Intersection points of international and European law* (Amsterdam Law School Research Paper No. 2014–39) (pp. 34–40).

de Waele, H. (2015). The secession conundrum – Through the looking-glass. *European Constitutional Law Review, 11*(3), 609–616.

de Waele, H. (2017). Independence and separatist movements – Europe between integration and disintegration. In A. Grimmel (Ed.), *The crisis of the European Union: Challenges, analyses, solutions* (pp. 104–115). London: Routledge.

de Witte, B. (2012). The European Union as an international legal experiment. In J. H. H. Weiler & G. de Búrca (Eds.), *The worlds of European constitutionalism* (pp. 19–56). Cambridge: Cambridge University Press.

Fehér, F. (1987). *The frozen revolution: An essay on jacobinism*. Cambridge: Cambridge University Press.

Ferreres Comella, V. (2014). The Spanish constitutional court confronts catalonia's "right to decide" (comment on the judgment 42/2014). *European Constitutional Law Review, 10*(3), 571–590.

Haljan, D. (2014). *Constitutionalising secession*. Oxford: Hart Publishing.

Hartwig, I., & Nicolaides, P. (2003). Elusive solidarity in an enlarged European Union. *EIPAScope, 3*(2), 19–25.

Held, D. (1995). *Democracy and the global order: From the modern state to cosmopolitan governance*. Stanford: Stanford University Press.
Helie-Lucas, M. A. (1991). *The original sin and internationalism or some musings on cultural relativism*. Combaillaux: WMLM.
Kochenov, D., & van den Brink, M. (2016). *Secessions from EU member states: The imperative of union's neutrality* (University of Edinburgh Europa Working Paper No. 2016/04).
Kymlicka, W. (2001). *Politics in the vernacular: Nationalism, multiculturalism, and citizenship*. Oxford: Oxford University Press.
Laborderie, V. (2014). La fin de la Belgique et ses impossibilities: L'hypothèse d'une independence flamande à l'épreuve des faits. *Outre-Terre – Revue européenne de géopolitique, 3*(2), 114–123.
Philpott, D. (1998). Self-determination in practice. In M. Moore (Ed.), *National self-determination and secession* (pp. 79–102). Oxford: Oxford University Press.
Popelier, P. (2015). Secessionist and autonomy movements in flanders: The disintegration of Belgium as the chronicle of a death foretold? In E. M. Belser, A. Fang-Bär, N. Massüger, & R. Oleschak Pillai (Eds.), *States falling apart? Secessionist and autonomy movements in Europe* (pp. 215–246). Bern: Stämpfli Verlag.
Siroky, D. S., & Cuffe, J. (2015). Lost autonomy, nationalism and separatism. *Comparative Political Studies, 48*(1), 3–34.
van Creveld, M. (1999). *The rise and decline of the state*. Cambridge: Cambridge University Press.
van den Driest, S. F. (2013). *Remedial secession: A right to external self-determination as a remedy to serious injustices?* Antwerp: Intersentia.
Weiler, J. H. H. (2012). Catalonian independence and the European Union. *European Journal of International Law, 23*(4), 910–912.

Chapter 10
The EU Falling Apart? Theoretical Discussions of Brexit, Grexit and Other Exit Scenarios

Tim Oliver

1 Introduction

The possibility of Britain exiting the European Union had long hung-over UK–EU relations. British politicians had often warned of and in some cases actively threatened the possibility of Britain quitting. They had done so often enough to sound like the boy who cried wolf in the Aesop fable. But as the fable and now Brexit teaches us, the wolf eventually appeared. The EU, like the UK government, was caught largely unprepared for the result, with little contingency planning for dealing with the outcome. For both sides the experience has been a sharp learning curve.

That a member of the EU is set to withdraw has also posed difficult questions for the study of European integration. Academic discussion of Brexit has so far focused largely on the UK. There exists a wealth of literature examining the UK–EU relationship ranging from studies of the history of UK–EU relations to a burgeoning literature on the referendum result itself (George 1998; Geddes 2013; Goodwin and Ford 2017). The political debate in the UK has also led to numerous proposals and discussions about the various options for the future of UK-EU relations (Booth and Howarth 2012). The British government and Westminster Parliament have also been a source of much respected analysis and debate. The 2010–2015 Conservative-Liberal Democrat coalition government's 'Review of the Balance of Competences' produced the most detailed analysis ever undertaken by a member state of its relations with the EU (Emerson 2015).

Discussion elsewhere in the EU on the possibility of a UK exit remained muted until the result was known (although see Möller and Oliver 2014; Irwin 2015). This in part reflected an unwillingness by decision makers elsewhere in the EU to

T. Oliver (✉)
London School of Economics and Political Science, London, UK
e-mail: T.L.Oliver@lse.ac.uk

A. Grimmel, S.M. Giang (eds.), *Solidarity in the European Union*,
DOI 10.1007/978-3-319-57036-5_10

become involved in the UK's referendum debate out of a fear their involvement would inflame British Eurosceptic opinion. It also reflected how any planning for a Brexit would be taken by some in the UK (and elsewhere in the EU) as a sign that the rest of the EU thought Brexit a real possibility, a move that would have risked further fuelling support for leaving the EU. However, it also reflected a taboo over discussing or contemplating a reversal in the direction of European integration, which has generally been forward moving rather than backward moving (Oliver 2013). At the same time, debate in the UK has also been largely oblivious to what impact Brexit could have on the EU and Europe more broadly. How Brexit unfolds, for example, in terms of what new UK–EU relationship emerges will be determined as much by how the rest of the EU responds as it will by Britain's response. This means that despite their more comprehensive debate, Britons can often overlook the crucial dimension of how the rest of the EU might react or be changed.

One of the questions overhanging the future of the EU is whether it will integrate or disintegrate (Wright 2013; Zielonka 2014). Brexit has added to this question but not caused it. The 2017 sixtieth anniversary celebrations of the signing of the Treaty of Rome have long been threatened with being overshadowed by problems in the Eurozone and Schengen, to say nothing of longer-running tensions over whether the EU has become too big and unwieldy (Dempsey 2016). Britain's vote, so the worry goes, could prove contagious, paving the way for Grexit and triggering votes in other member states where Eurosceptics have taken inspiration from Britain's decision. Far from being a cathartic moment liberating the EU of a country often termed 'an awkward partner' (George 1998), Brexit could instead clear the way for more referendums elsewhere in the EU. Given the poor record of EU governments at winning referendums, Britain could be a harbinger of what is to come rather than an example of British exceptionalism.

While there exists a wealth of literature and theories on European integration, European disintegration and theories of how it might happen have received only limited attention. Many students, to say nothing of decision makers or members of the general public, recoil at the mention of the word 'theory'. It can suggest abstract rather than practical thinking, the sort one suspects is best left in the academy's Ivory Tower. Yet we all use theoretical approaches and do so everyday as a way of making sense of our world and our lives in it. Theories are tools we use to narrow down the chaos and complexities of life so we can focus on what is the most important. One way to think of theory is of it as a torch that we use to light up only that which we think is important or necessary. From the insights it provides, we can explain and understand much more.

To discuss what Brexit could mean for the EU, this chapter looks into some of the theoretical discussions about European disintegration. Before this, the chapter begins by setting out how Brexit fits into the wider challenges facing the EU. While opinion is divided as to whether the EU is falling apart, the state of the Union is not one that should leave us feeling wholly optimistic. The chapter then moves onto explore the work on theoretical approaches to European disintegration by Douglas Webber (2014), Hans Vollard (2014) and Ben Rosamond (2016). Their works share some common themes. They also help answer one of the most important questions: what exactly is meant by 'European disintegration'.

2 The Brexit Challenge to the EU

How can we understand the challenge that Brexit presents to the EU? One of the simplest ways would be to look at what Britain contributes and therefore what it would take away when it leaves. The EU would lose 12.8% of its population (Eurostat 2016), an economy that contributes 19.4% of the EU's total exports (excluding intra-EU trade) (Open Europe 2012) and is 17.6%—or around one sixth—of the EU's economic area (Irwin 2015). Within the EU Britain runs a large trade deficit with the rest in goods and services that in 2014 was £61.6 billion (ONS 2015). The EU, especially states such as Germany, would need to make up for the UK's yearly net contribution to the EU budget, which in 2015 was £8.5 billion (HM Treasury 2015, p. 40). In security the EU would lose one of its two serious military powers and a permanent member of the UN Security Council. Britain has been a more constructive player in the EU's development than it is willing to credit itself with, and while its willingness to question EU proposals might frustrate others, it has in the past allowed other member states to hide behind it their own objections. A British withdrawal might also take with it Britain's more obstructive contributions that led to it being labelled 'an awkward partner' (George 1998). But Britain is not the only member state who can be awkward. It is worth remembering that the title of George's classic book on Britain's awkward relations with the EU begins with the indefinite article 'an' not the definite article 'the' (Daddow and Oliver 2016). Furthermore, just because a country is awkward or sometimes unpopular does not make it ineffective. The UK had successfully pursued a range of policy agendas in the EU and secured a wider range of opt-outs from EU policies than any other member state.

This is not to deny that Britain has or can be awkward. From the rest of the EU's perspective, the most awkward challenge Britain has ever presented it with is Brexit. Brexit presents both the UK and the EU with 14 negotiations and debates that can be divided into three groups: internal UK, UK–EU and internal EU (Oliver 2016). A fourth set of negotiations can be identified which involve how the rest of the world relates to the UK and EU over Brexit, but they can be grouped into the three aforementioned groups. These negotiations are summarised in the tables below.

UK Brexit negotiations

Negotiations	Participants	Key issues
1. Brexit narrative	UK political parties, media and academia	What the vote by the UK populace meant
2. Government, Parliament and the Judiciary	Ministers, MPs, Lords and Supreme Court	Who defines the Brexit process
3. Party politics	Conservatives, Labour, UKIP and Liberal Democrats	Positioning the parties to manage Brexit
4. A united kingdom?	UK government, Scottish government and Parliament, Northern Ireland Government and Assembly, Welsh Assembly and Government and London and local governments in England	Role of the devolved administrations in Brexit, the place of London and England in the negotiations and the stress of leaving the EU on the UK's existing quasi-federal structure
5. UK and the world	UK bilateral relations with the non-EU world, especially in the context of new trade deals	UK relations with the USA, emerging powers such as China and India and full membership of the World Trade Organisation (WTO)

The negotiations within the UK revolve largely around defining what Brexit should mean in terms of new relations to be sought with the EU along with debates about the UK's unity, political economy, democracy and place in the world. The EU referendum highlighted a large number of political issues facing the UK that span from issues of growing inequality through to changing identities.

UK–EU Brexit negotiations

Negotiations	Participants	Issues
1. UK–EU: Article 50 and an exit deal	European Parliament, European Commission, the UK and the EU 27 governments	Exit agreement for the UK, budget contributions and the status of UK and EU citizens
2. Brexit transition	UK, EU 27 heads of government, European Parliament and the European Commission	Possible transition arrangements for the UK out of the EU
3. New relationship	UK, political systems of EU 27, European Parliament and the European Commission	Agreement between the UK and EU over a new relationship, including a potential free trade deal
4. Brexit and the 27 other member EU states	EU 27 governments and their domestic political structures, European Parliament and the European Commission	Remaining EU member states need to reach agreement over what to offer the UK and over what timeframe, potentially with countries ratifying any agreement individually
5. Foreign, security and defence cooperation	UK and EU27 (especially France and Germany)	How to continue cooperation on international matters

UK–EU negotiations revolve around a deal for the UK to exit the EU and move to a new relationship. Exiting the EU may be the easiest stage of Brexit, albeit one overshadowed by tensions over the UK's budgetary contributions and the future status of UK nationals in the EU and EU nationals in the UK. The divisions the EU budget can often open up in EU politics, along with sensitivities surrounding immigration, mean we should not overlook the possibility that these will bring negotiations crashing to a halt. Agreeing to a new relationship—with options ranging from UK membership of the European Economic Area (EEA) through to a free trade deal or no deal at all (also known as a 'hard Brexit')—is likely to be more complicated and time-consuming. Agreeing to a deal, and possibly a transition stage of several years to implement the deal, will require the not so easily acquired agreement of the EU's remaining 27 members (including, possibly, the need for domestic ratification processes ranging from parliamentary votes to referendums) and the European Parliament. Depending on the nature of the deal reached, the European Court of Justice may be asked afterwards to rule on whether it contravenes the EU's treaties. It is often forgotten that in the early 1990s such a ruling struck down the original agreement reached between the EU and the EEA (Robinson and Barker 2016).

EU Brexit negotiations

Negotiations	Participants	Issues
1. Rebalancing the union	EU 27, European Parliament, Commission and the ECJ	The new balance of power within the post-Brexit EU, the Eurozone's place in the EU and European integration, disintegration or muddling through
2. EU in a multipolar Europe	EU, Norway, Switzerland, Iceland, Lichtenstein, Turkey, Ukraine, non-EU Balkan countries and the UK	The future of the EU's relations with non-EU European countries, EU-EEA/European Free Trade Association relations and European geopolitics
3. EU in a multipolar world	EU, UK, USA, Russia, China, UN and NATO	EU's place in an emerging multipolar world
4. EU's daily business	EU as a union of 28 member states until the UK exit becomes formally effective	How to let the UK and the rest of the EU continue normal non-Brexit business until the UK withdraws

Finally, the EU itself will need to negotiate how it will change to reflect the withdrawal of ones of its largest member states. The balance of power in the Union could shift, with implications for numerous policy areas and the EU's place in Europe and the wider world. Brexit will therefore shape the EU's unity and its political and economic direction. Two interconnected questions arise. First, will the EU become easier to manage and lead? Second, who and what ideas will benefit from Britain's withdrawal and how will this influence the EU's direction and outlook?

3 Is the EU Falling Apart?

The above 14 negotiations bring with them positive opportunities for the UK, UK-EU relations and the future of the EU. Such opportunities, however, must be set next to the possibility they will bring acrimony, frustration and a breakdown in relations within the UK and between the UK and the EU. They could also lead to strained relations within the remaining EU itself, potentially leading to the most profound outcome of the British vote to leave: the disintegration of the EU itself. Such a scenario might sound far-fetched, not least because the EU has faced numerous crises before from which it has emerged stronger and more integrated. Assuming the EU will always overcome its problems is myopic, especially given it has so far muddled through each crisis rather than solved them for the longer term (Wright 2013). The EU currently faces several defining challenges. As Rem Korteweg (2015) colourfully described the situation, the EU appears to be circled by the four horsemen of the apocalypse: War haunts relations with Russia; Famine brings hardship and misery to Southern Europe in particular through the ongoing problems of the Eurozone; Death's harvest of refugees and economic migrants in the Mediterranean puts pressure on Schengen; while Pestilence spreads Euroscepticism and populism from Britain. With his somewhat critical attitude towards the EU, a fifth horseman—President Trump—may have now appeared on the horizon.

Does this mean the EU is collapsing? It is easy to be pessimistic. Through the passage of time, the EU has lost the memories of the horror of war and communist tyranny that once helped drive it forward. Differences between East and West, North and South and growing inequality within states have created a Europe that appears deeply divided and prone to the rise of populists. Despite numerous attempts to enhance its power and institutions, the EU can instead appear unwieldy and incapable of delivering in the way it once did when it created such things as the Single Market. Even in areas of EU competence such as trade—where together the EU forms a trading superpower equal to that of the USA or China—the Union's past success appears to be on the wane with initiatives such as the Transatlantic Trade and Investment Partnership (TTIP) increasingly shunned rather than embraced. The EU's inability to solve the problems facing the Eurozone has led to a series of political, economic and social problems that leave it looking weak not only to the rest of the world but to its own citizens.

Despite this opinion polling shows that Europeans have not given up on the idea of the EU. The EU continues to oversee an area of the world that is amongst its most prosperous, stable, secure, cultured, innovative, integrated and peaceful. While NATO—and especially the US commitment to Europe—should always be given credit for its role in securing European peace, the integration and reconciliation the EU has helped create have underpinned Europe's peace in a way military security on its own could not have. The EU itself can be more effective than it is often given credit for. The aforementioned UK government 'Review of the Balance of Competences' concluded that the balance of powers between the EU and UK was about right and of benefit to the UK (Emerson 2015). Despite this, Europeans appear to be growing deeply sceptical of many of the EU's policies and ability to confront the longer-running problems the EU faces in the Eurozone, its declining demographics, productivity and ability to secure itself. The problem for decision makers, however, is that what Europeans want to see done to solve the EU's various problems varies across the EU. This helps explain why numerous reports into the problems facing the EU and what needs to be done have so far failed to find a way forward. These proposals have yet to secure sufficient political will from decision makers across the EU. One problem may be an attachment to 'EU mythology', such as an unquestioning commitment to ideas such as 'ever closer union' and an obsession with creating processes over securing positive outcomes.

4 Theoretical Discussions of European Disintegration

The idea of European integration reversing is not entirely new. Some of the earliest discussions of European integration included the idea of 'spill back' (Lindberg and Scheingold 1970). Theories of European integration have also developed in ways that consider integration in a variety of ways. One such example is 'differentiated integration' which examines how parts of the EU integrate at different speeds (Leuffen et al. 2012). However, differentiated integration focuses on why some member states integrate in some areas and others do not. Theories that look instead at disintegration are few and far between. This in part reflects an approach in academia to integration that has focused on internal changes to the EU but which, until recently, meant little attention was paid to the viability of the Union itself. Developments in the past few years have led to a number of publications considering the idea of disintegration.

4.1 Brexit as Integration Turned Upside-Down

Douglas Webber's 2014 article 'How likely is it that the European Union will disintegrate? A critical analysis of competing theoretical perspectives' offers one way of analysing Brexit by applying it to the various theories of European integration he examines. Webber's approach is to review these competing theories, 'comparing the explanation they offer for this process and evaluating to what extent the variables that each theory identifies as having driven this process are still present, have waned or have disappeared'. In short, he explores the idea of European disintegration as integration in reverse. He summarises his approach in the table set out below which has been adapted to show the possible role of Brexit.

Theory (and key authors)	Main independent variable(s)	(Potential) Disintegrator	Theory-based prognosis	Role of Brexit
Realism (Mearsheimer)	Distribution of military power	European multipolarity after collapse of NATO	Disintegration unlikely as long as the USA maintains military presence in Europe	Brexit encourages the USA to give up on NATO and EU
Classical intergovernmentalism (Moravcsik I)	Preferences/ interests of three big EU powers	Divergence of interests of big 3 powers	Disintegration unlikely provided France and Germany cooperate	Brexit destabilises Franco-German relationship
IR Institutionalism (Keohane)	Cooperation-facilitating role of institutions (EU)	Decline of members' common interest and hegemonic dominance/will	Disintegration increasingly conceivable	Brexit leads the way
Historical institutionalism (Pierson; Thelen and Steinmo)	Ever-tighter institutional constraints	(Generally externally induced) Crises or critical junctures	Disintegration likely only in very exceptional circumstances	Brexit alone insufficient, but could form part of/trigger exceptional circumstances
Liberal intergovernmentalism (Morvcsik II)	Big 3 powers and economic interdependence	Declining economic interdependence and divergent big 3 economic interests	Disintegration very unlikely—interdependence remains very strong	Brexit impact limited by continuing UK–EU interdependence
Neo-functionalism/ transactionalism (Stone, Sweet and Sandholtz)	Spillover/transactional exchange ad society	Decline of transnational exchange and society; de-institutionalisation	Disintegration virtually excluded—institutionalisation prevents even crisis-induced collapse	Brexit has no impact
Comparative federalism (Kelemen; McKay)	Judicial, partisan and sociocultural safeguards vs. explosion of federal state	Weakness of common identity and integrative pan-European political parties	Growing risk of disintegration with growing transfer of power from national to EU level	Brexit highlights weakness of common identity

Adapted from Webber (2014, p. 11)

Webber identifies two weaknesses in the various theoretical approaches he covers. As he summarises it, they 'have an insufficiently comparative inter-spatial as well as inter-temporal focus'. First, they fail to sufficiently take into account the role of domestic politics in the member states. In many member states the last decade has witnessed a major upsurge in 'anti-European' political attitudes and movements, thus ending the 'permissive consensus' (Hooghe and Marks 2009) that previously allowed integration to proceed. Secondly, they overlook the powerful 'semi-hegemonic' role of Germany as the state that is politically, economically and geographically central to underpinning integration and therefore whether Germany will be able or willing to continue to play this role.

These weaknesses are important for assessing the implications of Brexit. First, to what extent will the UK's domestic politics and Euroscepticism feed into the contemporary domestic politics of other member states? Second, will Brexit add to or trigger, as Webber terms it (but never elaborates on), a crisis 'made in Germany' for the EU? Such a crisis would be both unprecedented and potentially fatal for current European integration. To address these issues, we would need to examine the appeal of Brexit in each member state and in particular its impact on Germany. In many member states the appeal of Brexit was generally quite limited, in no small part due to attention being on other crises such as the Eurozone or Schengen. However, as mentioned earlier, if Brexit proves contagious and triggers votes in other member states, then the commitment of key states, and crucially Germany, could be called into question.

Britain's isolated position over recent issues may limit the impact of Brexit, which means the EU's future will rest more with other states. Britain has been somewhat indifferent to EU cooperation to deal with the migration problem in large part due to its non-membership of Schengen. Its non-membership of the Euro and aloofness from efforts to stabilise the single currency have left it with little if any influence over the future of the Eurozone or much of an appeal within it. London's limited interest in dealing with the crisis in Ukraine (through either the EU or NATO) has cast doubts over Britain's importance to European security. Britain's importance to other EU powers, especially France and Germany, has declined with them increasingly able to relate to one another without having to factor in Britain's needs (Krotz and Maher 2016). Finally, the Conservative Party's divisions over Europe, which have been crucial to shaping UK–EU relations, are not to be found in the governing parties of any other leading EU member state. Overall this means the UK has for a long time not been seen as a necessary partner. As such the formal impact on the EU of Brexit could be limited by the UK's passive role in EU cooperation and integration. That said, that does not mean its decisions and behaviour have no effect. As we saw earlier, Brexit is a long and complex set of negotiations some of which could easily become entangled with negotiations over some of the other problems facing the EU. Britain might not be viewed as a necessary partner, but Brexit is making it somewhat more relevant by confronting the EU with the need to think about it.

4.2 Brexit and Partial Exits

Hans Vollaard (2014) begins his analysis of how to explain European disintegration by reviewing various approaches that could be taken to the topic. In doing so he reviews theories of European integration (including when they are put in reverse), international relations, comparative federalism, optimum currency areas and imperial decline. Each he finds problematic because they fail to address the sui generis nature of the EU and how it has changed European politics. The focus of some approaches on the nation state leaves them offering limited insights given that the EU's disintegration may not necessarily lead to a return to a Europe of nation states in some form of reversal of integration to life before the emergence of the EU. They can also offer too many factors to explain why a union such as the EU might collapse, with factors ranging from cultural and linguistic homogeneity to economic inequalities. As Vollaard (2014, p. 6) points out when exploring ideas of imperial decline, some 210 wide-ranging factors have been identified to explain the collapse of the Western Roman Empire. Using such ideas to identify which factors are essential for the EU's survival therefore becomes too difficult given the sheer number to take into account.

Instead Vollaard turns to Bartolini's (2005) theoretical framework on polity formation. For Vollaard (2014, p. 7), Bartolini's key notion is mutual dependence 'between the external consolidation and the internal structuring of a political formation. Without a certain measure of closure, a political centre cannot keep resources and actors inside in order to allocate goods and values to enforce actors' behavioural conformity'. Without this internal organisation, a polity will struggle to maintain its boundaries and unity. External consolidation can vary in terms of permeability (opportunities for exit and enter) and congruence (the number of boundaries such as legal or economic). This means 'partial exits' can be imagined where a state or other actor remains part of the polity while developing links with another political formation (Vollaard 2014, p. 7). Bartolini applied his theory to European integration, with Vollaard (2014, p. 8) explaining that 'the process of European disintegration means that actors and resources cannot be locked in as well by the EU, and that the subsequent (partial) exits weaken political structuring within the EU, and the EU's capacity to enforce boundaries and behavioural conformity, to foster loyalty and to allocate goods and values'. Drawing on Bartolini's framework, Vollaard (2014, pp. 9–13) examines four testable propositions on the way the EU would disintegrate.

Brexit enters most clearly when Vollaard (2014, p. 12) discusses his fourth proposition on how a lack of exit options outside the EU causes Eurosceptic dissatisfaction to induce partial exits within the EU. In a way that reminds us of Webber's (2014, pp. 352–354) argument of the importance of looking at the domestic politics of each member state because how a partial exit might unfold will vary according to the political context in each state. 'The stronger Eurosceptic dissatisfaction, the less voice options at the EU level, the lower European loyalty, the lower the perceived costs to leave the EU and the better the provision of values and goods by non-EU integrative schemes, the more likely exit from the EU is' (Vollaard 2014, p. 13). Euroscepticism might therefore be on the rise across the EU, but this is not necessarily the determining factor. Compared to the UK, the costs of exiting (as opposed to some partial exits in the form of opt-outs) are too high for many EU states, not least those within the Eurozone. Many EU states lack the options the UK has available to it such as the membership of the UN Security Council, G7, close relations with the USA and the Commonwealth and its wider global economic, social and political links. As a result, Brexit will lead to a truncated union, but not complete disintegration. Instead further 'partial exits' can be imagined, perhaps for states where Eurosceptic opinion is boosted by Brexit, but this would lead to further differentiated integration or a two-speed Europe as opposed to complete disintegration.

4.3 Disintegration as an Indeterminate Process in a Wider Crisis

Looking at the wider global and European context—especially political economy—is something Ben Rosamond (2016) highlights when considering Brexit and the idea of European disintegration. As we noted earlier, Brexit is not an event as much as a process, and for Rosamond the idea of disintegration should be seen in a similar way. It need not be some critical juncture in the EU's development that produces a clearly defined outcome. Instead it is better thought of as an 'indeterminate process' (Rosamond 2016, p. 868) and one that should be 'understood within a much broader set of transformations'. Brexit takes place in a context that includes the possible stagnation of the EU, the rise of populists (not least that of Donald Trump), the financial crisis and repeated failings by technocratic elites, growing frustrations amongst national publics—especially those in the working class and, increasingly, the middle class—who do not feel empowered or feel excluded and tensions between large swathes of society and elites living in global metropolises such as London or New York.

Brexit must be seen as a symptom of a wider crisis in democratic capitalism identified by authors such as Wolfgang Streeck (2016). As Burgoon et al. (2017) argue, the past few years has seen the decline in a post-Cold War agenda pursued by both Europe and the USA that push forward the freer movement of people, goods, services, capital and ideas across national boundaries. Support for that agenda has declined across the West, both at the level of national policy and at the level of party politics, a development closely linked to the rise of populist parties in Europe and the USA. This does not mean the EU, transatlantic cooperation, Western internationalism and capitalism as we know it are doomed. The USA, the UK and the rest of Europe remain each other's most reliable partners. However, in understanding why Brexit happened, what is now unfolding within the UK, in UK–EU relations, within the remaining EU and in the wider West, it is clear that some of the political economic agendas that have sustained the relationships are being challenged in ways the leaders of each cannot ignore.

The biggest challenge the UK, the rest of the EU and the USA face in addressing these common problems will be finding some common purpose to overcome them. As Simon Tilford (2017) recently argued, it is not globalisation on its own that has caused Brexit or the long list of other problems Britain, the EU and the USA face. It has been the unwillingness of states to take responsibility—either themselves or through shared cooperation—for managing the challenges globalisation poses, not least the challenge of better managing the distribution of the unprecedented wealth and opportunities that globalisation has brought. That may not bode well for the future. Failure to agree will leave decision makers on both sides of the English Channel, across Europe and on either side of the North Atlantic to instead pursue inward looking policies that drive themselves further apart.

5 Conclusion

Brexit is the defining issue of British politics and one of several defining issues of European politics. Not an hour goes by without the emergence of a new speech, piece of gossip, minutes of a debate, statement or policy proposal. Following it can be an arduous task. It often leaves those seeking to understand Brexit feeling like they face an overwhelming challenge. One can only sympathise with the civil servants, diplomats and other decision makers now tasked with implementing Brexit. Implementing Brexit will depend on what 'Brexit' means, something that will only emerge as the process of Brexit unfolds. Through speeches and government reports, Theresa May's and the UK government's position might have slowly clarified, or at least we might have seen the negotiation starting points. Despite this, much remains uncertain, not least because a great deal depends less on what happens to the UK—or what the UK government wants—and more on what happens in the remaining EU. Brexit has added to an already long list of challenges facing the EU. It has triggered a series of overlapping negotiations in the UK, between the UK and EU, within the EU and between the UK, EU and the wider world. These are negotiations which could easily lead to strained relations between and within the various states institutions involved. The possibility that these negotiations might collapse should not be overlooked. Nor should we assume that it will only be UK–EU negotiations that will prove difficult and prone to bitter arguments. Brexit poses a challenge to the EU's unity, the response to which will depend on how the rest of the EU responds and not how Britain does. Given the potential costs involved, it remains to be seen whether all sides can adopt an approach to negotiations of the 'do no harm' principle.

The biggest question overhanging any breakdown in relations is whether this will in time lead to the disintegration of the EU. Such a scenario might still sound outlandish, but history—not least that of Europe—is littered with failed unions (Davies 2011). Britain's vote to leave the EU has added to the tensions within the union that is the UK. Scotland, Northern Ireland and the capital city of London have found themselves at odds with the rest of the union they form a part of. Yet the UK is a more integrated single market than the EU and one often bound together by a wider variety of common institutions (military, law, crown, BBC, a welfare state, transport, media), culture (language, comedy, science) and a history of shared struggle (empire, war, exploration) than the EU can claim. Granted, unity across the UK in each of these areas can vary greatly. There are also important differences in the types of union the UK and EU seek to be. But it is worth pausing to appreciate that if a union like the UK can shatter, then so too can the EU.

The idea of the EU disintegrating has remained something of an understudied topic in European studies. From the few theories and theoretical discussions so far put forward, it is possible to identify several factors to keep in mind when studying Brexit. First, the internal politics of EU member states remains key to the EU's politics and unity. The way Brexit plays out within the domestic politics of each state will therefore be crucial. Second, the politics of Germany in particular and its place in the EU are of central importance. As Webber argued, the EU has yet to see a crisis 'made in Germany'. It remains unclear whether Brexit can trigger this on its own or if it will do so only should it align with other problems in a way that becomes too much of a burden for Germany. Third, the extent to which some member states can exit varies according to how bound they are into the EU and what external options are available to them. Britain's ability to exit the EU has sometimes been compared to the mythical Hotel California sung about by The Eagles: that you can check out anytime you like, but you can never leave. Thanks to its position—economically, politically, internationally and geographically—Britain may indeed be able to check out more easily than other member states whose choices are limited to 'partial exits'. Fourth, the wider economic, political and security context in which Brexit unfolds will shape both the UK and the EU. Brexit or European disintegration should not be studied without taking into account the wider challenges facing the West, capitalism and multilateralism. Finally, Brexit and the response of the EU cannot be framed as a single one-off event. It will be a process that is potentially an open-ended one that will lack any clear ending for the UK, UK–EU relations or the EU itself.

References

Bartolini, S. (2005). *Restructuring Europe: Centre formation, system building and political structuring between the Nation-State and the European Union*. Oxford: OUP.

Booth, S., & Howarth, C. (2012). *Trading Places: Is EU membership still the best option for UK trade?* London: Open Europe.

Burgoon, B., Trubowitz, P., & Oliver, T. (2017). Globalization, domestic politics, and transatlantic relations. *International Politics*, forthcoming late 2017.

Daddow, O., & Oliver, T. (2016). A not so awkward partner: The UK has been a champion of many causes in the EU. *LSE Brexit Vote blog*. Available: http://blogs.lse.ac.uk/brexitvote/2016/04/15/a-not-so-awkward-partner-the-uk-has-been-a-champion-of-many-causes-in-the-eu/

Davies, N. (2011). *Vanished Kingdoms: The history of half-forgotten Europe*. London: Allen Lane.

Dempsey, J. (2016, December 14). Judy asks: Is the EU's architecture collapsing? *Carnegie Europe blog*. Available: http://carnegieeurope.eu/strategiceurope/66439

Emerson, M. (Ed.). (2015). *Britain's future in Europe: Reform, renegotiation, repatriation or secession?* Brussels: Centre for European Policy Studies.

Eurostat. (2016). *Population change—Demographic balance and crude rates at national level*. Available: http://appsso.eurostat.ec.europa.eu/nui/show.do?dataset=demo_gind&lang=en

Geddes, A. (2013). *Britain and the European Union*. Basingstoke: Palgrave Macmillan.

George, S. (1998). *An awkward partner: Britain in the European Community*. Oxford: Oxford University Press.

Goodwin, M. J., & Ford, R. (2017). Britain after Brexit: A nation divided. *Journal of Democracy, 28*(1), 17–30.

HM Treasury. (2015, December). *European Union finances 2015: Statement on the 2015 EU budget and measures to counter fraud and financial mismanagement*. Cm 9167. https://www.gov.uk/government/uploads/system/uploads/attachment_data/file/483344/EU_finances_2015_final_web_09122015.pdf

Hooghe, L., & Marks, M. (2009). A postfunctionalist theory of European integration: From permissive consensus to constraining dissensus. *British Journal of Political Science, 39*(1), 1–23.

Irwin, G. (2015). *Brexit: The impact on the UK and the EU*. London: Global Counsel. Available: https://www.global-counsel.co.uk/sites/default/files/special-reports/downloads/Global%20Counsel_Impact_of_Brexit.pdf

Korteweg, R. (2015). *The four horsemen circling the European Council summit*. London: Centre for European Reform. Available: http://www.cer.org.uk/insights/four-horsemen-circling-european-council

Krotz, U., & Maher, R. (2016). Europe's crisis and the EU's 'big three'. *West European Politics, 39*(5), 1053–1072.

Leuffen, D., Rittberger, B., & Schimmelfennig, F. (2012). *Differentiated integration*. Basingstoke: Palgrave Macmillan.

Lindberg, L., & Scheingold, S. (1970). *Europe's would-be polity: Patterns of change in the European community*. Hemel Hempstead: Prentice-Hall.

Möller, A., & Oliver, T. (Eds.). (2014). *The United Kingdom and the European Union: What would a "Brexit" mean for the EU and other States around the World?* Berlin: Deutsche Gesellschaft für auswärtige Politik e.V.

Oliver, T. (2013). *Europe without Britain: Assessing the impact on the EU of a UK withdrawal*. Berlin: SWP. Available: https://www.swp-berlin.org/fileadmin/contents/products/research_papers/2013_RP07_olv.pdf

Oliver, T. (2016). Brexit: The many roads to a crisis? *LSE Brexit Blog*. Available: http://blogs.lse.ac.uk/brexit/2016/09/21/brexit-the-many-roads-to-a-crisis/

ONS. (2015, June 26). *How important is the European Union to UK trade and investment?* Office for National Statistics. http://webarchive.nationalarchives.gov.uk/20160105160709/http://www.ons.gov.uk/ons/rel/international-transactions/outward-foreign-affiliates-statistics/how-important-is-the-european-union-to-uk-trade-and-investment-/sty-eu.html

Open Europe. (2012). *Right speech, right time?* London: Open Europe. Available: http://www.openeurope.org.uk/Content/Documents/Pdfs/EuropeSpeech.pdf

Robinson, D., & Barker, A. (2016, November 21). "Many ways" Brexit may go to EU courts, top ECJ judge says. *FT*. Available: https://www.ft.com/content/6609025a-adbc-11e6-ba7d-76378e4fef24

Rosamond, B. (2016). Brexit and the problem of European disintegration. *Journal of Contemporary European Research, 12*(4), 864–871.

Streeck, W. (2016). *How will capitalism end? Essays on a failing system*. New York: Verso.

Tilford, S. (2017). Crisis of capitalism? Perhaps, but don't blame it on globalisation. London: CER. http://www.cer.org.uk/insights/crisis-capitalism-perhaps-dont-blame-it-globalisation

Vollaard, H. (2014). Explaining European disintegration. *Journal of Common Market Studies, 52*(5), 1142–1159.

Webber, D. (2014). How likely is it that the European Union will disintegrate? A critical analysis of competing theoretical perspectives. *European Journal of International Relations, 20*(2), 341–365.

Wright, T. (2013). Europe's lost decade. *Survival, 55*(6), 7–28.

Zielonka, J. (2014). *Is the EU doomed?* Cambridge: Polity Press.

Chapter 11
"Inconvenient Solidarities": Extreme-Right Online Networks and the Construction of a Critical Frame Against Europe

Manuela Caiani and Elena Pavan

> *Leaders of far-right and outsider parties across Europe have been celebrating Britain's decision to leave the EU, with some demanding their own voteson whether to leave the bloc. Marine Le Pen, the leader of the National Front in France, said British people had given Europe and the world "a dazzling lesson in democracy".*
> *In Germany, Beatrix von Storch, a member of the right-wing Alternative for Germany (AfD) party, which takes an anti-Eurozone and anti-immigration stance, told national broadcasters she "cried for joy" at the news of the result. Party leader Frauke Petry wrote on Twitter: "The time is ripe for a new Europe" (http://www.independent.co.uk/news/world/europe/brexit-eu-referendum-latest-far-right-celebrations-news-marine-le-pen-a7101371.html).*

1 Introduction

In recent years, the use of information and communication technologies (from here on in, ICTs) for political participation has received ever-increasing attention, particularly with regard to the transformation of authoritarian contexts such as North Africa, where citizens and civil society organisations appeared to have scant room for manoeuvre (Eggert and Pavan 2014). In analysing and commentating relevant political events such as the so-called Arab Springs, the diffusion of *Occupy!* and the Spanish *acampadas*, academics and observers have placed much emphasis on the democratic potential that characterises communication on the Internet, particularly considering the possibilities this medium offers for overcoming traditional obstacles to collective mobilisation in a quick and economical manner (Bennett and Segerberg 2013), to construct transnational networks of "outrage and hope" (Castells 2012) and to transform "passive consumers" or simple

M. Caiani (✉) • E. Pavan (✉)
Institute of Humanities and Social Sciences, Scuola Normale Superiore, Pisa, Italy
e-mail: manuela.caiani@sns.it; elena.pavan@sns.it

A. Grimmel, S.M. Giang (eds.), *Solidarity in the European Union*,
DOI 10.1007/978-3-319-57036-5_11

"voters" into "global citizens" that are "user as producer, contributing to online debates and interacting directly with others" (Bruszt et al. 2005: 150).

The continual expansion of telecommunications infrastructure, the pervasive spread of mobile devices and the progressive redefinition of modes of communication in ways ever more horizontal, creative and interactive favour wide participation, diversified and organised through communication networks that are "crucial elements of information, sociability, and support" (Rainie and Wellman 2012: 13). Within these networks, ideas, knowledge and countercultural practices circulate and are modified continually, challenging traditional hierarchical models (Warkentin 2001), facilitating the hybridisation of organisational modes (Chadwick 2013) and repertoires of political action (Lievrouw 2011) and favouring the emersion to new forms of power and leadership (Padovani and Pavan 2016). Based on weak, but none the less relevant, ties (Rainie and Wellman 2012: 13), online communication networks become fully fledged "networked publics" (Boyd 2011): collective actors motivated and sustained over time by "feelings of belonging and solidarity, however evanescent those feelings may be" (Papacharissi 2016: 4) due to the ephemeral and extemporaneous quality of communicative acts in online space.

Before the general attention towards the positive effects induced by the collective and participatory use of ICTS, work focusing on the "dark side" of digital communications has been rare (Caiani and Parenti 2013). Just as scholars have begun to speak of "bad social capital" to underline the not uniformly positive externalities of associational activities (Berman 1997; Foley and Edwards 1997), so the need for a thorough investigation of the negative aspects of online communication has been ever more often invoked. Specifically, a growing number of studies underline how ICTs are becoming a strategic tool for groups and sympathisers on the extreme right (e.g. Bartlett et al. 2011). In addition, analyses in the field of political violence and terrorism studies show how isolated individual "consumers" may find a collective identity through frequenting extreme-right websites, convincing themselves that they are not alone but part of a wider community, even if only a "virtual" one (Post 2005). In this sense, the possibilities to create and circulate content, like the construction of ties between individuals and groups, are not only resources available to "civil" society: they also constitute real added value for extremist collective forces (Chase-Dunn and Boswell 2004; Whine 2012).

Empirical studies that aim to substantiate the "numerous theoretical arguments regarding the ways in which technologies could contribute to social ills, including violent conflict escalations, overwhelming flows of misinformation, and political polarization" (Garrett 2006: 217–218) are nevertheless rare. In this context, one aspect that is particularly crucial but still relatively little explored is the nexus that exists between extreme-right politics, the use of ICTS and the rampant Euroscepticism that has rapidly spread within and beyond Europe. On one hand, recent analyses conducted using Eurobarometer data suggest that digital media play a leading role in the creation of negative attitudes to projects of European integration (Conti and Memoli 2016), but stop short of investigating how this intersects with the growing Euroscepticism of the radical right. On the other, the internationalisation of processes has been identified by many scholars as one of the major causes of the recent revitalisation of the extreme right in Europe (e.g. Hermet 2001; Mény and Surel 2000). Anti-Europeanism and nationalism are also considered two crucial elements in the new populism of the right (Kriesi 2008). The European question and more generally the (bad) management of the crisis by national governments have in fact created conditions favourable for the extreme right to construct nationalist calls that, at minimum, seriously question belonging to the European Union (EU) and integration within this supranational institution (Bustikova 2009). The role played by ICTs in the public diffusion of these calls, along with their role in the possible creation of bridges between opposition agendas emanating from various sectors of the extreme right in Europe, remains mostly unexplored.

In response to this situation, we focus in this article on the use that extreme-right organisations make of ICTs to build online networks through which they develop common conversations, oppose current processes of European integration and propose alternative visions to overcome critical issues linked to the actual "state of the Union" and guide future developments. More specifically, we explore the way in which the websites of parties, groups and movements on the radical right are connected within systems of online relations underpinned by hyperlinks, the most basic form of relationship within the public space of the web, and fed by the publication of digital content that contributes to the formation of frames critical of and proposing reform for today's political Europe. As Padovani and Pavan (2016) note, the invisibility of these networks does not lessen their relevance, particularly in relation to the structuration of the cognitive and symbolic components of political processes and participation. In this sense, the exploration of online networks provides a highly useful entry point to understand the ways in which the use of ICTs supports and favours the creation of what we call "inconvenient solidarities", that is to say, alliance structures that oppose and distort current efforts towards transnational democratisation, particularly at the European level.

Through the combined use of diverse research techniques, and in particularly digital and network analysis research methods, in this article we map and examine the structures and content of online networks generated by extreme-right organisations in six European countries—Austria, France, Germany, Italy, Spain and the United Kingdom—in order to achieve a twofold objective. On one hand, we intend to uncover and, as a consequence, systematically render analysable the "conversations" that result from the strategic use that extreme-right groups make of digital communications to build contacts and bridges in the online space. On the other, we intend to explore the way in which these conversations contribute to the production of frames critical of and proposing reform for Europe and, more specifically, whether a nexus exists between the structure of relations built online by various sites and the capacity to transmit more or less homogenous and shared opposition and reform frames. The adoption of a complex and comparative perspective, considering the structure and content of online networks in several countries at once, allows us to capture the heterogeneity of ways in which ICTs contribute both structurally and cognitively to the construction of systems of "inconvenient solidarities" within single national contexts as well as the transnational level more systematically. In that sense, rather than testing hypotheses, our study seeks to provide an analytical structure and possible methodological approach to analyse in more detail the implications that derive from the strategic use of ICTs for the construction of a collective opposition to processes of integration and democratisation in Europe.

The article is structured as follows. Section 2 illustrates our research approach and the data considered in our analyses. Section 3 presents the results of the analyses conducted on the structures of online networks in the six countries considered and proposes a classification within a typology of online conversations. Section 4 illustrates the results of the content analysis undertaken, beginning with the websites of the principle actors in each online network, and locates these in relation with the types of conversation identified previously. In the concluding section, we recap on the results obtained and propose possible research paths.

2 Methodology

To map the structures and content of online networks between extreme-right sites in the six countries considered, we adopt a multi-method approach. In particular, we use certain techniques rooted in so-called digital methods (Rogers 2013), a set of tools and research procedures developed specifically for the analysis of digital objects (e.g. hyperlinks and search engines), in combination with analytical techniques that aim to investigate the patterns of relations between social actors (Borgatti et al. 2013).

With regard to the structures of online networks, we map the hyperlinks between extreme-right websites using Issue Crawler (IC) software, one of the main tools used in web crawling (Rogers 2013).[1] Beginning from a list of website addresses of extreme-right organisations in each country (URL),[2] the software searches for and traces the hyperlinks between them.[3] Because the construction of a hyperlink from

[1]http://www.issuecrawler.net

[2]Although the use of social media (such as Facebook and Twitter) is increasing among radical right-wing groups in Europe (see Bartlett et al. 2011), in this study we focus on organisations' websites as we are principally interested in the meso-organisational level of the use of Internet for propaganda and the organisation of the extreme right. The organisations considered in this study constitute a subset of the "dark side collection" (Caiani and Parenti 2013), which maps extreme-right organisations with websites in the six countries using a snowball technique. More specifically, in this study we consider the websites of the "dark collection" that remained active throughout the period in which the research was undertaken (July–September 2015). For a list of URLs used as a departure point for each country, see Appendix 1.

[3]Mapping hyperlinks through IC rather than manually as was the case in the "dark side collection" allows us to trace links between sites more systematically and to reduce possible researcher inferences during the mapping and coding procedure. In each case, it should be noted that IC is

one site to another can be interpreted as a voluntary expression of recognition and involvement within dynamic digital relations (Rogers 2013), we consider the online networks mapped through IC as a proxy for the structures of online conversations that the organisations from each country establish among themselves and that, in turn, constitute the infrastructure on the basis of which they develop inconvenient solidarities.

Once mapped, the six online networks are analysed using network analysis techniques at both the macro (i.e. the entire web) and micro (i.e. single actors or "nodes") levels in order to identify possible "modes of conversation" online between extreme-right organisations. At the macro level, we examine the levels of cohesion, activity and centralisation in online networks, which are among the principal dimensions used to distinguish the ways in which collective actors organise and coordinate through networks (Diani 2003; Cinalli and Füglister 2008). At the micro level, instead, we identify those actors occupying the most central positions for each network (Freeman 1979), and in particular we identify the nodes that receive the highest numbers of hyperlinks and, thus, more recognition from other nodes in the network. Recent approaches to the study of power dynamics in online space (in particular, Padovani and Pavan 2016) suggest that the most central actors are, by virtue of the general recognition they enjoy, more capable of "programming" the content of online conversations. In this sense, identifying the nodes that play a programming role within online networks and examining how homogenous or heterogeneous the central nucleus within which they gather helps to further characterise the modes of organisation and coordination adopted by right-wing groups to "inhabit" digital space.[4] Finally, we classify the six networks within a typology distinguishing between various "conversational modes" on the basis of the combinations of characteristics of the networks and the levels of homogeneity of the programmers' nuclei.

With regard to the content circulating within the online networks, we concentrate in particular on anti-European criticisms and on possible alternative visions proposed by programmers through the pages of their sites. In this view, we compile a list of keywords in the corresponding language of each country that denote both critical aspects of the current "state of the Union" and proposals for moving forward which we consider as proxies for the critical and reform frames of the various programmers.[5] The concept of the frame is directly imported from social movement studies with a view to analysing the cognitive and symbolic component

---

not able to process pages containing Javascript nor can it navigate within social platforms. The maps produced using IC do not therefore represent the totality of online hyperlink structures. They do, however, constitute a good starting point to explore "who speaks to whom" in the online public sphere (Pavan and Diani 2016).

[4]To evaluate the level of homogeneity of the central nuclei of online networks, we consider each site as representative of a determined extreme-right group or organisation following a classification used in previous work—in particular in Caiani and Parenti (2013).

[5]The keywords used to uncover frames critical of the EU are "Eurocracy", "Troika", "Eurocrats", Brussels bureaucrats", "European dictatorship", "Brussels politicians", "Brussels technocrats" and

(Melucci 1996) of extreme-right opposition to Europe. In studies on the dynamics of collective participation, frames are in fact defined as cognitive instruments, typically elaborated by leader organisations, that allow them to make sense of and elaborate external reality and to place strategies to change it in context (Snow and Benford 1992). More specifically, frames can seek to identify critical and problematic aspects (i.e. diagnostic frames) as well as possible solutions to solve them (i.e. prognostic frames) (Snow et al. 1986).

The keywords used are derived from a previous in-depth qualitative study of the discourse on Europe elaborated by the extreme right in Germany, Italy and the United States (Caiani et al. 2012) in order to capture salient features of the diagnosis and prognosis of the "EU problem" elaborated by extreme-right organisations in the various countries considered. To trace the presence of these keywords within programmers' sites, we use GoogleScraper, a tool for the automated analysis of online content.[6] For each word, the tool interrogates all of the URLs that compose the online networks of the six countries considered and reports the number of web pages containing the words. This number can be considered an indicator of the quantity of attention given by an extreme-right site to a specific critical or reformist argument. In this sense, focusing on programmers and pinpointing the elements that structure their criticisms and alternative proposals allow us to begin to better understand the symbolic and cognitive bases that imply a joint convergence among the various organisations in the different countries considered, as well as the potential for the development of collective action against Europe at the transnational level.

3 Systemic, Aggregated and Weak Conversations: How Extreme-Right Organisations Interact Online

In what ways do the sites of extreme-right organisations in the six countries examined talk to each other? To begin to answer this question, it is important to first understand how the online networks are structured. With this end in mind, we first examine the level of cohesion of the online networks, which indicates how easily communications flow between the various actors (Diani 2003: 306), and their levels of internal activity and indicator of how far the nodes of a network are "engaged" in maintaining the unity of a system of relations (Cinalli and Füglister 2008). The first element through which to evaluate levels of cohesion is the *number of components* that structure the network. A component is defined as a portion of the network in which all the nodes are reachable either directly or indirectly (Borgatti et al. 2013): the higher the number of components, the higher the level of

"Totalitarian super state". The keywords used to uncover reformist frames are "Europe of the peoples", "Europe of sovereign states", "Europe of nations" and "United States of Europe".

[6]https://tools.digitalmethods.net/beta/scrapeGoogle/

fragmentation of the network and, as a consequence, the conversation that develops through it. Second, we consider the level of *compactness* of the network, a measure of cohesion calculated as the harmonic mean of the entries in the matrix for distance between the nodes. The values of compactness vary from 0 to 1, where 0 indicates a situation of total disconnection and 1 a completely connected network within which conversations between sites develops more easily. To evaluate the levels of activity within the networks, we consider the average degree, that is, the average number of link nodes within the network are involved in: the higher this value, the higher the number of hyperlinks sent and received by the various sites, and, as a consequence, online conversation is more "lively". Third, by looking at the level of *centralisation* of online networks, we explore how far the conversations between the extreme-right sites tend to be concentrated around a restricted group of particularly "prestigious" actors (Diani 2003: 306). Higher levels of centralisation signal that online conversations are developing around a few specific nodes that receive a lot of hyperlinks and are thus "points of reference" (centralisation of indegree) or send a lot of hyperlinks and are thus "systematic builders" of online conversations (centralisation of outdegree).

As shown in Table 11.1, the networks among French sites and British sites are the most cohesive structures. In both cases, the networks are formed of a single component and tend to be more compact compared to those of other countries (the compactness scores are, respectively, 0.244 and 0.159) but also more active (the average degrees are, respectively, 18.41 and 14.72). The German network also shows relatively high levels of compactness and activity (respectively, 0.118 and 16.67) despite being split into two components. In addition, in all three of these networks, the high levels of activity are accompanied by high levels of centralisation (both indegree and outdegree). Together, these elements suggest that the online conversations that take place within these networks tend to be rather fluid (though less so in the German case), lively and built around sites that function as collective reference points but also depend on the operation of a few nodes that are particularly engaged in the construction of links with others.

Table 11.1 Characteristics of extreme-right online networks on the six countries examined

	Austria	France	Germany	Italy	Spain	United Kingdom
Size	27	36	16	25	21	22
N. ties	44	133	21	34	26	42
Density	0.0627	0.1056	0.0875	0.0567	0.0619	0.0909
N. components	2	1	2	5	1	1
Compactness	0.105	0.244	0.118	0.091	0.079	0.159
Average degree (normalised)	11.11	18.41	16.67	8.33	11.90	14.72
Indegree centralisation	9.47%	24.41%	26.22%	7.12%	9.25%	20.41%
Outdegree centralisation	21.45%	47.92%	33.33%	24.48%	30.25%	45.35%

On the contrary, the Italian network appears as the most fragmented, broken into five components and with low levels of compactness and activity. In Spain, however, despite the connection in a single component, levels of internal activity and compactness (11.90 and 0.079, respectively) remain relatively low. Finally, the Austrian network can be placed at an intermediate level, since it is composed of a single giant component that includes the majority of nodes and a dyad (that is a subgroup formed by two nodes). In this case, the level of compactness nears that of the German network, but, analogously to that seen in the Italian and Spanish cases, levels of centralisation are lower than elsewhere, especially as regards the centralisation of indegree. This suggests that the online conversations in these three countries lack common points of reference and are also less dependent on the activities of specific nodes, thus resulting more horizontal and evenly distributed compared to those in France, Germany and the United Kingdom.

As mentioned in the previous section, the second aspect that we believe useful in defining the modes of online conversation here is the level of homogeneity that characterises the nucleus constituted by the nodes that receive wider recognition from other members of the network and are thus most able to "programme" the content of online conversations. Among the various ways of measuring the centrality of a node within a system of relations, the number of links received by other members of the network (indegree) is typically associated with the level of recognition and prestige an actor enjoys (Freeman 1979). In the case of online networks, the indegree of a site corresponds to the number of hyperlinks received from other members of the network, and the programmers can be identified as those sites that have a higher indegree score than the average plus a standard deviation (Padovani and Pavan 2016).

Looking at the programmers in each of the six networks, we notice that the levels of homogeneity within the nuclei vary among the different countries. As shown in Table 11.2, the nucleus of the French network is composed almost exclusively of political movement sites such as Polémia and Novopress (with indegrees of 12 and 9, respectively). The nucleus of the British network is also extremely homogenous, though composed instead almost totally by the sites of political parties like England First (indegree of 6). In Austria too, the nucleus of the online network, though smaller as suggested by the low level of centralisation of indegree, is rather homogenous, formed by political movement sites as well as the FPO (Freiheitliche Partei Österreich) party. In Germany, however, the centre of the online network appears to be a more pluralist environment, populated by the sites of political movement, subcultural organisations (like the Autonomen Nationalisten Ostfriesland) and the most important German extreme-right political party, the NPD (National Democratic Party of Germany). Finally, the Italian and Spanish networks differ from the others by the extreme heterogeneity that characterises the nuclei of the programmers. In addition, within these wider nuclei, it is not possible to identify a category of extreme-right organisation sites that are more often taken as a reference point than others.

Combining the results obtained from the exploration of the structures of the networks with those from the study of their centrality, we can seek to identify the

Table 11.2 Programmers in the six extreme-right online networks

	Organisation	Type	Indegree
AT	Unzensuriert	PM	4
	ÖLM, Österreichische Landsmannschaft	PM	3
	FPÖ, Freiheitliche Partei Österreich	PP	3
	Zur Zeit	PM	3
FR	Polémia	PM	12
	Novopress	PM	9
	Synthèse National	PM	8
	Rivarol	PM	8
	Alsace d'abord	PM	7
	Làgrif	PM	7
	L'association Terre et Peuple	CULT	7
DE	Autonomen Nationalisten Ostfriesland	SUB	5
	Aktionsbüro Thüringen	PM	2
	Freies Pommern	PM	2
	NPD Die Volksunion	PP	2
	Junge Freiheit	PM	2
IT	RSI, Repubblica Sociale Italiana	NR	3
	Federazione Nazionale Combattenti della Repubblica Sociale Italiana	NR	3
	Tabula Rasa	PM	3
	Il museo delle divise fasciste	COMM	2
	Movimento Nazional Popolare per l'Unità dell'Area	PM	2
	Noreporter.org	SUB	2
	Decima Mas Network	NR	2
	Casa Pound Italia	SUB	2
	Guardia Nazionale Repubblicana Legione Tagliamento	NR	2
	Raido	SUB	2
	Italia Libera	NR	2
ES	Grupo Edenia	COMM	3
	Movimiento Social Republicano	PM	3
	Libreria Europa	COMM	3
	Ciudad Libre Opinion	SUB	3
	Nuevo Orden	NAZI	2
	Union Nacional de Trabajadores	PM	2
	Falange Española de las JONS	PP	2
	RDN—Red de Distribucion Nacional	COMM	2
	Velsas Shop	COMM	2
UK	England First Party	PP	6
	British People's Party	PP	4
	Aryan Unity	PP	4
	Civil Liberty	PP	3
	Imperium Europa	NAT	3
	British National Party	PP	3

PM political movement, *PP* political party, *CULT* cultural organisation (new age, neo-mystical, catholic), *SUB* subcultural organisation (skinhead, musical and sport groups), *NR* nostalgic revisionist, *COMM* commercial and publishers, *NAZI* neo-Nazi, *NAT* nationalistic and patriotic organisations

Table 11.3 Modes of conversation in the six extreme-right online networks

Country	Type of conversation	Level of activity	Level of fragmentation	Level of compactness	Convergence Towards the inside	Convergence Towards the outside	Level of homogeneity
AU	Aggregated	Medium	Low	Medium	Low	Low	High
FR	Systemic	High	None	High	High	High	High
DE	Aggregated	High	Medium	Medium	High	Medium	Medium
IT	Weak	Low	High	Low	Very low	Very low	Low
ES	Weak	Medium	None	Low	Low	Medium	Low
UK	Systemic	High	None	High	High	High	High

different ways in which the sites of the extreme-right organisations and groups converse online. Table 11.3 synthesises the principal characteristics of the six networks examined and classifies them in three main types. The French and British networks host what may be called *systemic conversations,* characterised by a high level of activity and compactness, as well as by high levels of convergence around a narrow group of "reference points" and "builders" of online conversations, and by the presence of a rather homogenous central nucleus of programmers. On the contrary, the Spanish and Italian networks sustain *weak conversations,* characterised by medium to low levels of activity and compactness, as well as a limited capacity to converge around a defined, homogenous central nucleus. In an intermediate position, the networks of the Austrian and German sites supply relational infrastructures for *aggregated conversations*, whether the obstacles to communication found in the Italian and Spanish cases in terms of low activity and compactness are not present but, in general, the type of conversation is less fluid and organised than that generated by the French and British sites. *Aggregated conversations* tend in fact to be fragmented, but nevertheless display medium to high levels of activity; the components that form them have medium levels of compactness, and the central nuclei are diversified, but not totally heterogeneous as in the case of weak conversations. Next to these common characteristics, the conversations between Austrian and German differ in terms of a tendency to converge around specific actors: in the Austrian case, they tend to lack both common "reference points" and "systematic builders" as in Italy and Spain; while the German case comes closer to the online conversations of French and British sites.

4 Pro- and Anti-EU Frames in Extreme-Right Online Networks

What criticism the programmers of the six countries do at the current situation of the EU through their websites? And what alternative visions do they propose? Are there aspects around which they converge and that supply a symbolic basis to reinforce systems of inconvenient solidarities among extreme-right organisations?

Or do the programmers use their sites to spread diversified and heterogeneous criticisms and projects for reform? Can we infer a nexus between the online "modes of conversation" identified earlier and the way in which extreme-right sites in the different countries elaborate their critical and reform frames of Europe?

Figures 11.1 and 11.2 provide a graphic synthesis of the results of the automatic content analysis carried out using GoogleScraper. Each country is represented by a group of small circles, each of which signifies the keywords that the programmers in the corresponding online network associate with critical (Fig. 11.1) and reform (Fig. 11.2) frames of the current project for a unified Europe. The size of the circles is proportionate to the number of pages identified by the software for each of the keywords. In this sense, for each country, circles with a larger diameter correspond to those aspects most emphasised by the programmers through the pages of their sites.

In general, the results suggest that opposition to current processes of European integration is a question discussed with many nuances in the online conversations between extreme-right sites. Indeed, all of the critical aspects of associated frames criticising and proposing reforms to the current political Europe are present, albeit to varying degrees, in the sites of the programmers of all the online networks considered. The political and institutional aspects see rather heated critical arguments, particularly when speaking of relations between member states and the Union. For example, the theme of "European dictatorship" is traced in the websites of the programmers in all of the countries and constitutes the main critical aspect in France, Austria and Italy. Still, the programmers of the six online networks also share a preoccupation with the (bad) behaviour of politicians linked to Europe. For

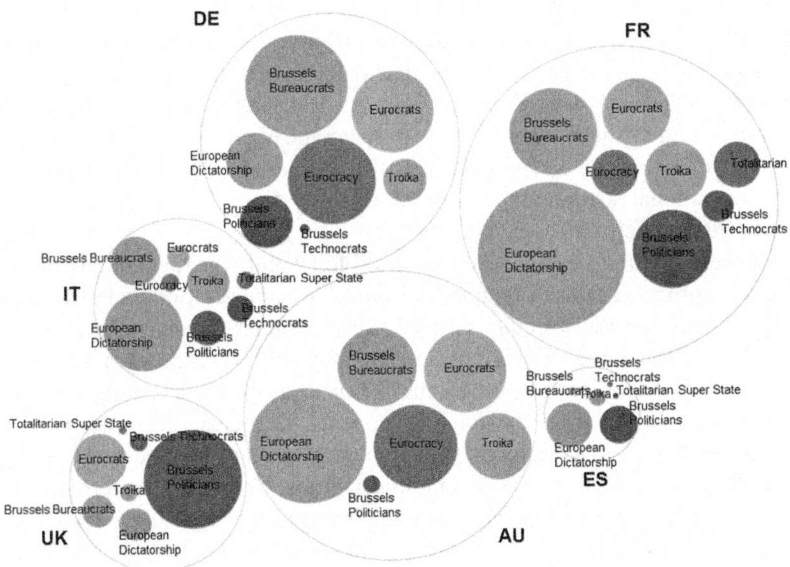

Fig. 11.1 Composition of frames critical of the EU in programmers' sites in the different countries

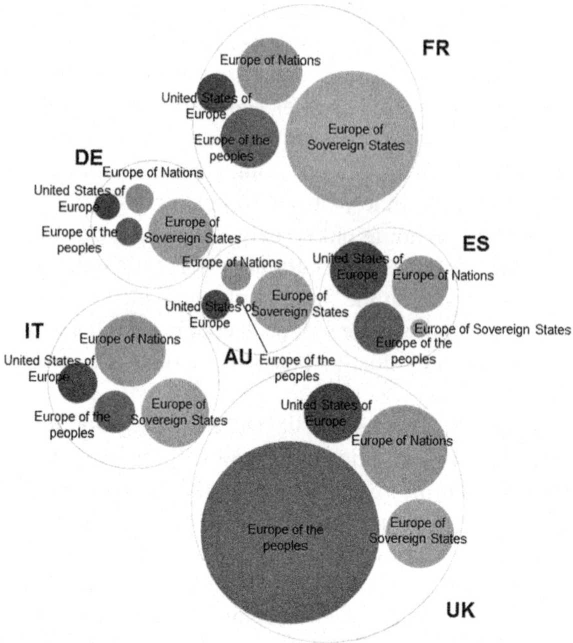

Fig. 11.2 Composition of frames for the reform of the EU in programmers' sites in the different countries

example, reproofs aimed at "petty politicians" and "Brussels bureaucrats" are present and relevant in all conversations and in particular those driven by British and German programmers. In addition, a legitimacy problem seems to emerge with particular reference to the distance of EU institutions from citizens and their general opacity. This problem is often presented by resorting to old "conspiracy theories" typical of extreme-right ideology (see Caiani and della Porta 2011), as suggested by the diffusion of the keyword "Eurocracy" in the web pages of the German and Austrian programmers. In response to these problematic elements, the programmers of the six networks propose two main visions: the restoration of a system centred on state-level or national sovereignty and breaking away from the European institutions to restore Europe to its own "peoples".

Beyond these common traits, it is also possible to pinpoint specificities in the various frames proposed, linked both to the "mode" of conversation underway and to the peculiarities of the specific national context under consideration. In the French case, which as we saw is characterised by the presence of a systemic conversation, though not ignoring criticisms of European politicians, programmers tend to convey in particular on a vision of Europe as "European dictatorship" and, albeit to a lesser degree, as a "Eurocracy". For example, in a page published as early as 2011, Polémia (the main French programmer) writes: "What the western oligarchy calls 'democracy' in reality means the negation of sovereignty, the negation of liberty, the negation of citizenship, the negation of people. It is in fact a new form of oriental despotism, incarnated in a remote and untouchable power, which signifies dominion over an empire of Helots".[7] A degree of convergence is also noted when speaking of possible alternatives: the programmers seem to agree in particular on the fact that the only solution to the centralised "European dictatorship" is a return to the "Europe of the Nations" where authority is diffused and national authority is re-established. For example, the Polémia site identifies the transition to a Europe of the nations in a post from March 2015 as "the only basis possible to allow the renewed construction of a European project".[8]

A degree of convergence on criticisms and proposals for reform can also be found among the British programmers, also involved in a systemic conversation. In this case, however, the diverse nature of the sites that are present within the central nucleus of this online network (with a prevalence of political parties) leads to convergence around arguments that differ from those in the French case. While the French programmers identify the EU as an institutional target, the British agree in identifying the problem as principally one of civil servants and policy makers, often defined as "petty Brussels politicians", with the emphasis on their (bad) behaviour and the lack of respect for British voters and citizens. For example, the British People's Party site in a page published as early as 2006 decries that "Europe works by corrupting politicians with high salaries and investing a lot, pushing them to vote for Europe against the interests of their own voters".[9] In a similar vein, in 2015, a post on the site of the British National Party discussing the migrant crisis asks for "the arrest of politicians colluding with the invaders".[10] In light of this common preoccupation, the British programmers converge in proposing the alternative of a "Europe of peoples", more genuine and far from the corrupt European civil servants.

In the other four countries, where the online conversations are less fluid and less organised compared to those in France and the United Kingdom, the programmers tend to articulate the "EU problem" in a more heterogeneous manner. Looking again at Fig. 11.1, we can note in particular that in Austria, like Germany, Italy and Spain, the programmers recognise both European institutions and politicians as two sides of the same "EU problem" and use two main "master frames"[11]: on one hand, the idea of the EU as a "European dictatorship" and, on the other, politicians seen as "Brussels bureaucrats". Notwithstanding this, in this case too, the "modes of conversation" online that characterise the different networks seem to play a role in the construction of shared critical frames. In the cases of aggregated conversations in Austria and Germany, we can note that the idea of a "European dictatorship" is associated with

[7]http://www.polemia.com/la-democratie-totalitaire-ou-comment-le-despotisme-oriental-sinstalle-en-europe/

[8]http://www.polemia.com/leuro-arme-de-destruction-massive-des-nations/

[9]http://www.bpp.org.uk/nationsdeath.html

[10]http://www.bnp.org.uk/news/national/europe-being-systematically-and-intentionally-ruined

[11]A "master frame" is a view that is elastic, flexible and inclusive enough to be adopted by different actors in multiple contexts and stages of mobilisation (Benford 2013; Snow and Benford 1992).

that of "Eurocracy" and "European bureaucracy". In line with this, politicians are also portrayed as "Eurocrats", that is, as working for inefficient and centralised institutions. In Italy and Spain, however, where weaker conversations take place within contexts of fragmented frames without direction, no specific implementation of master frames is found, with the sole exception of the idea of "petty Brussels politicians" preferred by the Spanish programmes to that of "bureaucrats". Just as these four online networks tend to traffic more heterogeneous critical frames compared to those transmitted by the French and British networks of programmers, in their elaboration of reform frames, no real convergence around any possible "solution" to the "EU problem" can be found. Nevertheless, in the aggregated conversations between Austrian and German sites, it is possible to note how the programmers tend to pay more attention to the idea of a return to a "Europe of the Nation States", while in the cases of weak conversations between Italian and Spanish sites, it becomes more difficult to identify a common focus by which to orient proposals for "another Europe".

5 Conclusions

In this article, we proposed an analytical and methodological approach to begin to investigate the ways in which the most radical right-wing organisations and groups use the communicative and relational potential offered by ICTs to build what we call "inconvenient solidarities". The latter are defined as systems of alliances between actors that oppose and distort current efforts towards transnational democratisation, particularly in relation to processes of European integration. Departing from the central role played by digital communication networks in contemporary political dynamics, we first examined the type of online structures formed by the sites of various extreme-right groups and organisations in six European countries. Second, departing from an exploration of content critical of and proposing reforms to the current European political edifice circulated by these networks, we examined how these online conversations contribute to the formation of collective frames that support forces opposing dynamics of European integration.

In this vein, we noted that ICTs do not always supply the same "structural" support for the construction of systems of inconvenient solidarities but allow online conversations in different "modes"—in some cases, more compact and fluid exchange systems are generated; in others, they are more fragmented and weak. In the same manner, we observed that ICTs do not always supply the same "cognitive" support to extreme-right opposition. More specifically, our results seem to suggest that when organisations' sites generate and are involved in more compact and organised conversations, as in the cases of France and the United Kingdom, this is accompanied by a greater capacity to spread critical and reform frames of Europe that are more homogeneous, centred on common and shared "priorities" and, as a consequence, better suited to sustaining collective and coordinated opposition strategies. In the opposite direction, the weaker the structure of the online conversation, as seen among Spanish and Italian sites, the lower the possibility to supply shared diagnoses and prognoses of the "European problem" that unite participants and motivate them to support a common opposition to the dynamics of European integration. Cases such as Germany and Austria appear to suggest instead that the more curated online conversations are, the greater the possibility to achieve coordination and to present a united front in pursuing an "inconvenient" opposition.

References

Bartlett, J., Birdwell, J., & Littler, M. (2011). *'The rise of populism in Europe can be traced through online behaviour' The new face of digital populism.* London: Demos.

Benford, R. D. (2013). Master frame. In D. A. Snow, D. Della Porta, B. Klandermans, & D. McAdam (Eds.), *The Wiley-Blackwell encyclopedia of social and political movements* (pp. 273–274). Hoboken: Blackwell Publishing.

Bennett, W. L., & Segerberg, A. (2013). *The logic of connecting action.* Cambridge: Cambridge University Press.

Berman, S. (1997). Social capital, civil society and contemporary democracy. *American Behavioral Scientist, 42*, 562–574.

Borgatti, S. P., Everett, M. G., & Johnson, J. C. (2013). *Analyzing social networks.* London: Sage.

Boyd, D. (2011). Social network sites as networked publics: Affordances, dynamics and implications. In Z. Papacharissi (Ed.), *A networked self* (pp. 39–58). New York: Routledge.

Bruszt, L., Vedres, B., & Stark, D. (2005). Shaping the web of civic participation: Civil society websites in Eastern Europe. *Journal of Public Policy, 25*(1), 149–163.

Bustikova, L. (2009). The extreme right in Eastern Europe: EU accession and the quality of governance. *Journal of Contemporary European Studies, 17*(2), 223–239.

Caiani, M., & Della Porta, D. (2011). The elitist populism of the extreme right: A frame analysis of extreme right-wing discourses in Italy and Germany. *Acta Politica, 46*, 180–202.

Caiani, M., Della Porta, E., & Wagemann, C. (2012). *Mobilizing on the extreme right: Germany, Italy, and the United States.* Oxford: Oxford University Press.

Caiani, M., & Parenti, L. (2013). *European and American extreme right groups and the internet.* Farnham: Ashgate.

Castells, M. (2012). *Networks of outrage and hope.* Cambridge: Polity Press.

Chadwick, A. (2013). *The hybrid media system. Politics and power.* Oxford: Oxford University Press.

Chase-Dunn, C., & Boswell, T. (2004). Global democracy: A world-systems perspective. *PRO, 20*, 15–29.

Cinalli, M., & Füglister, K. (2008). Networks and political contention over unemployment: A comparison of Britain, Germany, and Switzerland. *Mobilization: An International Quarterly, 13*(3), 259–276.

Conti, N., & Memoli, V. (2016). Media, cittadini, euroscetticismo. L'influenza dei mezzi di comunicazione nell'orientare gli atteggiamenti verso l'UE. *ComPol – Comunicazione Politica, 1*(2016), 45–64.

Diani, M. (2003). Networks and social movements: A research programme. In M. Diani & D. McAdam (Eds.), *Social movements and networks: Relational approachs to collective action* (pp. 299–318). New York: Oxford University Press.

Eggert, N., & Pavan, E. (2014). Researching collective action through networks: Taking stock and looking forward. *Mobilization: An International Journal, 19*(4), 363–368.

Foley, M., & Edwards, B. (1997). Escape from politics? Social theory and the social capital debate. *American Behavioral Scientist, 40*, 550–561.

Freeman, L. C. (2002[1979]). Centrality in social networks: Conceptual clarifications. In J. Scott (Ed.) *Social networks: Critical concepts in sociology* (vol. I, pp. 238–263). London: Routledge.

Garrett, R. K. (2006). Protest in an information society: A review of literature on social movements and new ICTs. *Information, Communication and Society, 9*(2), 202–224.

Hermet, G. (2001). Les Populismes dans le monde: Une histoire sociologique XIXe–XXe siècle. *Politique étrangère, 66*(3), 730–731.

Kriesi, H. (2008). Political participation and the mobilisation, political power of the vote. *West European Politics, 31*(1–2), 147–168.

Lievrouw, L. (2011). *Alternative and activist new media*. Cambridge: Polity Press.

Melucci, A. (1996). *Challenging codes. Collective action in the information age*. Cambridge: Cambridge University Press.

Mény, Y., & Surel, Y. (2000). *Par Le Peuple, Pour Le Peuple. Le populisme et les démocraties*. Paris: Fayard.

Padovani, C., & Pavan, E. (2016). Global governance and ICTs: Exploring online governance networks around gender and media. *Global Networks. A Journal Of Transnational Affairs, 16* (3), 350–371.

Papacharissi, Z. (2016). Affective publics and structures of storytelling: Sentiment, events and mediality. *Information, Communication and Society, 19*(3), 307–324.

Pavan, E. & Diani, M. (2016). Making computer and normative codes converge. A sociotechnical approach to smart cities. In *Proceedings of the Third International Conference on Internet Science*, INSCI 2016, Florence, Italy, September 12–14, ch. 23.

Post, J. M. (2005). Psychology. In Club de Madrid (Ed.) *Addressing the causes of terrorism* (pp. 7–12). Retrieved from http://www.clubmadrid.org/img/secciones/Club_de_Madrid_Volume_I_The_Causes_of_Terrorism.pdf

Rainie, L., & Wellman, B. (2012). *Networked. The new social operating system*. Cambridge: The MIT Press.

Rogers, R. (2013). *Digital methods*. Cambridge: The MIT Press.

Snow, D. A., & Benford, R. D. (1992). Master frames and cycles of protest. In J. Morris & E. Mueller (Eds.), *Frontiers in social movement theory* (pp. 136–152). London: Yale University Press.

Snow, D. A., Rochford, E. B., Warden, S., & Benford, R. (1986). Frame alignment processes, micromobilization, and movement participation. *American Sociological Review, 51*(4), 464–481.

Warkentin, C. (2001). *Reshaping world politics. NGOs, the internet and the global civil society*. Lanham: Rowman & Littlefield.

Whine, M. (2012). Trans-European trends in right-wing extremism. In A. Mammone, E. Godin, & B. Jenkins (Eds.), *Mapping the extreme right in contemporary Europe* (pp. 317–334). London: Routledge.

Chapter 12
Solidarity in the European Union: Fundamental Value or "Empty Signifier"

Andreas Grimmel

1 Introduction

The value of solidarity has a long history in Europe—stretching from early conceptions in Roman law, over reformist endeavours in nineteenth-century France and the European revolutions of 1848, to modern conceptions that go beyond the nation state. Against this backdrop, it comes as no surprise that solidarity was given a central place in the canon of values of the European Union (EU). It is now prominently featured in Article 2 of the Treaty of Lisbon and is mentioned in numerous political declarations as a guiding principle of the EU. This commitment to solidarity in the European integration process goes back to the early days of the European Coal and Steel Community (ECSC, 1951) and has accompanied the integration process ever since. As Sangiovanni reminds us, the preamble of the Treaty establishing the ECSC has already affirmed that "Europe can be built only through real practical achievements which will first of all create real solidarity". Later on, "'solidarity' appeared alongside 'cohesion' in both the Single European Act (1986) and the Maastricht Treaty (1992). The Treaty of Lisbon (2006) not only continues this commitment but also expands it, mentioning it both as a value binding together member states and as a value binding together the citizens of each and every member state" (Sangiovanni 2013, 1–2).

But does this obvious centrality and expansion of the value of solidarity in the textual and legal basis also mean that it takes a central role in the actions of the EU, its Member States and citizens? Can we infer from the fact of its recurring use that recognition of the concept of solidarity is mirrored by corresponding practice in the EU? Here, it will be argued that this is not the case. Although there is a link between

A. Grimmel (✉)
University of Hamburg, Hamburg, Germany

Institute for European Integration, Europa-Kolleg Hamburg, Hamburg, Germany
e-mail: andreas.grimmel@uni-hamburg.de

A. Grimmel, S.M. Giang (eds.), *Solidarity in the European Union*,
DOI 10.1007/978-3-319-57036-5_12

the concept and the corresponding actions that define the meaning of solidarity, the density of this link cannot be measured by relying exclusively on either the textual side or the practical side. Rather, both have to come together to fill solidarity—as a concept and value—with life and give it a central role in the integration process. This argument will be developed by building on the works of Ludwig Wittgenstein and discussing three of his most influential concepts: meaning in use, rule-following and private language. It will be claimed that such a Wittgensteinian perspective has the potential to arrive at an understanding of solidarity that discloses a major shortcoming of the value in the context of the EU, namely, a lack of commonality in terms of what solidarity *practically* implies, i.e. what it means *to act* in solidarity in actual cases. It will be further argued that the only way to overcome this shortcoming is to follow a somewhat pragmatic agenda in applying the value in concrete cases and, in doing so, making its common meaning explicit.

2 The Conceptual Weakness of Solidarity in the European Union

Solidarity is probably one of the most ambivalent values of the EU. On the one side, there are hardly any Member States or EU citizens who would disagree that it plays and has to play a vital role in the EU and the integration process. On the other side, what it actually means to act in a way that reflects solidarity is far from being common sense, and it is largely unclear what the concept implies in terms of the policies and practice of the EU. While meaningful in other contexts, the concept is quite simply lacking in content when it comes to its actual application in the EU. At least, there seems to be little in the EU's common value of solidarity that also results in common action—by either Europeans or Member States. On the contrary, there seem to be an abundance of different interpretations, and, as Barnard concludes, "the use made by the Union institutions of 'solidarity' shows that while the principle has been used in a variety of ways by the institutions, at no stage has there been any attempt to define the term. The EU institutions appear to apply the elephant test: you know it if you see it" (2010, 80). Of course, this is also true for other political and societal contexts, and it is not a phenomenon that is limited to the EU. In this regard, the conceptual blurriness of solidarity seems to be a general problem rather than one that would solely concern the integration process. However, the current crises that the EU is confronting have revealed the degree to which there is dissent among the European institutions, Member States' governments and also the "peoples of Europe" (TEU, preamble) about what solidarity actually means and how it should be translated into concrete measures.

The *Eurozone crisis* and the *refugee and migrant crisis* made this more than clear. There was not only discord about if and to what extent the value of solidarity matters to these crises. The need for concrete answers to the concrete challenges that the crises presented revealed how indistinct the meaning of the concept is in the

EU today and how open it is to conflicting and even opposed interpretations. In the extreme, however, a concept that is open to any possible interpretation is a concept without meaning, because any action can then be argued to be in line with the value. Solidarity in the EU is certainly more than this. But the lack of a common understanding and manifest action in the current crises has allowed the value to remain a weak concept in the context of the EU.

2.1 The Case of the Eurozone Crisis

Looking first at the Eurozone crisis, the concept was invoked by both the Greek government and its creditors, but both sides had a very different understanding of what solidarity practically implies. How divergent the approaches of solidarity have been (and continue to be) in this case can be especially seen in the exemplary statements of the former President of the European Council, Herman Van Rompuy, and the German government, on the one side, and the Prime Minister of Greece, Alexis Tsipras, in light of the bailout programmes, on the other. In the wake of the crisis, speaking at the opening of the academic year 2011–2012 at the European University Institute, Van Rompuy (2011) particularly emphasised "that solidarity consists . . . not merely in receiving but also in giving. Solidarity is a duty, not only a right. A lax national policy is therefore contrary to the spirit of solidarity". The German government, especially the Federal Finance Minister Wolfgang Schäuble, concurred with this appraisal by repeating that "solidarity is not a one-way street". The Greek Prime Minister, on the contrary, emphasised in his summary comments at the European Parliament on 8 July 2015 first and foremost the need for financial help by stating that it stems from solidarity, claiming that "lending is certainly a form of solidarity. There is no doubt about it. But we want a sustainable program, exactly because we want to be able to pay back what we have borrowed. And when we ask for debt reduction, we ask for this reduction exactly because we want to be able to make good on those loans and not to be constantly obliged to seek new loans in order to repay previous loans" (Tsipras 2015). Both positions can be seen as emblematic of the discussion that developed around the concept of solidarity during the Eurozone crisis.

While solidarity is portrayed as a right, but also a duty, for those countries in financial distress to engage in reforms in the first interpretation, it is primarily seen as a creditor–debtor relationship in the second one. What becomes apparent now in these statements is not only the fact that solidarity is a contested concept but also that the concept can have different implications in practice. Even though both might certainly be true, this is only part of the picture. It is also interesting to focus on the highly instrumental use of the concept of solidarity. Not only in these two exemplary statements but also in the entire debate about the financial crisis solidarity rarely stands for itself, i.e. is treated as an intrinsic value. Rather, it is used instrumentally for a certain argumentative purpose, particularly as a "rhetorical" backing for a certain political position, in the sense of a "strategic use of norm-based arguments" (Schimmelfennig 2001, 48), instead of guiding common action in a troublesome situation. The concept, therefore, largely remains a dependent variable of an independent political intent. It is, as Laclau says, "the result of political competition" (Laclau 1996, 35). As such, it necessarily becomes a "floating" or even "empty signifier" in that it is defined ex post. Solidarity was ascribed specific meanings based on political considerations rather than because a certain notion of solidarity was imposing itself on the situation.

2.2 *The Case of the Refugee and Migrant Crisis*

The same situation can be seen in the case of the refugee and migrant crisis, which has led to serious discord over the answer that the situation at the EU borders, especially in Greece and Italy and along the refugee trails, demands. Solidarity, again, was at the heart of the political debates. And, again, it was less a guiding principle and more a means of backing up pre-existing political positions or even to create rhetorical pressure (with the presidents of the EU institutions and those Member State governments that were willing to receive larger numbers of refugees and open up long-term prospects to them on one side and those EU members who generally refuse such engagement on the other side).

When the President of the European Commission, Jean-Claude Juncker (2015), stated that "Europe has clearly under-delivered" in the field of "common solidarity with regard to the refugees who have arrived on our territory", this evaluation was shared by many EU members. However, at the same time, others still remain reluctant to reform the EU's migration policy. The idea of "migrant quotas", as well as the argument that to accept migrants is an expression of solidarity, is especially rejected by central European states (cf. Inotai et al. 2015). The Visegrád Group (Czech Republic, Hungary, Poland, Slovakia), for example, insisted on an understanding of solidarity as "flexible solidarity", with no mandatory quotas, but voluntary contributions based on what Member States are able and willing to offer—e.g. financial contributions, manpower for border control or voluntary acceptance and accommodation of refugees. In this redefinition, solidarity mainly depends on criteria of (self-declared) capability and a large portion of political interest expressed in self-declared capabilities. The President of the European Parliament, Martin Schulz (2015), was refuting the position of the Visegrád Group when he claimed that "you can't cherry pick solidarity" and that "[t]here are ways to demand solidarity. [...] Those who want something will have to offer something in return—such as solidarity in the refugee question, for example". But this "tit for tat" strategy to "demand" solidarity was not undisputed either, and there is the question of whether enforcing solidarity, as Schulz proposed, recalls the impossibility of forcing someone to be free, since that then makes the core of the value disappear.

Since the Bratislava summit in September 2016, the redefinition of solidarity as "flexible solidarity" has been principally accepted alongside the political position, even by those who were pushing most strongly for a fair share in the relocation and settlement of refugees within the EU, like the German government and also the President of the Commission. In his opening statements to the 2016 debate on the state of the Union, Juncker resignedly declared: "I'm convinced much more solidarity is needed, but I also know that solidarity must be voluntary, it must come from the heart, it cannot be forced, it cannot be imposed". But these words already suggest a kind of consent that is, in fact, non-existent: "voluntary solidarity" as well as "flexible solidarity" would not only require political ability and political will but would also need accord in terms of *when* and *how* to apply solidarity in principle. However, exactly this accord is already fundamentally missing when looking at the political discussions concerning the refugee and migrant crisis, as the case of the Visegrád Group shows. Solidarity remains a blurry concept and the "floating signifier" (a concept with an unstable or highly variable meaning) that it already was in the Eurozone crisis.

2.3 Solidarity Lost?

All this might be seen as a rather pessimistic and disappointing portrayal of the current state of affairs and the significance of solidarity in the EU. However, there are sound reasons why we should not lose optimism given the EU's weakness in coping with the current problems, and it is undisputed that solidarity is needed more than ever to handle the ongoing crisis. However, it must not be overlooked that the current usage of solidarity in the European context makes it a weak concept, one that will hardly help to overcome any of the issues that the EU and its members face today or in the future. But why is it so problematic that there is little *commonality* in terms of the understanding of solidarity that finds its expression in the political discussions and also the practices of the EU? Could it not be argued that even though the concept seems to be open to divergent interpretations, and it is not clear when and how it is to be applied, it still has an important symbolic function for the cohesion of the EU and its decision-making? And is the mere reference to solidarity as a European value in the discussions not already a positive sign for its significance, or at least an indication of the concept's rising importance in EU politics?

To answer these questions, it becomes necessary to first understand the practical conditionality of values. By relying on a Wittgensteinian argument, it will be maintained here that the key to defining solidarity in the context of the EU will be to go beyond the abstract understanding of the concept that made it the "floating signifier" it is today. As long as there is no *common practice* that determines the meaning of the concept and makes it explicit, it is argued here that solidarity will not be unconditional but merely contingent upon individual interests and political positions.

3 Wittgenstein and the Need to Understand Solidarity as Concrete Practice

Wittgenstein never dealt with the meaning and application of solidarity in his philosophy of language, and indeed most other "grand concepts" of political theory were left largely unregarded by him. Nevertheless, numerous works in the field of political science have turned to Wittgenstein in order to clarify the relationship between the linguistic and practical dimensions of language, as well as the difficulties that arise in this field (e.g. Pitkin 1972; Onuf 1989; Tully 1989; Heyes 2003; Gunnell 2011; Robinson 2011; Grimmel 2015), and there are good reasons to do so with regard to the concept of solidarity. This is not so much the case in order to arrive at a specific definition of what solidarity "really" means, or should mean, but in order to understand how and when the textual or verbal use of the term becomes meaningful in the first place—and also in order to understand why and when a linguistic expression remains "floating" or even an "empty signifier".

Other than in the notion of Ernesto Laclau, however, such a signifier will not be understood here as "a signifier of the pure cancellation of all difference" (1996, 38), but rather as *lacking in a common practice that allows for a joint interpretation of the concept*. It is a signifier that leaves such questions as "what to do", "how to do it" and "when to do it" essentially open, because its concrete meaning is not sufficiently clear to lead to joint answers based on a common conceptual understanding. This thesis shall be argued in three steps by way of discussing Wittgenstein's considerations of meaning in use, rule-following and private language.

3.1 Meaning in Use

If we think about the meaning of solidarity, or any other concept, we tend to believe that there is something within the concept itself that defines its meaning and exists regardless of how the term is used by us. Every concept seems to offer some kind of guidance on how to apply it. This guidance, it could be assumed, is to be unveiled through mere reflection on what "really" makes up the concept. The meaning of the concept seems to give us everything needed to apply it.

Wittgenstein takes a radically different position here. For him, the meaning of concepts and rules is bound to the ways these are used in language (PI, § 43). Other than the picture theory of language, which (the later) Wittgenstein rejects, he draws our attention to the fact that there cannot be meaning without a practice that defines what it actually means to *follow* a certain rule or *apply* a certain concept. For Wittgenstein, meaning can never be the result of a private, merely reflective mental experience but has to be learnt and clarified by learning the use of concepts and rules, i.e. how these are practised in concrete cases. This notion of language dismisses an idea that he ascribes to Augustine: namely, "a particular picture of the essence of human language" in which "[e]very word has a meaning" that is "correlated with the word. It is the object for which the word stands" (PI, § 1).

Wittgenstein's approach is different here: rules and concepts do not stand for previously existing or corresponding objects or practices. Instead, as Bloor says, meaning comes into existence "in a step-by-step fashion as we go along. It is not progressively revealed by usage. It does not pre-exist, but is created in response to the sequence of contingencies attending each act of concept application. . . . Use is not to be explained by reference to meaning, because use does not come from meaning. Rather, meaning comes from use" (Bloor 1997, 136). In short, from a Wittgensteinian perspective, rules and concepts have to be understood as gaining and changing their meaning only through their regular practice and not through some kind of direct relation to the things they describe. But there is also a counter-side to this, namely, that we can recognise and refer to certain practices only because there are linguistic expressions attached to them. It is this very mutuality and circularity of linguistic expression, on the one side, and practice, on the other, that is at the heart of the idea of meaning in use, which the later Wittgenstein made a matter of principle.

At the same time, the need to make concepts and rules explicit through deeds makes the constitution and evolution of meaning a social matter through and through. Every understanding of rules and concepts already requires basic consent within a community of speakers about the application of linguistic expressions, which allows them to go along with (i.e. continue) their application:

> Here it is of the greatest importance that all or the enormous majority of us agree in certain things. I can, e.g., be quite sure that the colour of this object will be called 'green' by far the most of the human beings who see it. (RFM, 342)

From a Wittgensteinian point of view, there is no other criteria to say that something is green than the agreement that we share in calling something "green". Meaning and the practice that is accepted to be in accordance with a certain concept or rule essentially amount to the same thing. This does not mean, of course, that there cannot be dissents about meaning—this is often the case, rather than the exception, for such concepts that are more open to interpretation than those referring to basic colours.

What Wittgenstein wants to draw our attention to here is essentially this: that we have to accept certain judgements or measurements (PI, § 242) because there is such a fundamental agreement about their use that we cannot question them without losing the common grounds for communication. On the flip side, however, concepts and rules that largely lack such an agreement leave room for interpretation and diverging applications. This becomes especially apparent in those cases where the relevance of a concept (such as solidarity) is invoked in situations (such as the Eurozone crisis) that have not been faced before in a certain context of action (such as the EU). Here, questions arise as to if, why, how and to what extent the concept of solidarity is applicable and what it implies for the actors involved. Although there might be meaning in the use of solidarity in other contexts (such as on the level of the Member States) or other situations (such as emergency aid after a natural disaster), there is no precedent for solidary action in the present one.

One could now be inclined to conclude that all this is a matter of mere interpretation, just depending on how the meaning of a concept is interpreted in "new" and unprecedented cases. But it is not. Wittgenstein reminds us that "any interpretation still hangs in the air along with what it interprets, and cannot give it any support. Interpretations by themselves do not determine meaning" (PI, § 198). There simply is "a way of grasping a rule which is *not* an *interpretation*, but which is exhibited in what we call 'following'[1] the rule' and 'going against it' in actual cases" (PI, § 201). What Wittgenstein addresses here is crucial for our further discussion and for the argument about the significance of solidarity in the EU. This is true, at least with regard to two central aspects: first, the external dimension of following a rule and, second, the social conditionality of following a rule, as expressed in Wittgenstein's private language argument.

3.2 *Rule-Following*

The meaning of a concept is defined by the ways it is used. The application of a concept can, therefore, always be understood as following a rule, i.e. making use of it in a particular way. "A meaning of a word is a kind of employment of it. For it is what we learn when the word is incorporated into our language. That is why there exists a correspondence between the concepts 'rule' and 'meaning'" (OC, § 61–62). This might not be immediately obvious for those cases where "the enormous majority of us agree in certain things" (RFM, 342), as in the case of identifying basic colours. The reason here is that we do not normally reflect on such fundamental denominations anymore. Rather, we "follow the rule blindly" (PI, § 219) that lets us identify the colour (PI, § 53) or, of course, any other everyday matter. And even if we reflect on whether something is green or not, we again need a rule that allows for exactly this. As soon as we follow that rule, however, we no longer question how to follow it. Rather, we follow it blindly. One rule is replaced by another, and the question arises of which rule is the one that "truly" defines or should define what the concept—e.g. the name of a colour—means. From a Wittgensteinian viewpoint, this indeterminacy is no severe problem, since the meaning of a concept or sign is neither defined by the intention or belief of the individual following a rule (PI, § 202; OC, § 432) nor any kind of rule book but rather by *the ways how it can be used* (PI, §§ 432, 454).

[1]Sometimes, the German expression *der Regel folgen* has been translated into English as "obeying the rule", which seems to give it a more coercive connotation than it has in the original phrase. Here and in the following the translation, "following the rule" will be preferred, since it seems to be closer to the original manuscript.

All of this makes applying concepts and following rules an entirely external and practical business instead of a mere mental and theoretical exercise. The only possible way to determine the ways in which a concept can be used is to clarify its actual use, e.g. by actually using it. Solidarity, in the words of Wittgenstein, is exhibited in what we call "to act solidary" and "going against it" in actual cases (cf. PI, § 201). And what we call "to act solidary" can be explicated by either pointing to regular patterns of use *or* engaging in the regular use itself.

The visibility and identifiability of the act of rule application are, therefore, preconditions for linking certain patterns of action with a rule. Otherwise, there would be no way to determine what counts as following the rule, and there would also be no criteria to determine whether there is agreement about the implications of following the rule or not. Every "'inner process' stands in need of outward criteria" (PI, § 580).

For Wittgenstein, "'following a rule' is a practice that can be identified as such. And to *think* one is following a rule is not to follow a rule. Hence, it is not possible to follow a rule 'privately': otherwise thinking one was following a rule would be the same thing as following it" (PI, § 202). But who then decides what counts as following the rule and what remains the mere belief of following it? The answer to this question has to be found in the social dimension of language rather than in any kind of technique of cognition or reflection that could be fulfilled individually. This finally brings us to Wittgenstein's private language argument.

3.3 *Private Language*

The core of Wittgenstein's private language argument can be traced in the following line of thought: since the meaning of a concept cannot be detached from the rules that specify the ways how it can be used, there has to be some kind of authority or instance that decides whether a certain action is in line with the rule or not. This authority or instance, however, needs an external point of reference that allows for the identification of that rule: if the act of rule application is not visible and is, therefore, not identifiable as such, it would simply not make sense to talk about rule-following anymore, because there would be no criteria left to tell whether someone is following a rule or not. Everyone could claim to follow a rule every time it *seems* to him or her that the rule is followed.

Wittgenstein saw this problem, especially in such cases where the point of reference was an inner, private experience, such as feelings or moods, because there is no possibility of ostensive definitions here (except from the reactions that these inner experiences might cause). And there is no other way to tell that someone is following a rule other the *self-declaration* of following a rule. In such a private language, "[t]he words . . . are to refer to what can be known only to the speaker; to his immediate, private, sensations. So another cannot understand the language" (PI, § 243).

However, as Kripke pointed out, this problem only exists if we look at isolated actors, i.e. actors that do not interact with each other. "The situation is very different if we widen our gaze from consideration of the rule follower alone and allow ourselves to consider him as interacting with a wider community. Others will then have justification conditions for attributing correct or incorrect rule following to the subject, and these will *not* be simply that the subject's own authority is unconditionally to be accepted" (Kripke 1982, 89). Again, the crucial point in this argument is the verifiability of acts of rule-following, which can only be ensured in those cases where it is possible (a) to perceive an act as rule-following and (b) to compare the way a rule is used with other cases of rule-following. Both aspects are entirely social endeavours, just as the institution of language—its concepts, rules and grammar—is an entirely social phenomenon.

This is also the reason why Wittgenstein insists that rules do not come into existence through one use (PI, § 199), but rather through their repeated, constant, common—and, in this sense, regular—use within a community of speakers/actors. To be able to use concepts and follow rules means to have some kind of skill without having the final say about their "correct" use at one's disposal. Rather, the standards of what counts as following a rule largely depends on the other members of a community of speakers and their ability to understand an action as an expression of a certain rule. This is not because this community has a deeper insight in terms of what it "really" means to follow this or that rule or because rule-following would be some kind of majority decision. It is also not that there would be some kind of centralised instance in this community of rule-followers or that the sum of its members makes up such a centre. The crucial point is that language, as a social phenomenon, is largely based on human agreement, "not only in definitions but also ... in judgements" (PI, § 242), and "[i]n order to make a mistake, a man must already judge in conformity with mankind" (OC, § 156), as Wittgenstein says. We see ourselves, our interpretations and our actions through the eyes of the others (Foerster 1991). There is simply no individual, private or solipsistic use of language—its rules and concepts—at least as long as standards of correctness, comprehensibility and compliance apply. The reference to linguistic expressions necessarily presupposes commonly accepted standards—whatever these standards might be (for such standards cf. e.g. Apel 1973, 429; Habermas 1984, 354). Without these standards, there is no shared ground for mutual understanding, successful communication and common action. Meaning is a result of social interaction, and it depends on the commonalities that this life permits.

4 Making "Solidarity" Explicit

In our discussion of the concept of solidarity in the EU so far, we have arrived at a rather pessimistic conclusion by arguing that there is a clear lack of commonality in terms of what solidarity *practically* implies, i.e. what it means *to act* in solidarity in actual cases. We also saw that the concept of solidarity is used instrumentally in the current crises, namely, as a "rhetorical" backing for a certain political position instead of as a guide to common action in difficult situations. It has been argued that the concept, therefore, largely remains a dependent variable of certain political interests and intentions.

These aspects, we said, make the concept a weak one or even an "empty signifier", because there seem to be few facets of the EU's solidarity concept with the potential to actually shape *common* action within the EU. This brought us to the question of whether solidarity still has an important symbolic function for the cohesion of the EU and its politics—even though there are divergent interpretations. We also asked if the mere reference to solidarity as a fundamental value in the discussions of the EU may not be seen as a positive sign for its significance already, or at least as pointing to the concept's rising importance in the EU.

The digression into Wittgenstein's considerations of meaning in use, rule-following and private language helped us to develop a deeper understanding of how meaning and the use of concepts work together. Against this backdrop, we shall now turn back to our initial discussion and our open questions.

4.1 *Towards a Shared Meaning of Solidarity*

The meaning of a concept, as we have argued with Wittgenstein, essentially depends on its use. A concept that is not used is meaningless, because if a concept is not used it remains unclear when and how to apply it. And even if there is a meaning in use in other contexts, this does not mean that there is such a use in the context at hand. In the context of the EU, it is first of all interesting to see that solidarity is frequently evoked as a common value. The concept shows up over and over again in the treaties, political and legal texts, speeches and judgements of the European Court, as well as in general public discourses. This alone might be interpreted as a good indication of its significance in EU politics. But the routine references to solidarity do not automatically make it a *common* concept, since the ways in which the concept is used in the different Member States' and the EU's institutions do not necessarily define its use in European politics. The sum of different uses of solidarity within the EU is quite simply not tantamount to a common understanding of the concept on the EU level. Put differently, while the word "solidarity" might show up frequently in various EU contexts, this fact alone does not tell us anything about its impact on joint actions or its potential to shape the discussions.

The problem with the solidarity concept in the EU is that there is no *regular* common use of it. More concretely, the EU's concept of solidarity does hardly transfer to rules that are followed, or allow for rule-following. Rather, there is an abundance of divergent uses of solidarity that do not allow for stabilising expectations and guiding action. The reason for this lack of "regularity" has its roots in the instrumental use of the solidarity concept, as can be seen most obviously in both the

Eurozone crisis and the migrant crisis. Solidarity was used here as a mere backup for interest-based politics, either to build up pressure on other governments (like the German government on the Greek government, in case of the bailout and reform programmes) or to shield against others' claims (as the Visegrád states with its concept of "flexible solidarity").

It could now be argued that this instrumental use amounts to the same thing as acting solidary, just as long as actors refer to the concept of solidarity often enough. But this is a flawed argument, as our discussion of *private language and rule-following* revealed: either solidarity will be synonymous with the self-interested motives underlying its use (in that case, this would be the rule), or—and this is the private language case—solidarity will be invoked every time it seems right to particular actors, and it would, therefore, lack common criteria for when the term is used correctly. In the latter case, every actor could decide in splendid isolation whether an action reflects solidarity or not, since the only criteria left is that very private appraisal of rule-following. "[W]hatever is going to seem right to ... [an actor] is right. And that only means that here we cannot talk about 'right'" (PI, § 258), as Wittgenstein puts it. Solidarity certainly does not disappear in these cases, but its conceptual basis is either altered or even destroyed: the self-interested and private use of solidarity creates an arbitrary instead of a shared meaning of the concept.

4.2 How to Fill the Concept of Solidarity with Life

All this does not imply that solidarity cannot gain meaning on the level of the EU. On the contrary: the preconditions for a meaningful concept of solidarity are in place in Europe. However, they have not been brought to fruition yet. Three aspects are crucial here:

First, it has to be recalled that to fill the concept of solidarity (like every concept or value) with life depends not on what single actors or particular Member States of the EU make of it. Rather, it depends on what the *community* of actors using the concept *make of it together*, i.e. in their social interactions. The current crisis situation revealed that solidarity means many things to many different actors. Although this diversity of conceptual interpretations might not be considered a problem per se, the formation of meaning very much depends on whether there are ways of *using* a concept that are shared by the actors and that guide their actions. The evocation of solidarity is not enough to make it a meaningful concept in the context of the EU. Even though referring to solidarity is essential for the definition of the concept, it is only one necessary precondition. The other prerequisite is the *application* of the concept. Solidarity means *to act* in a solidary way. And what it means to act in such a way has to be made explicit within the community of those who consider it to be an important value to the EU and its politics. Here, there is much room for improvement for the EU and its Member States.

Second, one way to make solidarity explicit through its application is, first of all, to ask the question of whether solidarity is applicable to a concrete case and, second, what solidarity actually implies in the case at hand. This neither means that there will be a unanimous answer to the question right away nor that there will be consent at all. But this is not necessary either. The mere effort of finding an answer to the question by concretising "what it means to act in a way that reflects solidarity" is already enough to entail social learning and clarify what "following the rule" and "going against it" mean in actual cases (PI, § 201). It clarifies the common ground, unveils dissent and keeps actors from hiding behind the hollow saying that "solidarity matters" to the EU. This technique of exemplifying by continuously and persistently asking for the exact practical significance of a concept is largely neglected in the EU today.

Third, another way of making the meaning of solidarity explicit is through concrete action or by the deed, i.e. clarifying by example what solidarity *could* mean. This does not necessarily require that everyone agrees that a certain action expresses solidarity. But it constitutes the basis for a meaningful discussion about what counts as solidary, and what does not, through its attempt to develop outward criteria for the use of solidarity. Moreover, such explicatory action enables others to follow and jointly proceed from example to rule. The discussion of Wittgenstein's private language argument has shown that to use concepts and follow rules mean to have some kind of skill without having the final say about their "correct" use at your disposal. But it has also shown that the meaning of a concept is defined by the ways it is used and that the application of a concept can always be understood as following a rule, i.e. making use of it in a particular way. In this sense, Wittgenstein is right when he cites Goethe: "In the beginning was the deed" (OC, § 402). Without attempting to exemplify what solidarity means in the EU in practical terms, there will be no grounds for its use—neither now nor in the future.

5 Crisis as a Chance to Arrive at a Meaningful Concept of Solidarity

The crises the EU is confronting offer a major opportunity—an opportunity derived from the essential tasks that these crises necessitate—to ask what solidarity implies with regard to concrete problems. It offers the opportunity to ask what solidarity means in practice, rather than in the abstract theoretical vacuum.

However, this question has to be asked in a way that (a) does not allow to neglect the necessary answers, (b) discloses the instrumental uses of solidarity and (c) enables action. Does solidarity mean to resolve crises like the financial crisis or the refugee crisis together or to aid one another in difficult situations? If so, does it also mean paying to help those in trouble (self-inflicted or not) or sharing the responsibilities that arise from a situation in which migration concerns some Member States more than others? If so, in which cases and to what extent? Is there an obligation (morally and legally) to engage in joint actions? Is it possible to "opt out" from solidarity in certain cases? Can Member States decide on their own if and in which ways they want to show solidarity? Can they base this decision on their wider interests? May Member States demand specific efforts from others? What about EU institutions? May they even force their members to act? If so, in which cases?

This tentative list of conceptual questions could certainly be much longer, and it is true that to persistently ask "what solidarity means in practice" can always just be one element of making sense of the EU's concept of solidarity. However, it is an important one, because it makes it difficult to shy away from the search for the necessary answers. No less important is the practical side. Solidarity has to be built by us, and it has to be made explicit by the deed.

Admittedly, this insight is not new. On the contrary, it was a core element of the early European integration process, as stated by Robert Schuman in his visionary declaration on 9 May 1950: "L'Europe ne se fera pas d'un coup, ni dans une construction d'ensemble: elle se fera par des réalisations concrètes créant d'abord une solidarité de fait". The EU would do well to finally take Schuman's advice seriously and engage in the process of making solidarity explicit through the concreteness of the deed. The result will not (and cannot) be a clear-cut or final definition of solidarity that outlasts time and space. Rather, solidarity has to be thought of as the result of a process of constant conceptual application, ascertainment, adaption and refinement. Actions do not speak louder than words in this process, but they are absolutely necessary in order to develop a meaningful concept of solidarity. As long as there is no common practice that determines the meaning of the concept and makes it explicit, solidarity will not be unconditional but merely contingent upon individual interests and various political positions in the EU.

At the end, it might prove the highest hurdle to develop the necessary *will* to concretise and exemplify the concept of solidarity in actual cases, as well as the *effort* to do so. But there is simply no other way to bring the EU's fundamental value out of the conceptual vagueness and obscurity that characterise it today.

References

Apel, K. O. (1973). *Transformation der Philosophie: Das Apriori der Kommunikationsgemeinschaft* (Vol. 2). Frankfurt am Main: Suhrkamp.

Barnard, C. (2010). Solidarity and the Commission's "Renewed Social Agenda". In M. Ross & Y. Borgmann-Prebil (Eds.), *Promoting solidarity in the European Union* (pp. 73–105). Oxford: Oxford University Press.

Bloor, D. (1997). *Wittgenstein, rules and institutions*. London: Routledge.

Grimmel, A. (2015). Wittgenstein and the context of rationality: Towards a language practical notion of rational reason and action. *Journal of Language and Politics (JLP), 14*(5), 712–728.

Gunnell, J. G. (2011). *Political theory and social science: Cutting against the grain*. New York: Palgrave Macmillan.

Habermas, J. (1984). *Vorstudien und Ergänzungen zur Theorie des kommunikativen Handelns*. Frankfurt am Main: Suhrkamp.

Heyes, C. J. (2003). *The grammar of politics: Wittgenstein and political philosophy*. Ithaca: Cornell University Press.
Inotai, E., Segeš Frelak, J., & Schmidt, H. J. (2015). Die Visegrád-Staaten und die europäische Flüchtlingspolitik. *Aus Politik und Zeitgeschichte, 65*(47–48), 38–46.
Juncker, J. C. (2015). *State of the Union 2015: Time for honesty, unity and solidarity*. Strasbourg.
Juncker, J. C. (2016). *State of the Union 2016: Extracts from the opening statements*. Strasbourg.
Kripke, S. A. (1982). *Wittgenstein on rules and private language: An elementary exposition*. Oxford: Blackwell.
Laclau, E. (1996). *Emancipation(s)*. New York: Verso.
Onuf, N. G. (1989). *World of our making: Rules and rule in social theory and international relations*. Colombia: University of South Carolina Press.
Pitkin, H. F. (1972). *Wittgenstein and justice: On the significance of Ludwig Wittgenstein for social and political thought*. Berkeley: University of California Press.
Robinson, C. C. (2011). *Wittgenstein and political theory: The view from somewhere*. Edinburgh: Edinburgh University Press.
Rorty, R. (1989). *Contingency, irony, and solidarity*. Cambridge: Cambridge University Press.
Sangiovanni, A. (2013). Solidarity in the European Union. *Oxford Journal of Legal Studies, 33*(2), 213–241.
Schimmelfennig, F. (2001). The community trap. Liberal norms, rhetorical action, and the eastern enlargement of the European. *International Organization, 55*(1), 47–80.
Schulz, M. (2015, December 1) The situation in Europe is extremely concerning. Interview conducted by H. Knaup & P. Müller. *Spiegel Online*. Accessed September 19, 2016, from http://www.spiegel.de/international/europe/european-union-in-trouble-says-parliament-president-schulz-a-1065306.html
Tsipras, A. (2015). *Summary comments at the European Parliament*. Strasbourg.
Tully, J. (1989). Wittgenstein and political philosophy: Understanding practices of critical reflection. *Political Theory, 17*(2), 172–204.
Van Rompuy, H. (2011). *The economic and political challenges for Europe: Speech at the opening of the academic year 2011–2012 European University Institute*. Fiesole.
von Foerster, H. (1991). Through the eyes of the other. In F. Steyer (Ed.), *Research and reflexivity* (pp. 21–28). London: Sage.
Wittgenstein, L. (1953). *Philosophical Investigations [PI]*. New York: Macmillan.
Wittgenstein, L. (1956). *Remarks on the Foundations of Mathematics [RFM]*. Oxford: Blackwell.
Wittgenstein, L. (1969). In G. E. M. Anscombe & G. H. von Wright (Eds.), *On Certainty [OC]*. Oxford: Blackwell.

CPSIA information can be obtained
at www.ICGtesting.com
Printed in the USA
BVOW06*0213170717
489473BV00001B/3/P

9 783319 570358